Beginning Writing Skills

Beginning Writing Skills

Trace the broken lines. Color the pictures.

Skills: Writing from left to right; Association; Fine motor skill development

Beginning Writing Skills

Trace the broken lines. Color the shapes.

Beginning Writing Skills

Trace and color the picture.

Skills: Fine motor skill development; Eye/hand coordination

Beginning Writing Skills

Trace and color the picture.

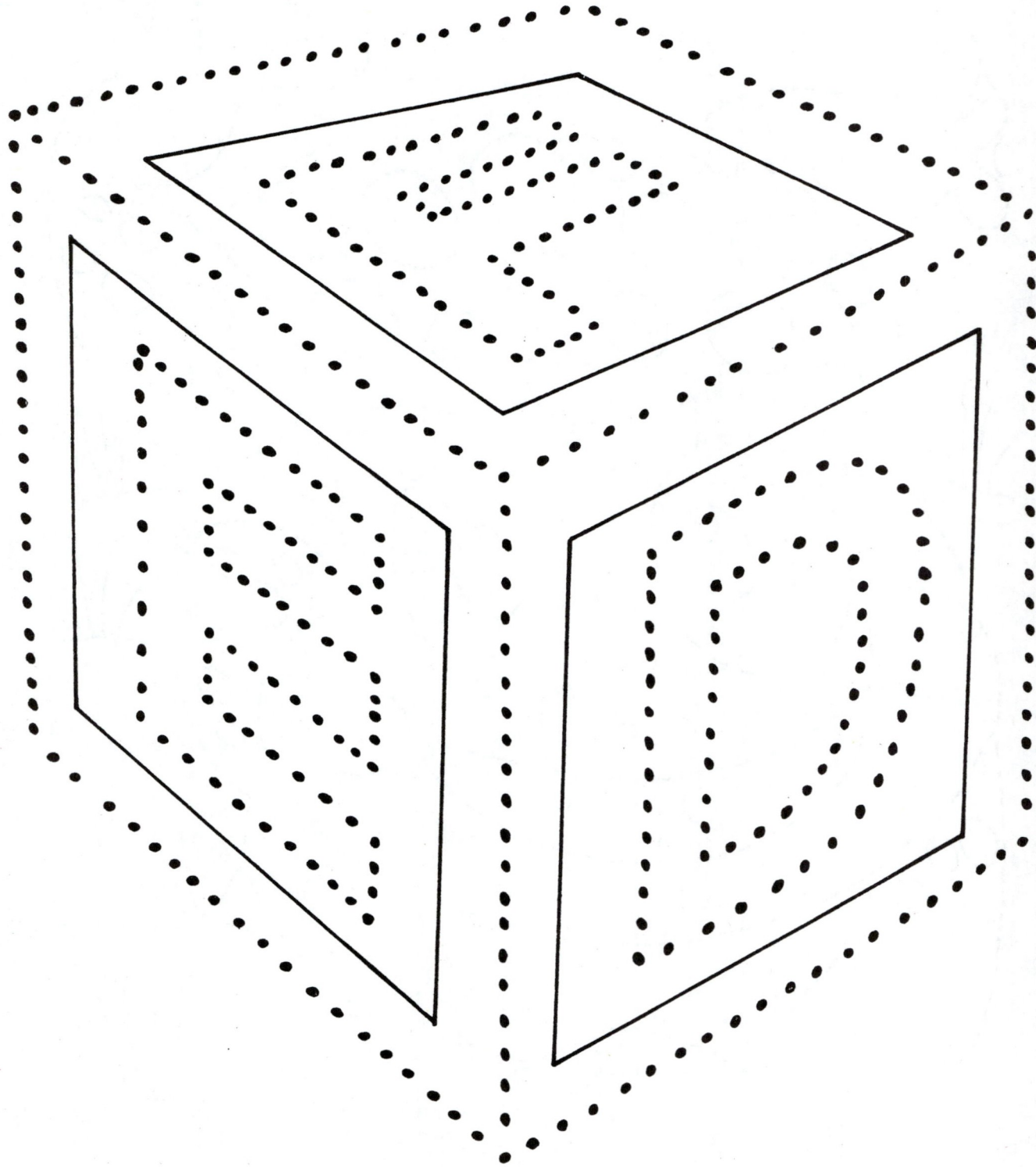

Skills: Fine motor skill development; Eye/hand coordination

Beginning Writing Skills

Trace and color the picture.

Skills: Fine motor skill development; Eye/hand coordination

Beginning Writing Skills

Trace and color the picture.

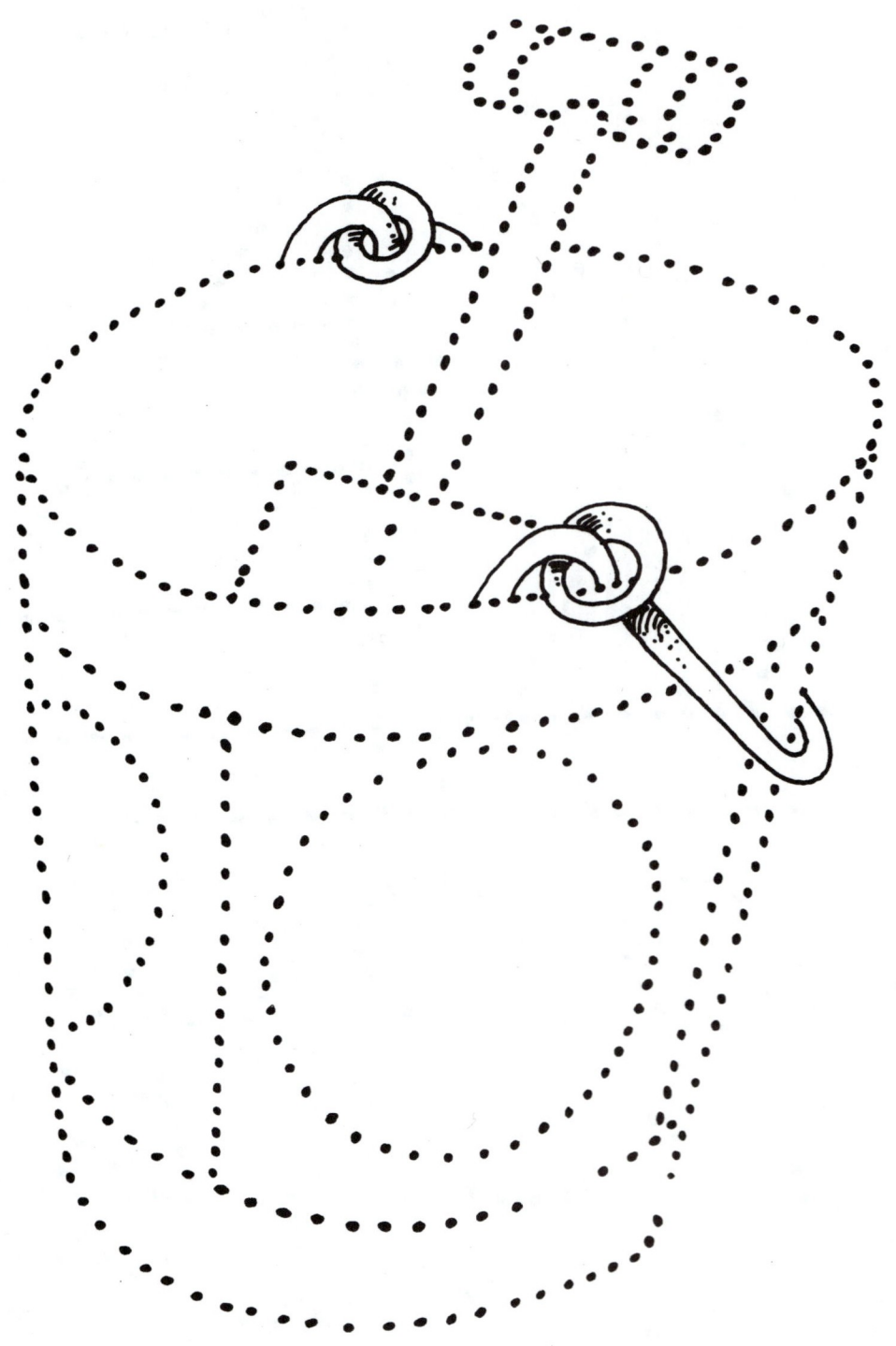

Skills: Fine motor skill development; Eye/hand coordination

Beginning Writing Skills

Trace the broken lines.

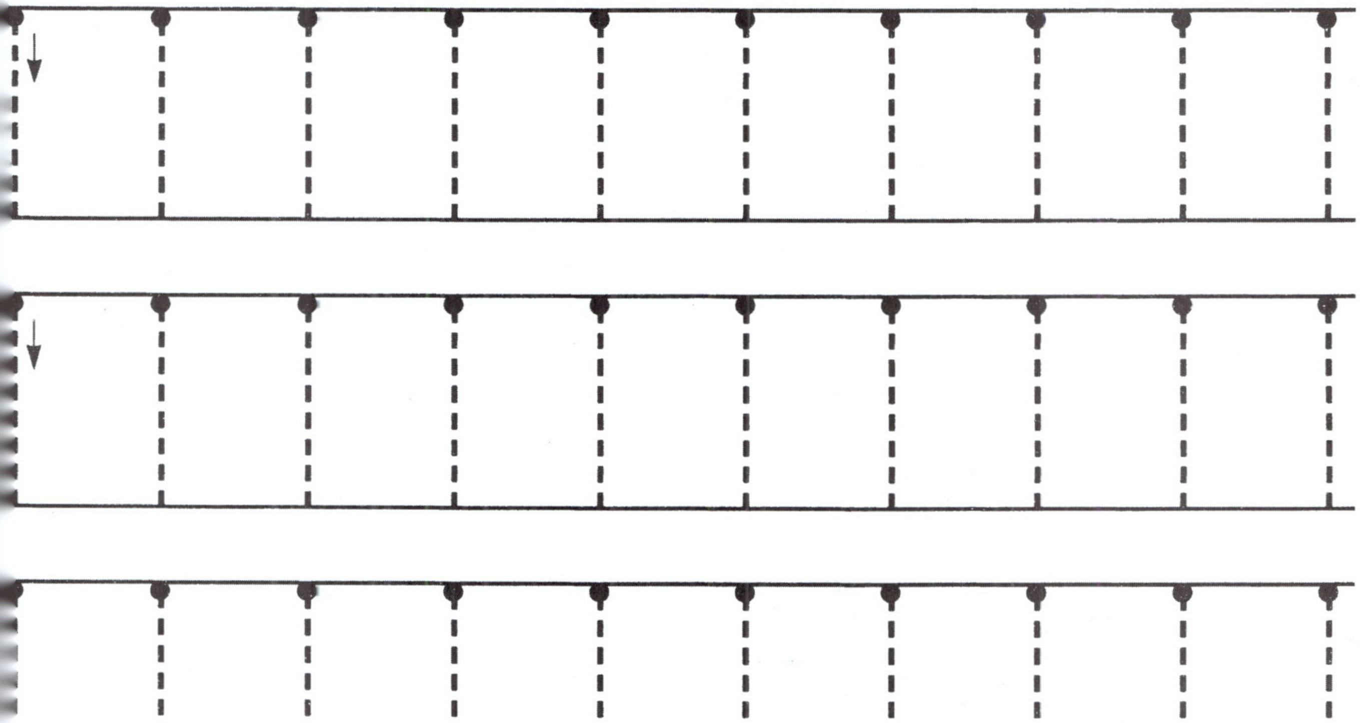

Skills: Fine motor skill development; Eye/hand coordination; Forming vertical lines

Beginning Writing Skills

Trace the broken lines.

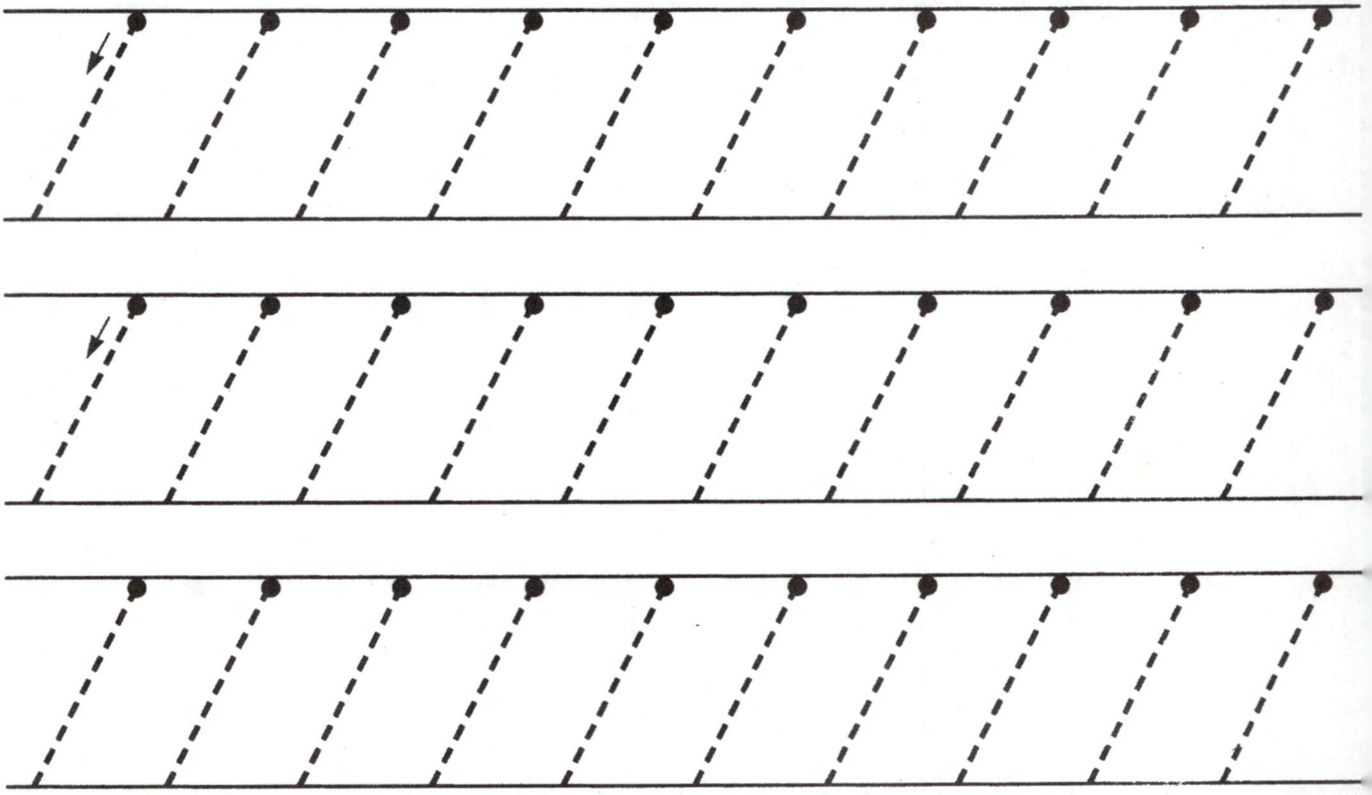

Skills: Fine motor skill development; Eye/hand coordination; Forming diagonal lines

Beginning Writing Skills

Trace the broken lines.

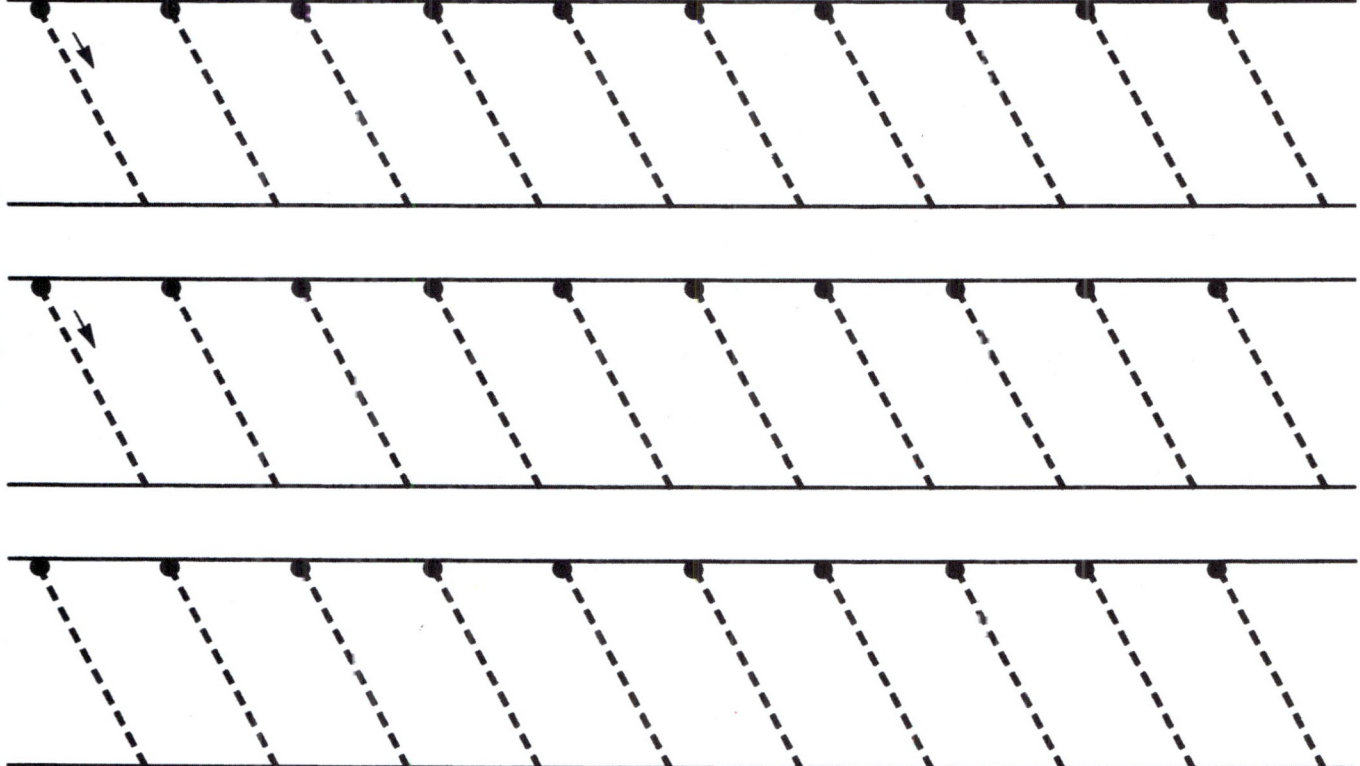

Skills: Fine motor skill development; Eye/hand coordination; Forming diagonal lines

Beginning Writing Skills

Trace the broken lines.

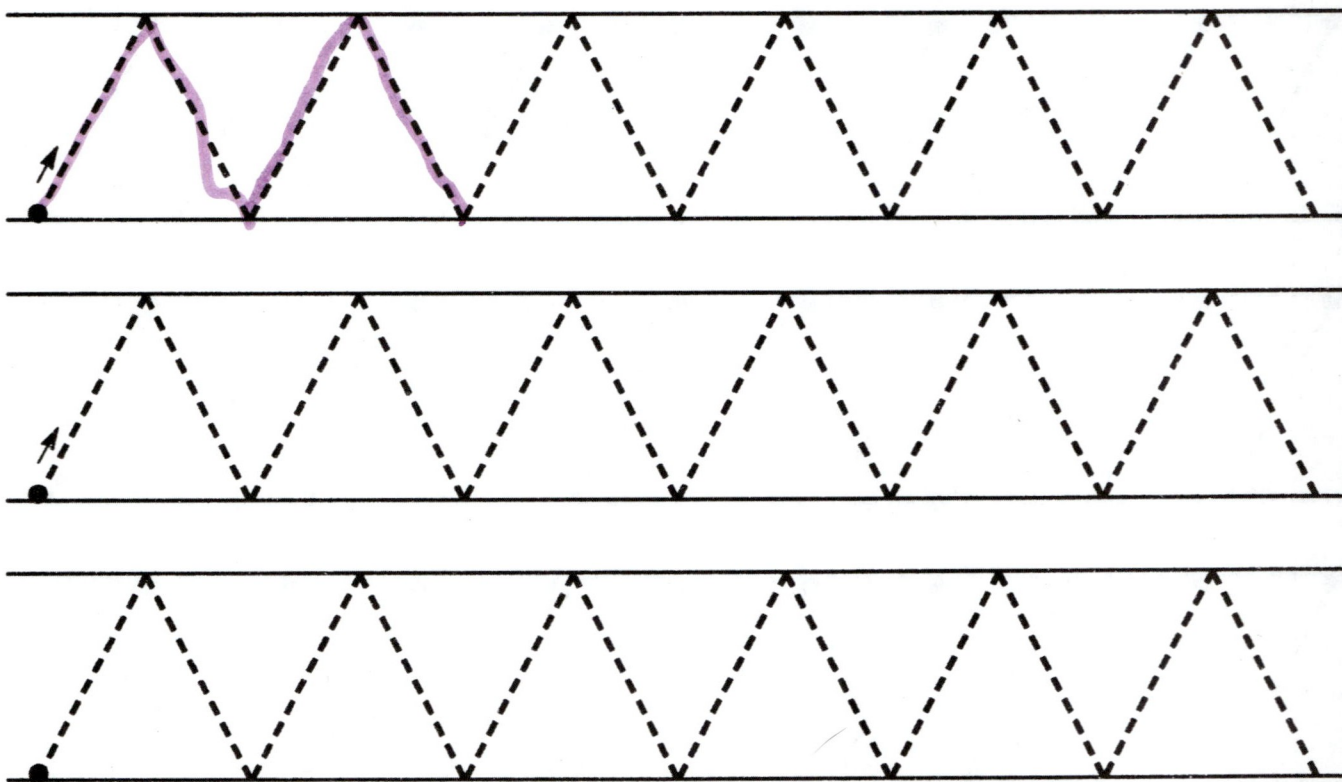

Skills: Fine motor skill development; Eye/hand coordination; Forming diagonal lines

Beginning Writing Skills

Trace the broken lines.

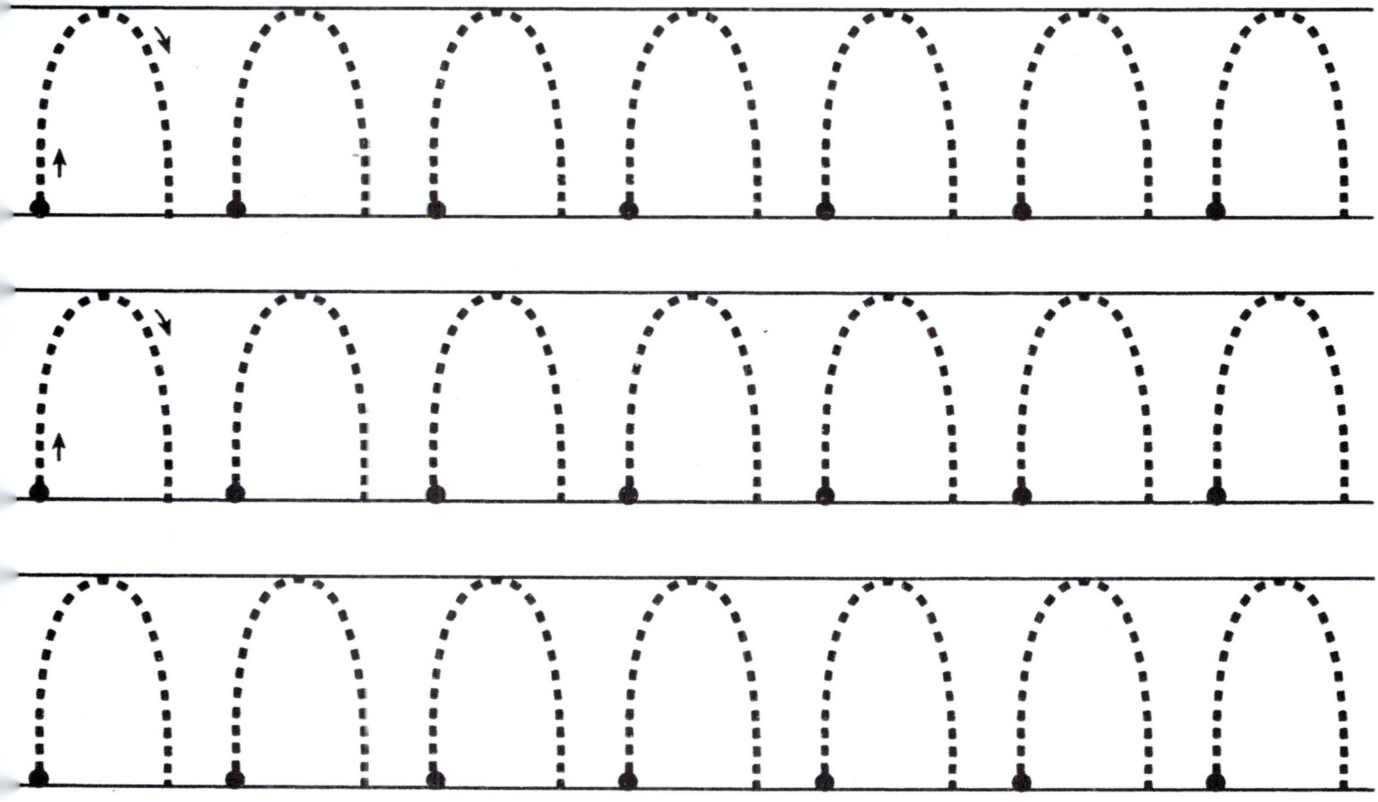

Skills: Fine motor skill development; Eye/hand coordination; Forming open curves

Beginning Writing Skills

Trace the broken lines.

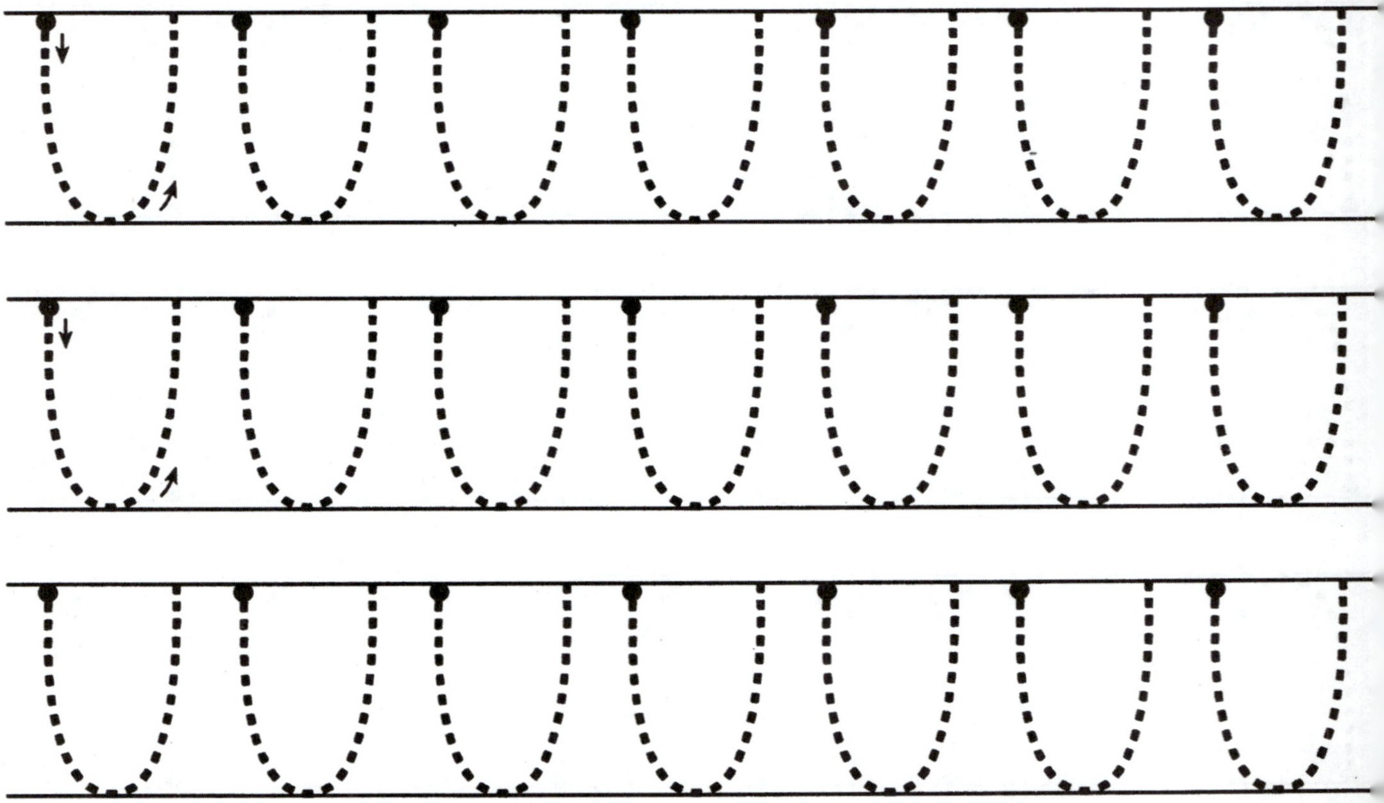

Skills: Fine motor skill development; Eye/hand coordination; Forming open curves

Beginning Writing Skills

Trace the broken lines.

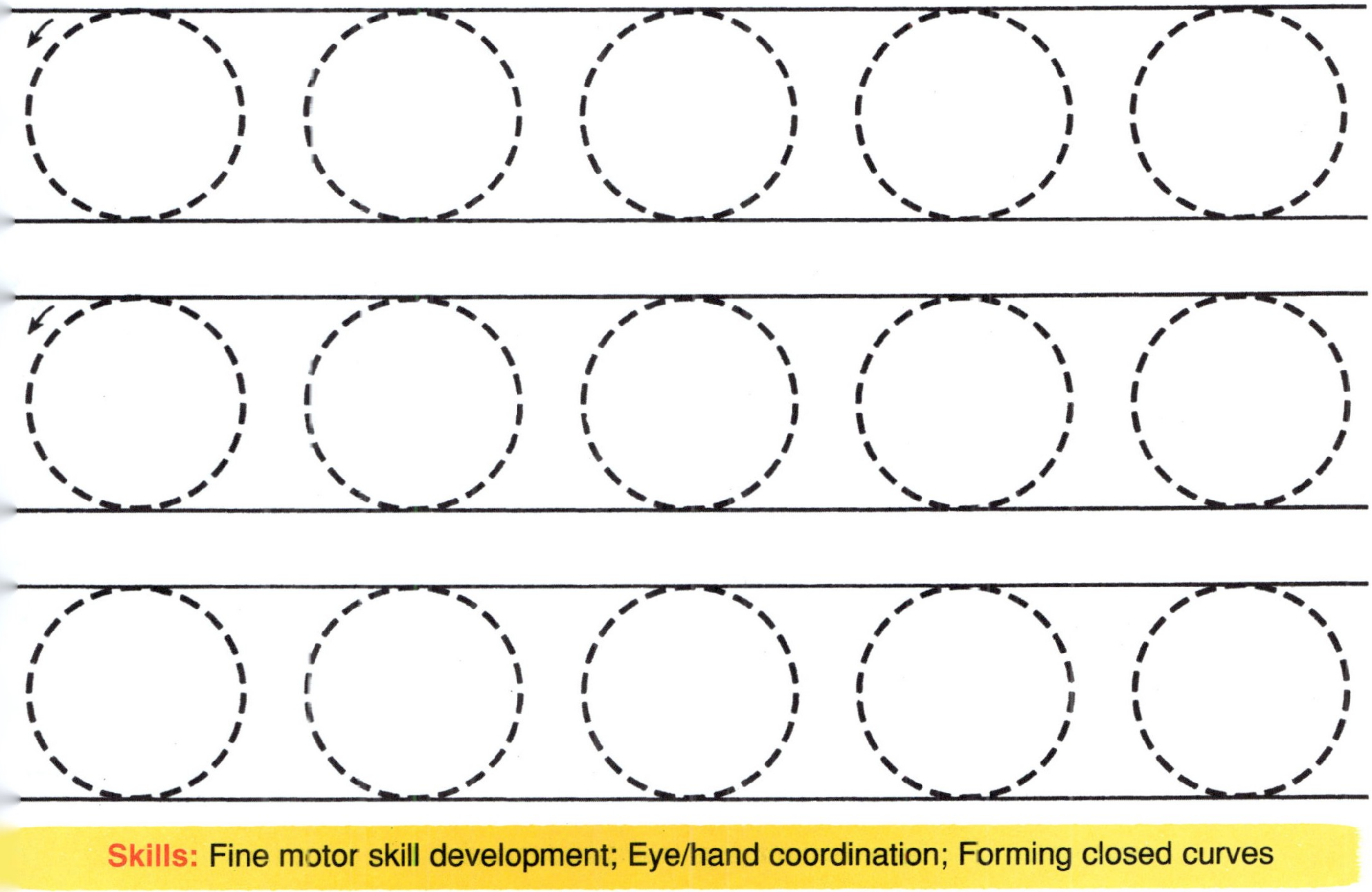

Skills: Fine motor skill development; Eye/hand coordination; Forming closed curves

Beginning Writing Skills

Trace the broken lines.

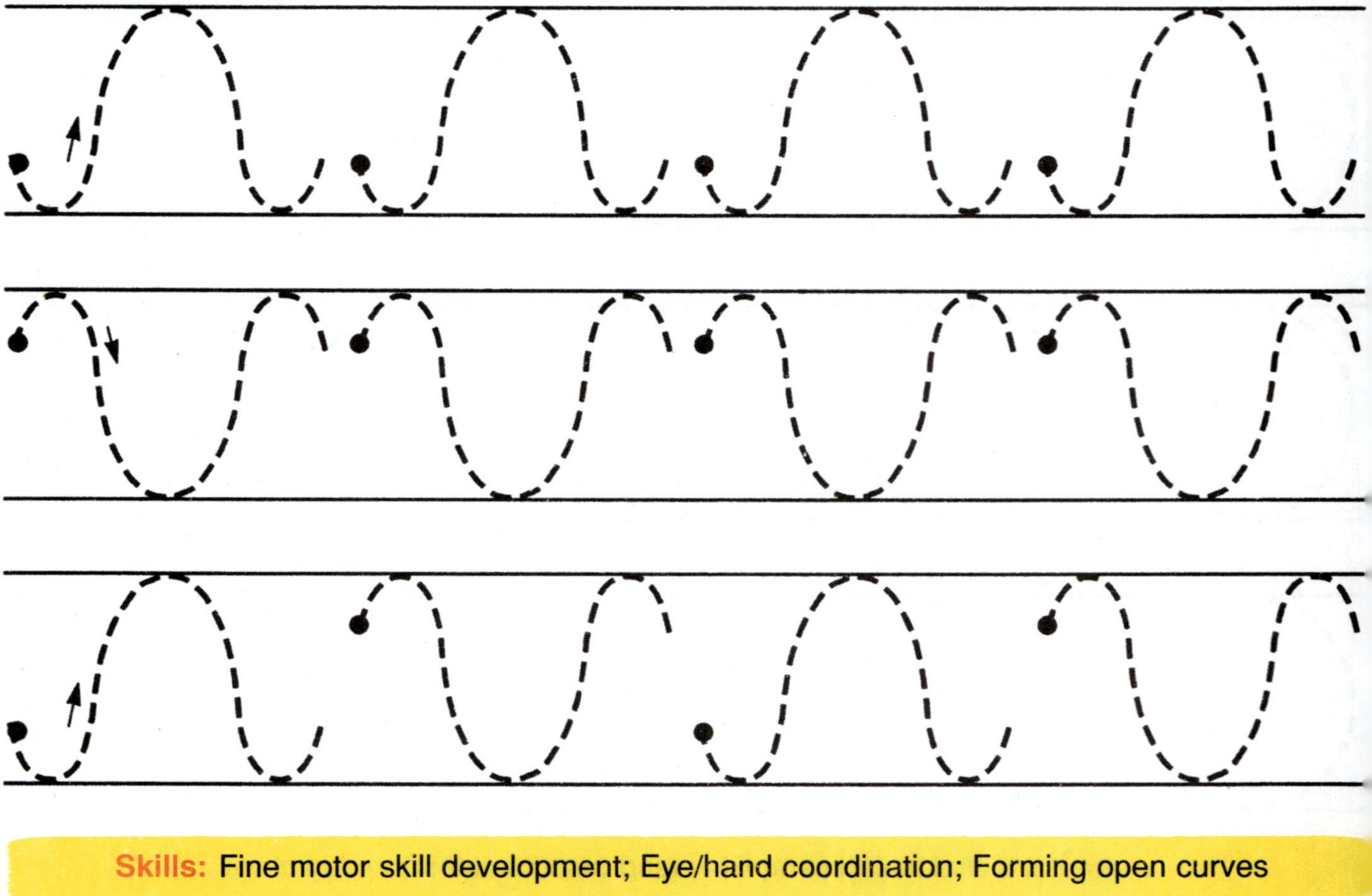

Skills: Fine motor skill development; Eye/hand coordination; Forming open curves

Beginning Writing Skills

Trace the broken lines.

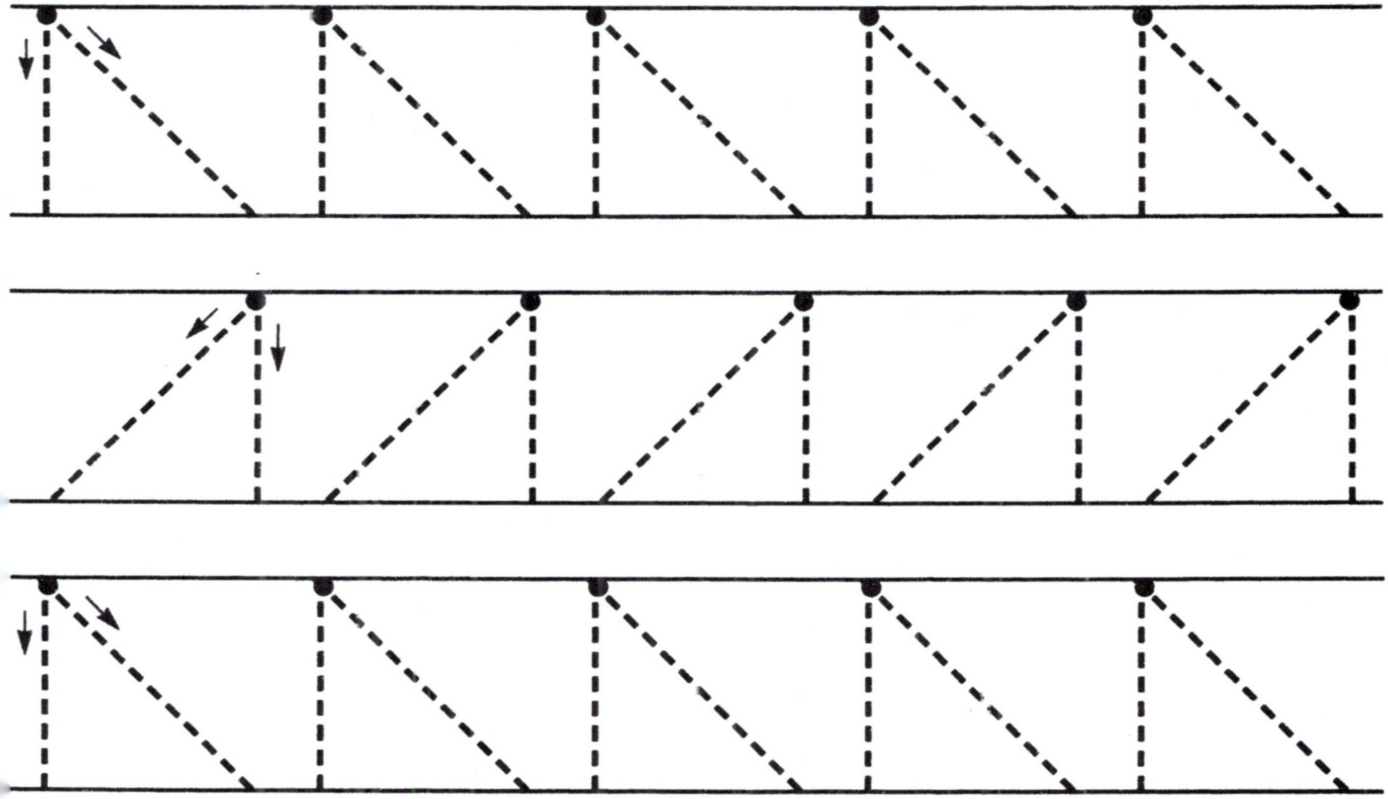

Skills: Fine motor skill development; Eye/hand coordination; Forming vertical and diagonal lines

Beginning Writing Skills

Trace the broken lines.

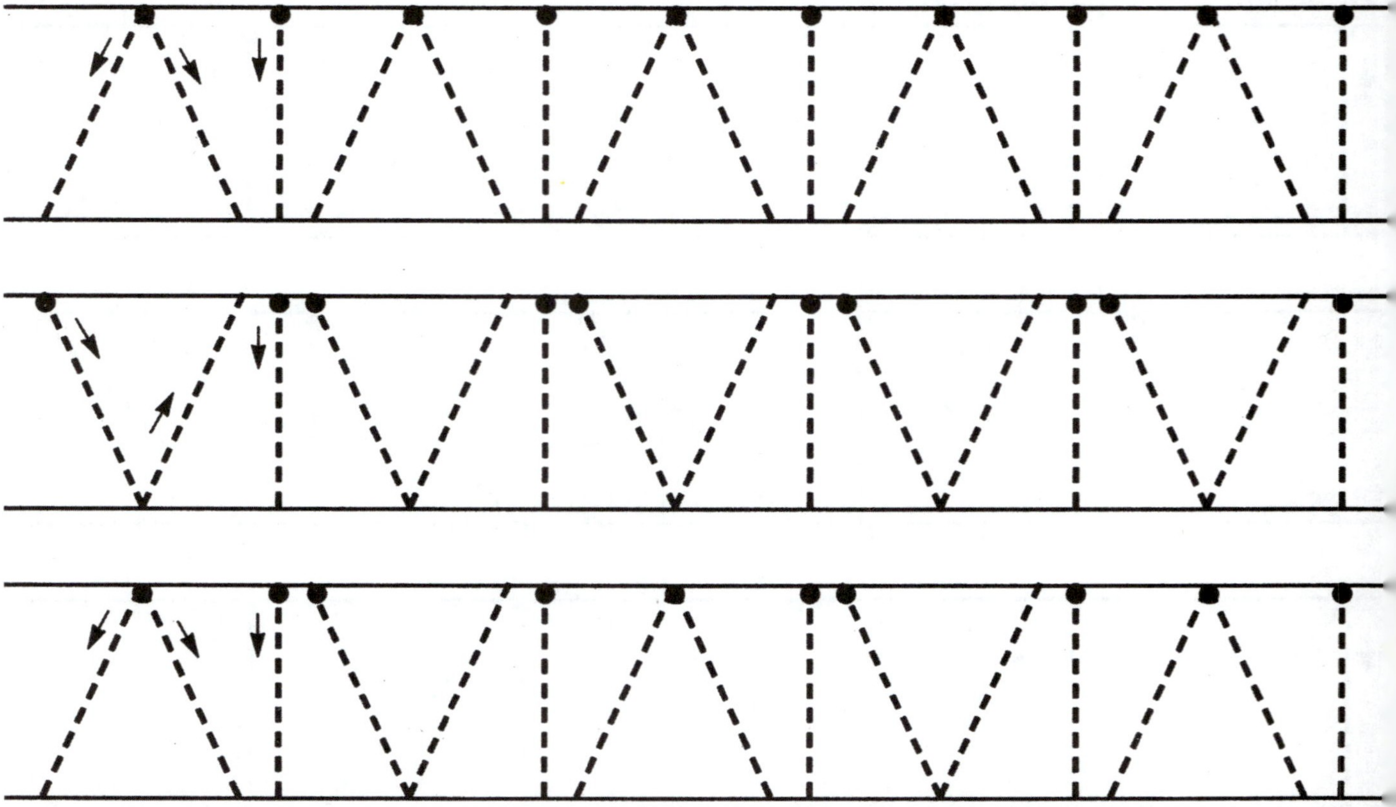

Skills: Fine motor skill development; Eye/hand coordination; Forming vertical and diagonal lines

Beginning Writing Skills

Trace the broken lines.

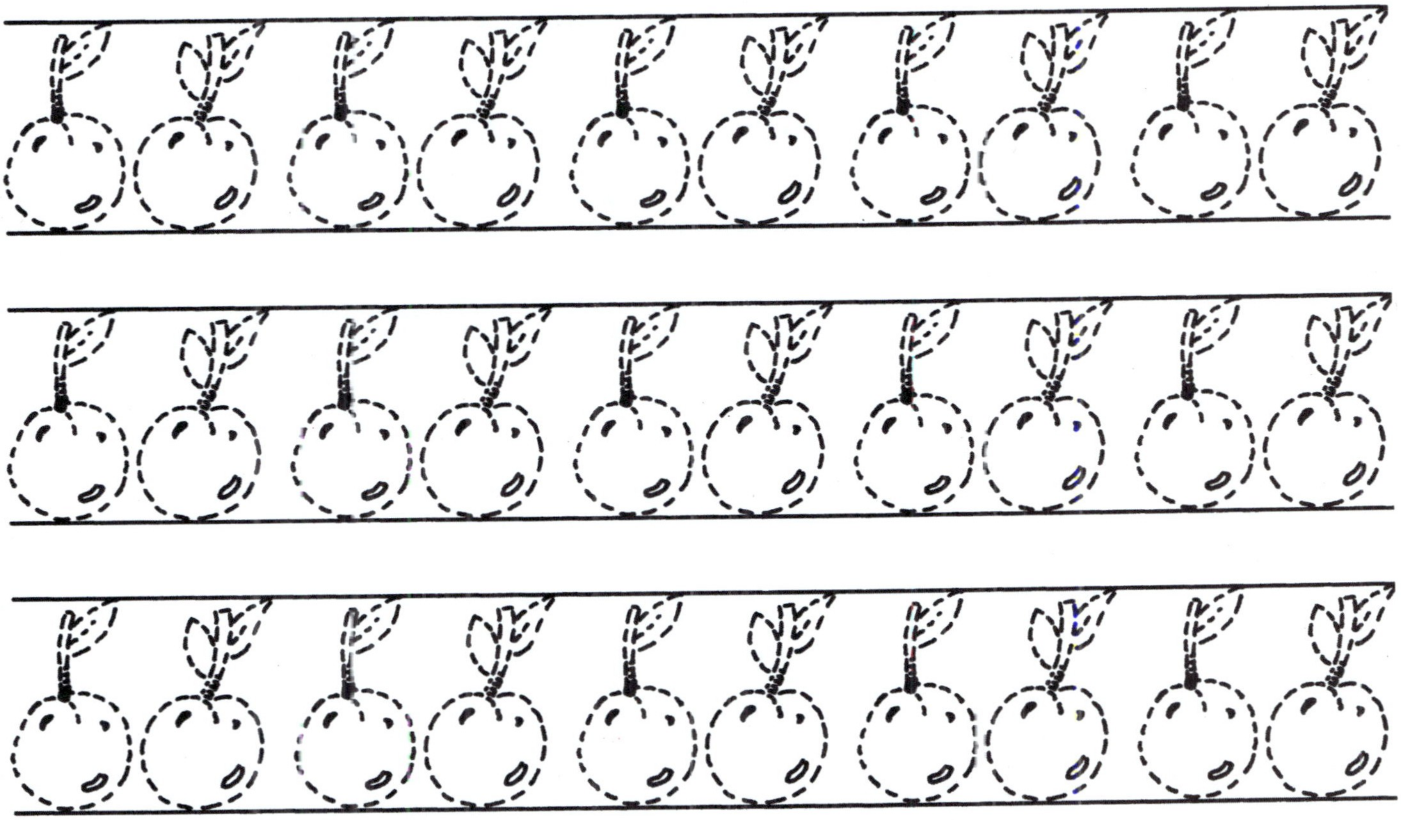

Skills: Fine motor skill development; Eye/hand coordination; Forming closed curves

Beginning Writing Skills

Trace the broken lines.

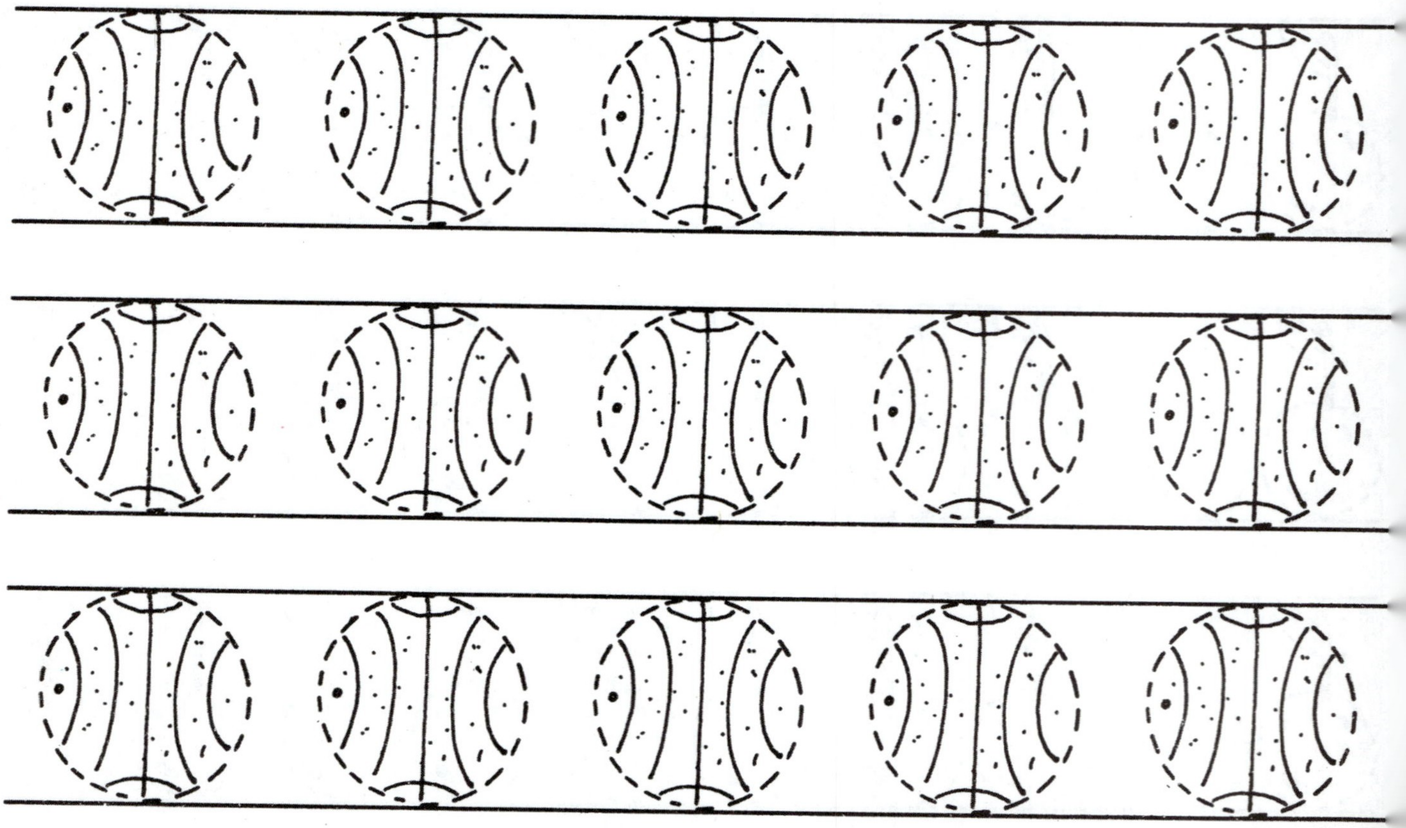

Skills: Fine motor skill development; Eye/hand coordination; Forming closed curves

Beginning Writing Skills

Start at the dots. Trace the broken lines. Finish the page.

Skills: Fine motor skill development; Eye/hand coordination; Forming diagonal lines

Beginning Writing Skills

Start at the dots. Trace the broken lines. Finish the page.

Skills: Fine motor skill development; Eye/hand coordination; Forming horizontal lines

Beginning Writing Skills

It is fun to play outside! Start at the dots. Trace the broken lines.

Skills: Fine motor skill development; Eye/hand coordination; Forming open curves

Beginning Writing Skills

Trace each letter. Point to something in the picture that begins with A.

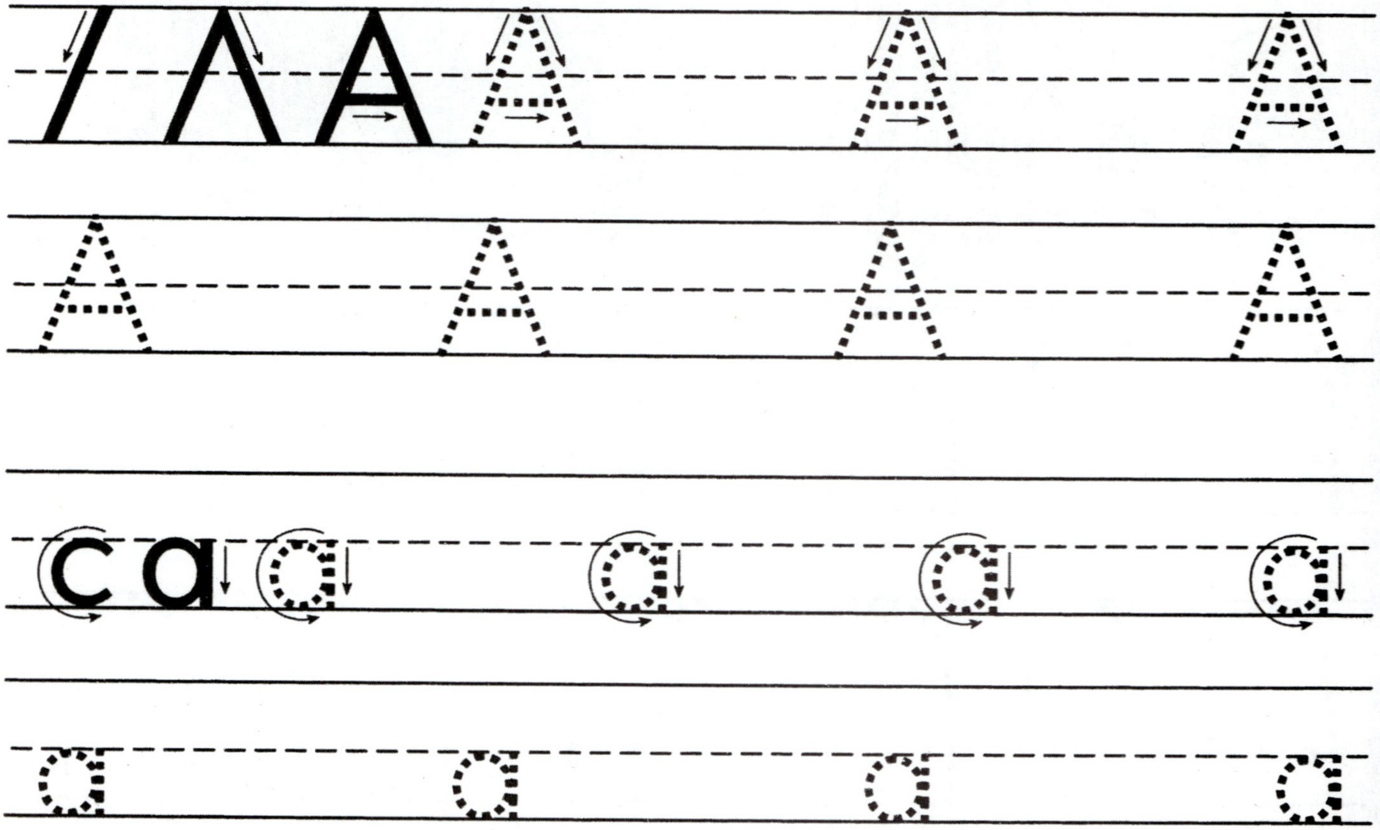

Skills: Fine motor skill development; Eye/hand coordination; Forming upper/lowercase letters

Beginning Writing Skills

Trace each letter. Point to something in the picture that begins with B.

Skills: Fine motor skill development; Eye/hand coordination; Forming upper/lowercase letters

Beginning Writing Skills

Trace each letter. Point to something in the picture that begins with C.

Skills: Fine motor skill development; Eye/hand coordination; Forming upper/lowercase letters

Writing Skills

Trace each letter. Point to something in the picture that begins with D.

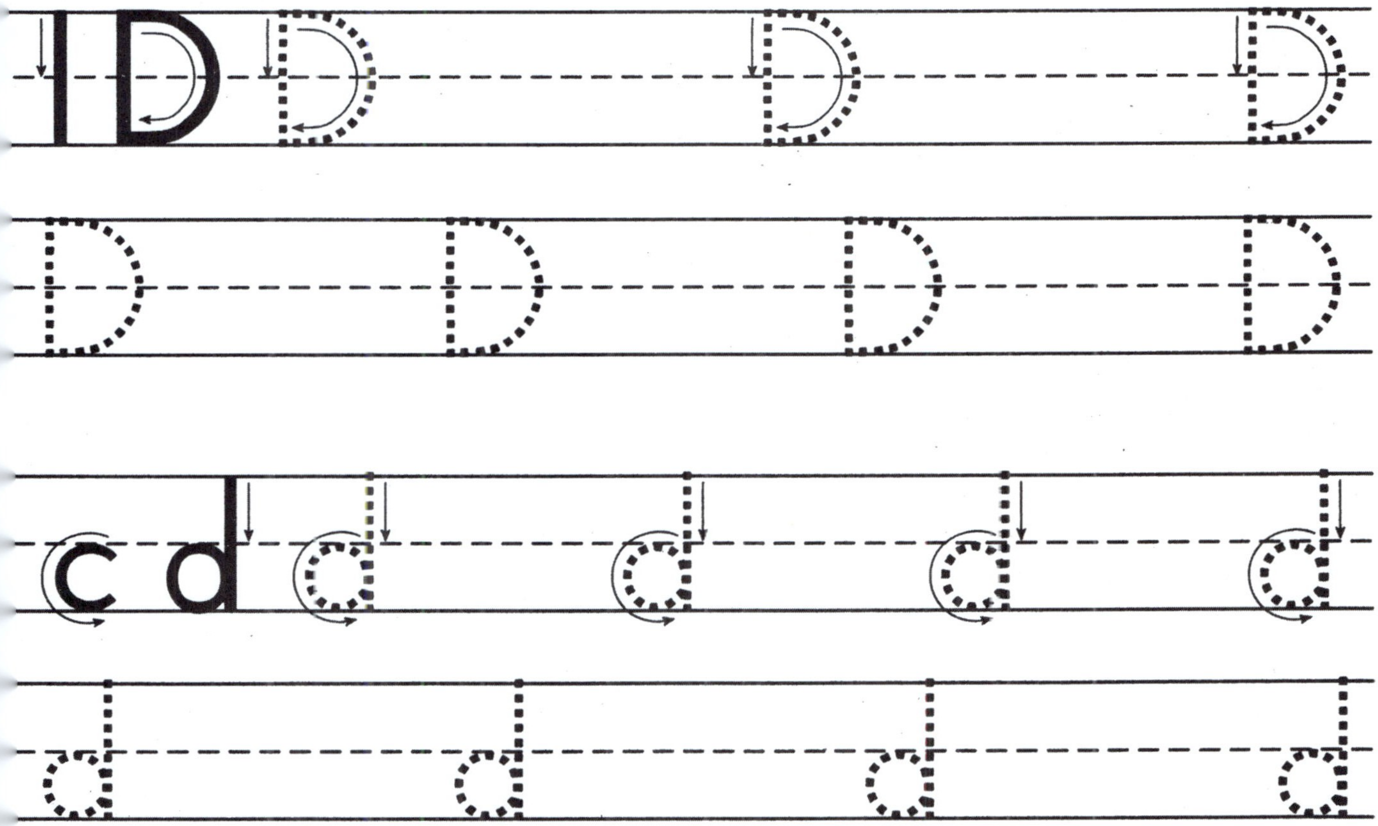

D D D D D

D D D D D

c d d d d d

d d d d

Skills: Fine motor skill development; Eye/hand coordination; Forming upper/lowercase letters

Beginning Writing Skills

Trace each letter. Point to something in the picture that begins with E.

Skills: Fine motor skill development; Eye/hand coordination; Forming upper/lowercase letters

Beginning Writing Skills

Trace each letter. Point to something in the picture that begins with F.

Skills: Fine motor skill development; Eye/hand coordination; Forming upper/lowercase letters

Beginning Writing Skills

Trace each letter. Point to something in the picture that begins with G.

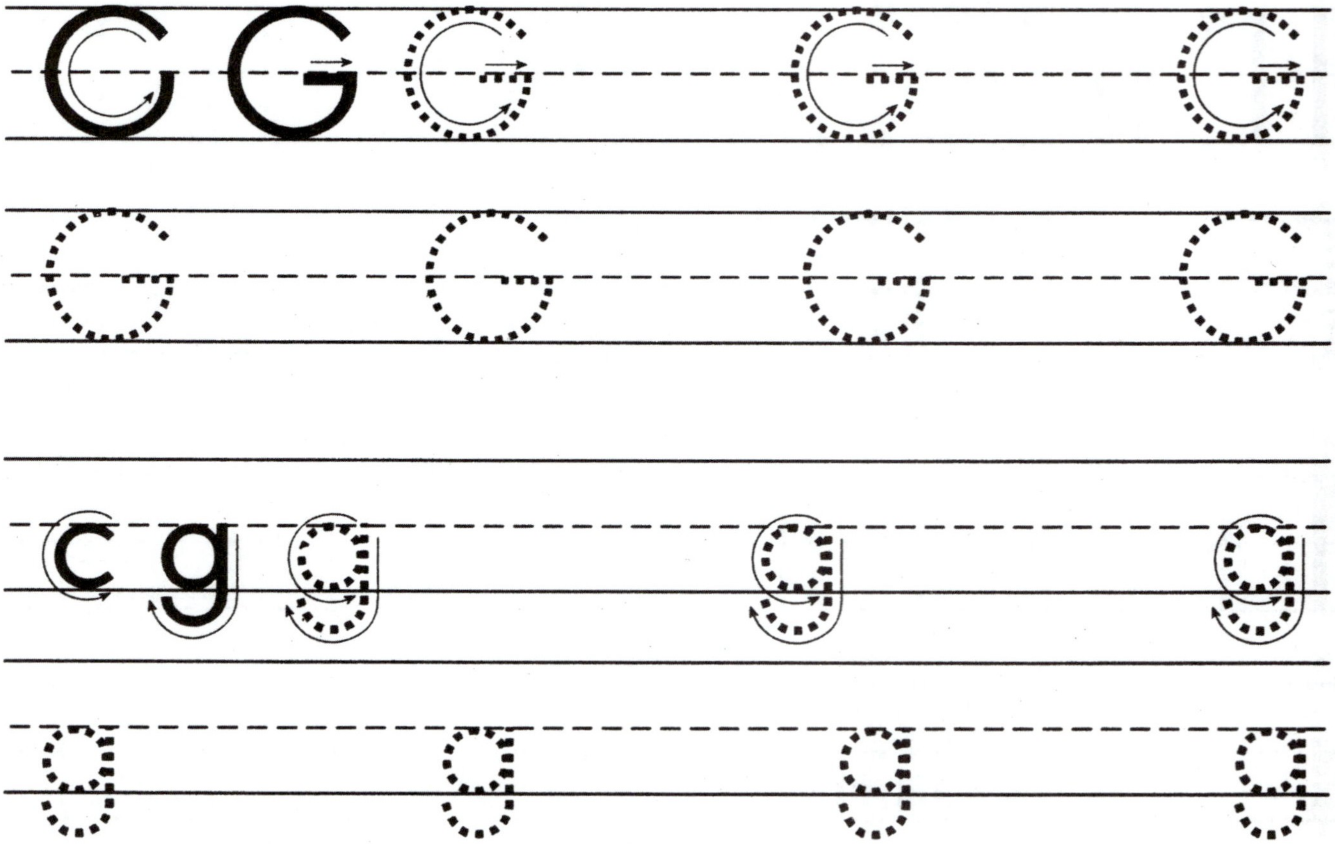

G G G G G

G G G G

C g g g g

g g g g

Skills: Fine motor skill development; Eye/hand coordination; Forming upper/lowercase letters

Beginning Writing Skills

Trace each letter. Point to something in the picture that begins with H.

Skills: Fine motor skill development; Eye/hand coordination; Forming upper/lowercase letters

Beginning Writing Skills

Trace each letter. Point to something in the picture that begins with I.

Skills: Fine motor skill development; Eye/hand coordination; Forming upper/lowercase letters

Beginning Writing Skills

Trace each letter. Point to something in the picture that begins with J.

Skills: Fine motor skill development; Eye/hand coordination; Forming upper/lowercase letters

Beginning Writing Skills

Trace each letter. Point to something in the picture that begins with K.

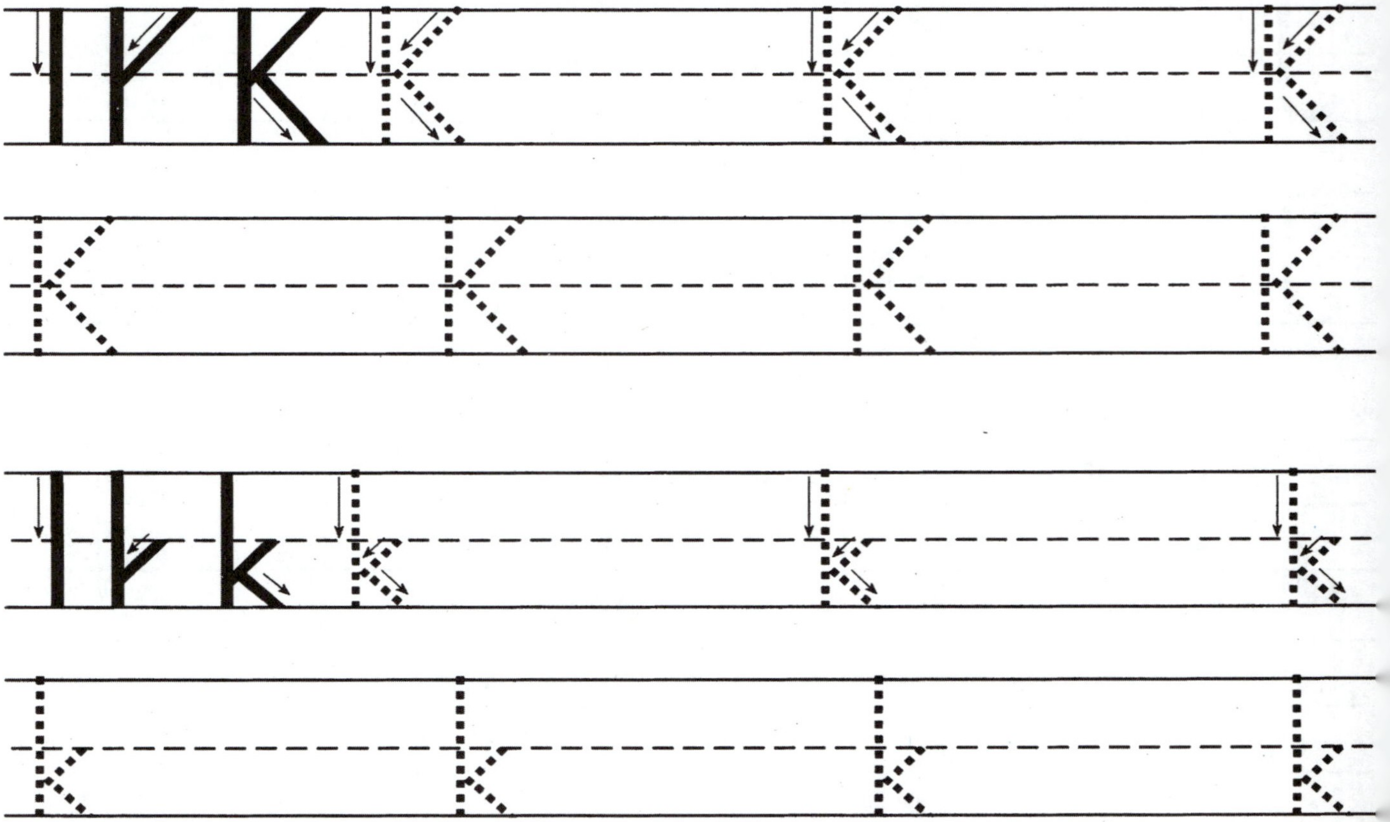

Skills: Fine motor skill development; Eye/hand coordination; Forming upper/lowercase letters

Beginning Writing Skills

Trace each letter. Point to something in the picture that begins with L.

Skills: Fine motor skill development; Eye/hand coordination; Forming upper/lowercase letters

Beginning Writing Skills

Trace each letter. Point to something in the picture that begins with M.

Beginning Writing Skills

Trace each letter. Point to something in the picture that begins with N.

Skills: Fine motor skill development; Eye/hand coordination; Forming upper/lowercase letters

Beginning Writing Skills

Trace each letter. Point to something in the picture that begins with O.

Skills: Fine motor skill development; Eye/hand coordination; Forming upper/lowercase letters

Beginning Writing Skills

Trace each letter. Point to something in the picture that begins with P.

P P P P

P P P P

p p p p p

p p p p

Skills: Fine motor skill development; Eye/hand coordination; Forming upper/lowercase letters

Beginning Writing Skills

Trace each letter. Point to something in the picture that begins with Q.

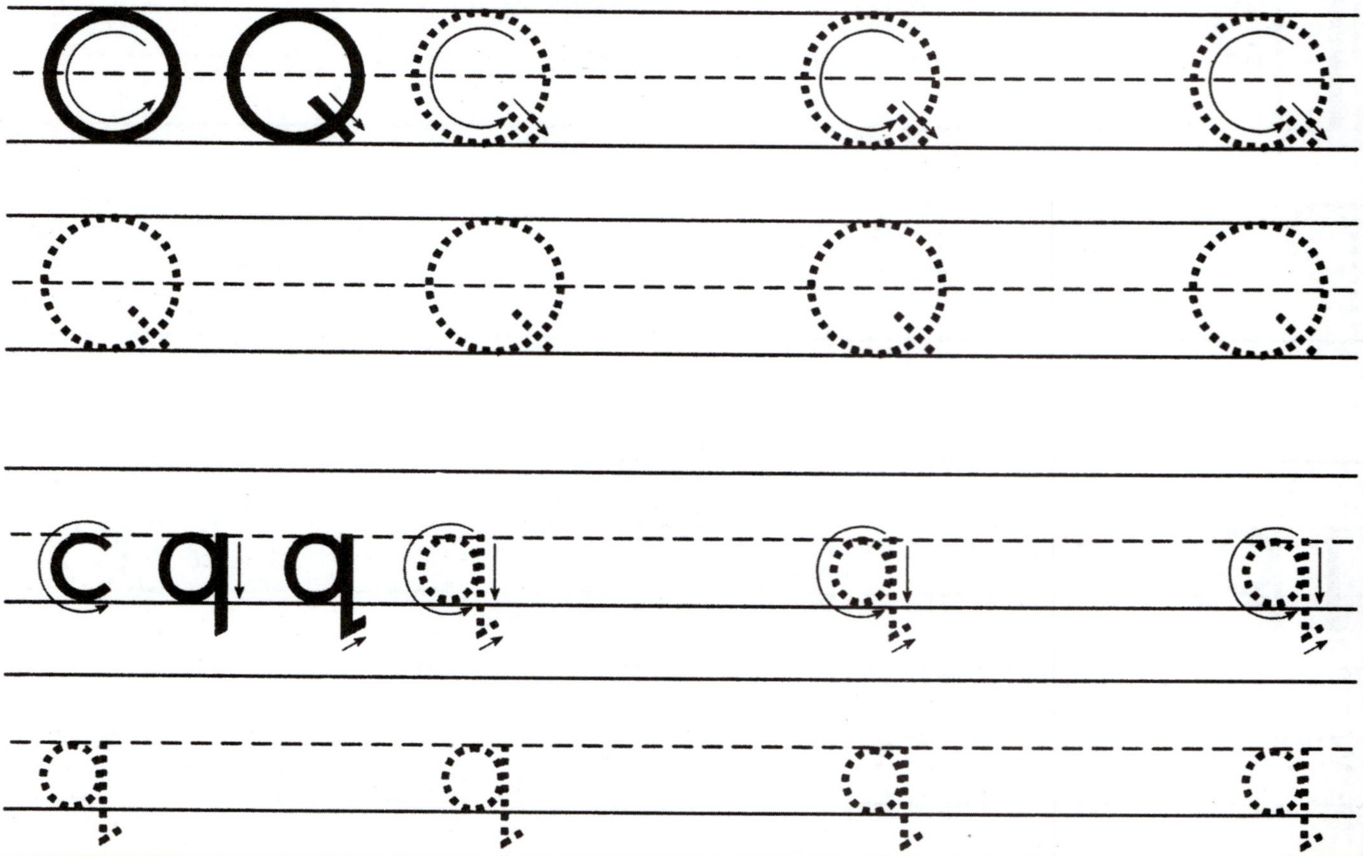

Skills: Fine motor skill development; Eye/hand coordination; Forming upper/lowercase letters

Beginning Writing Skills

Trace each letter. Point to something in the picture that begins with R.

PR R R R

R R R R

r r r r r

r r r r

Skills: Fine motor skill development; Eye/hand coordination; Forming upper/lowercase letters

Beginning Writing Skills

Trace each letter. Point to something in the picture that begins with S.

S S S S

S S S S

s s s s

s s s s

Skills: Fine motor skill development; Eye/hand coordination; Forming upper/lowercase letters

Beginning Writing Skills

Trace each letter. Point to something in the picture that begins with T.

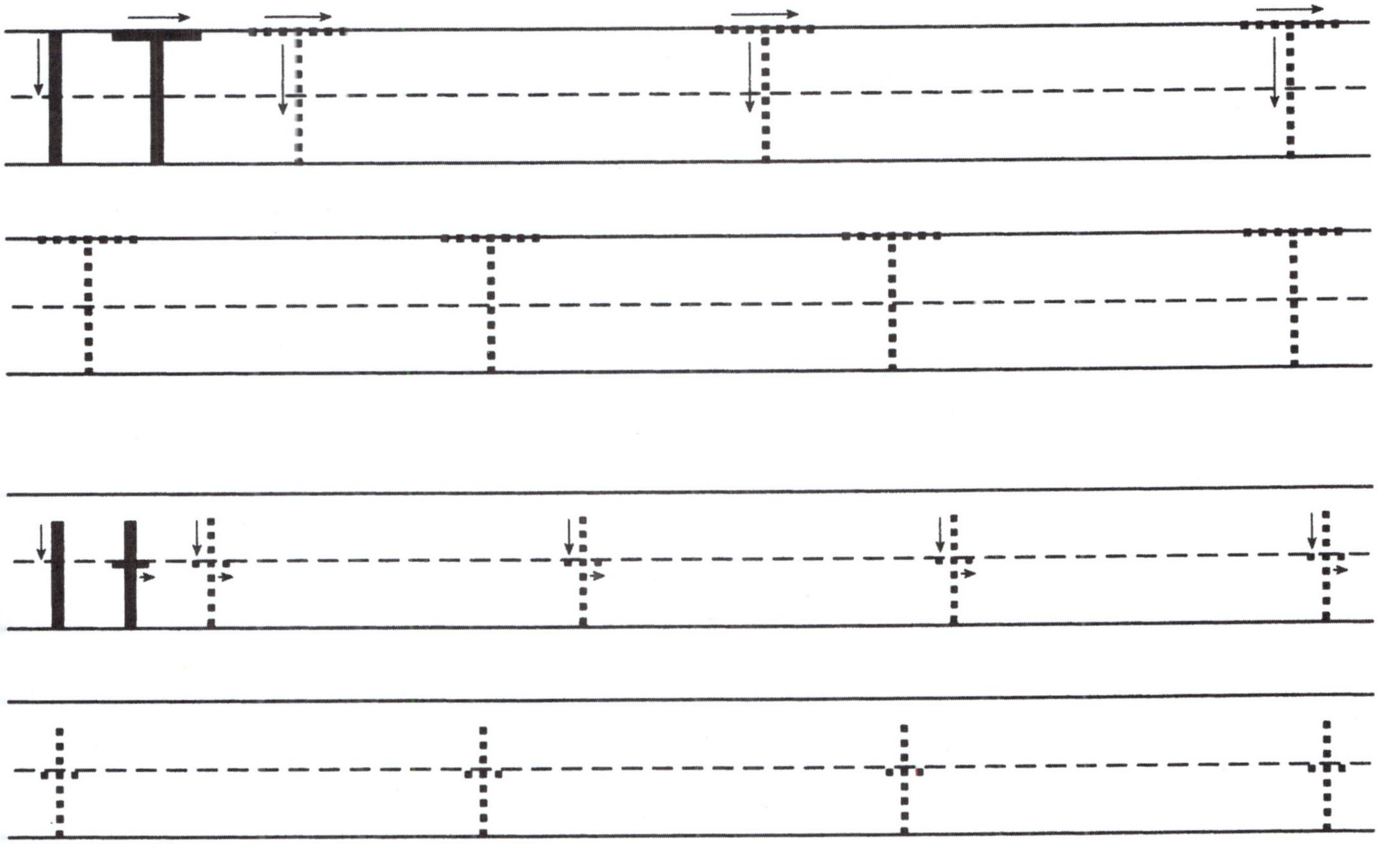

Skills: Fine motor skill development; Eye/hand coordination; Forming upper/lowercase letters

Beginning Writing Skills

Trace each letter. Point to something in the picture that begins with U.

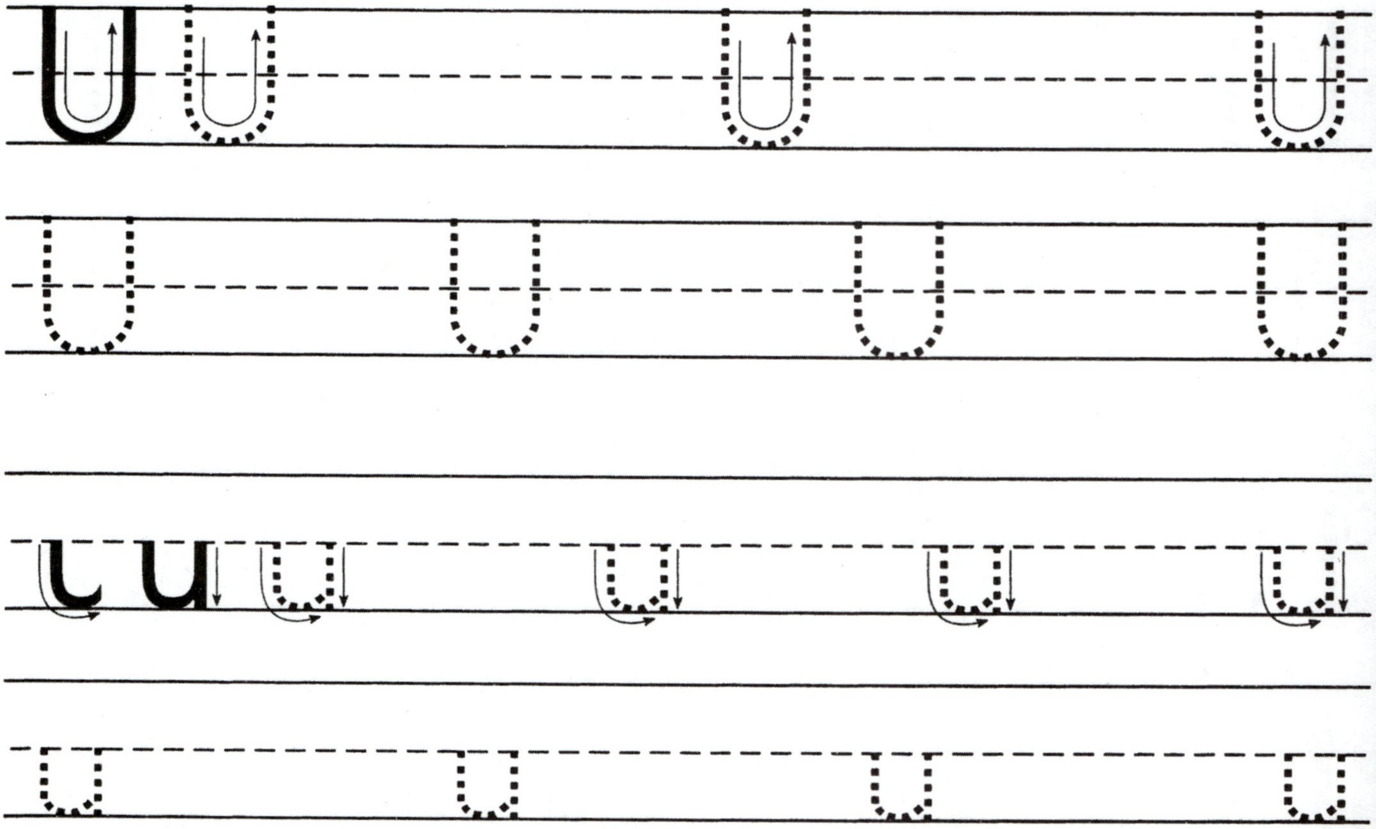

Skills: Fine motor skill development; Eye/hand coordination; Forming upper/lowercase letters

Beginning Writing Skills

Trace each letter. Point to something in the picture that begins with V.

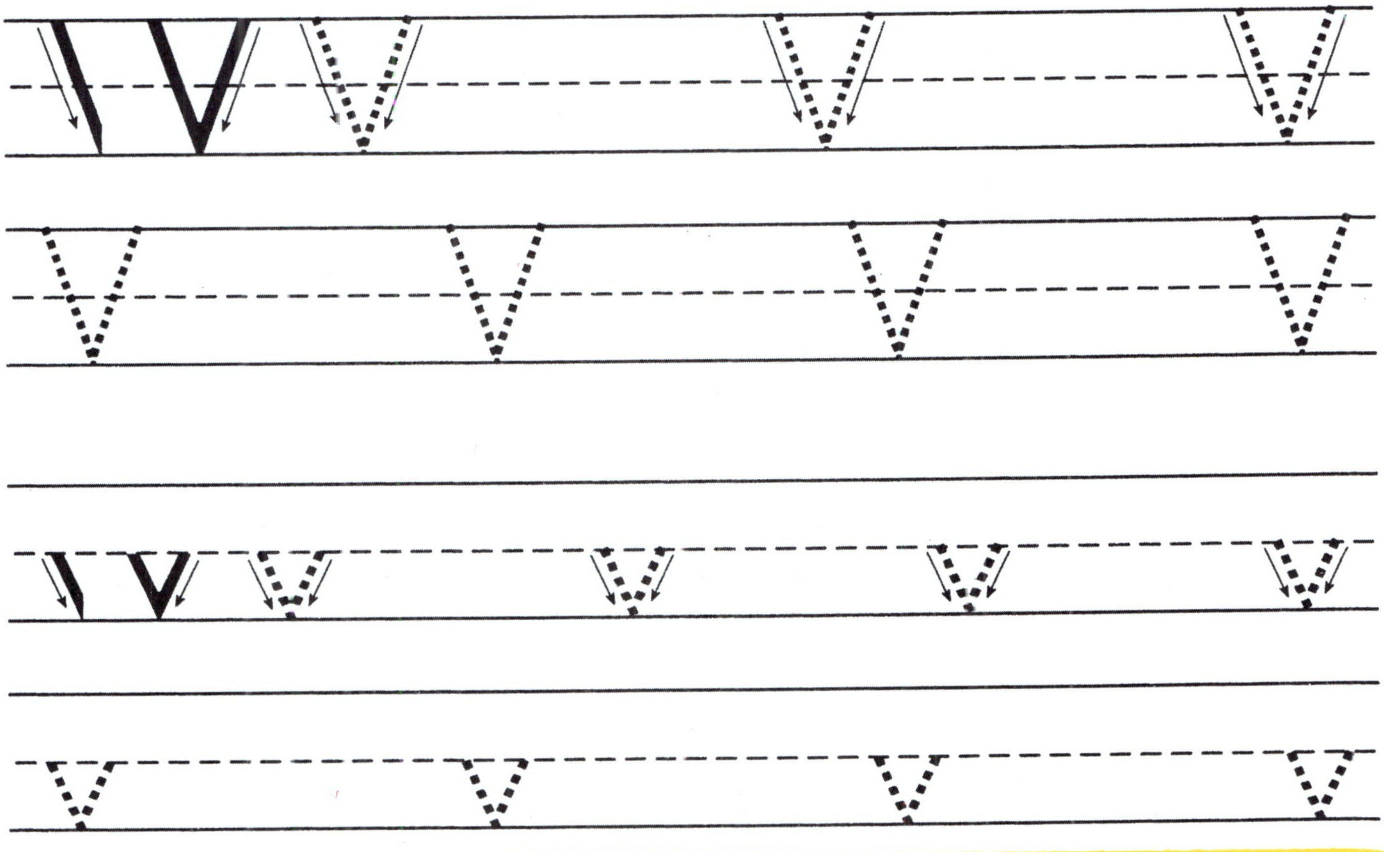

Skills: Fine motor skill development; Eye/hand coordination; Forming upper/lowercase letters

Beginning Writing Skills

Trace each letter. Point to something in the picture that begins with W.

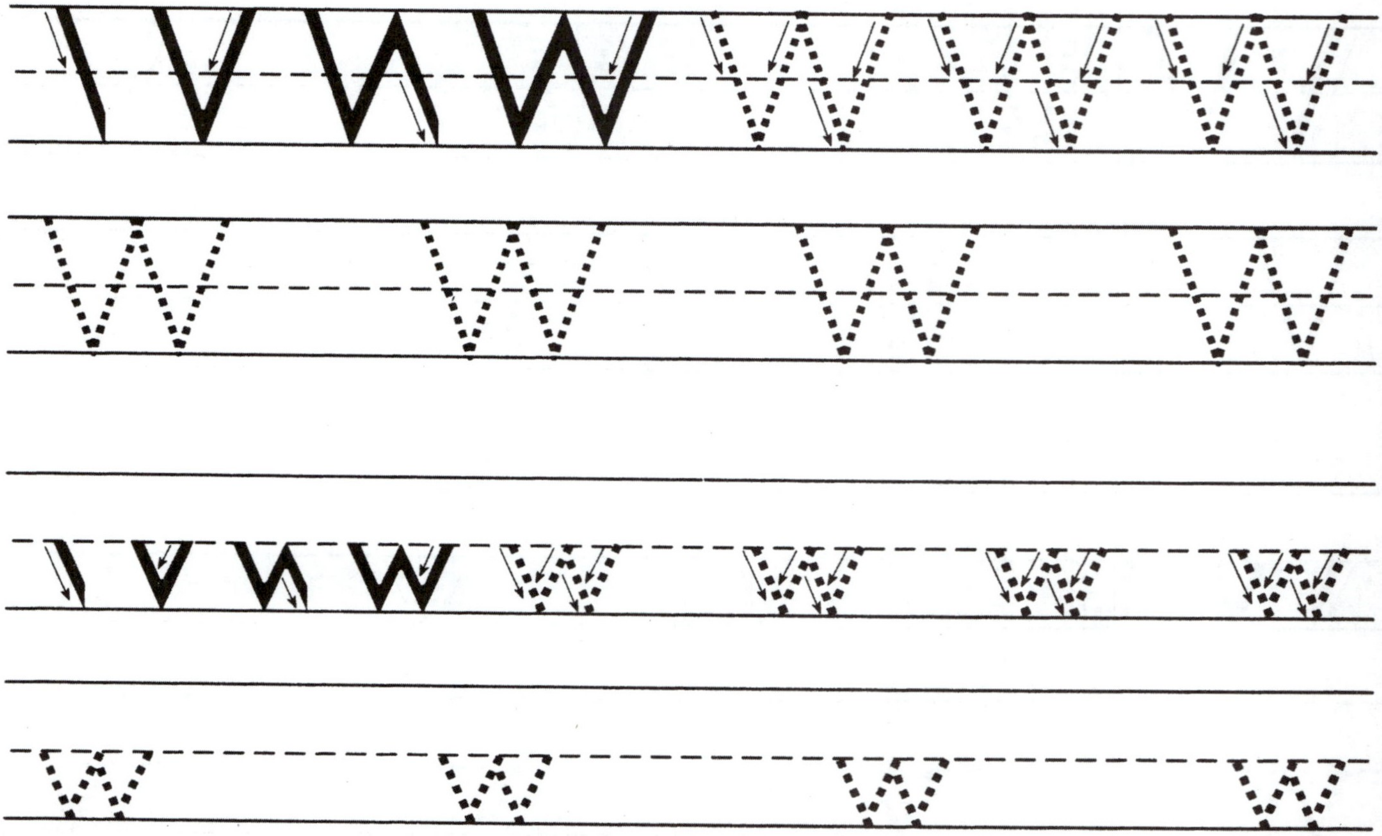

Skills: Fine motor skill development; Eye/hand coordination; Forming upper/lowercase letters

Beginning Writing Skills

Trace each letter. Point to something in the picture that begins with X.

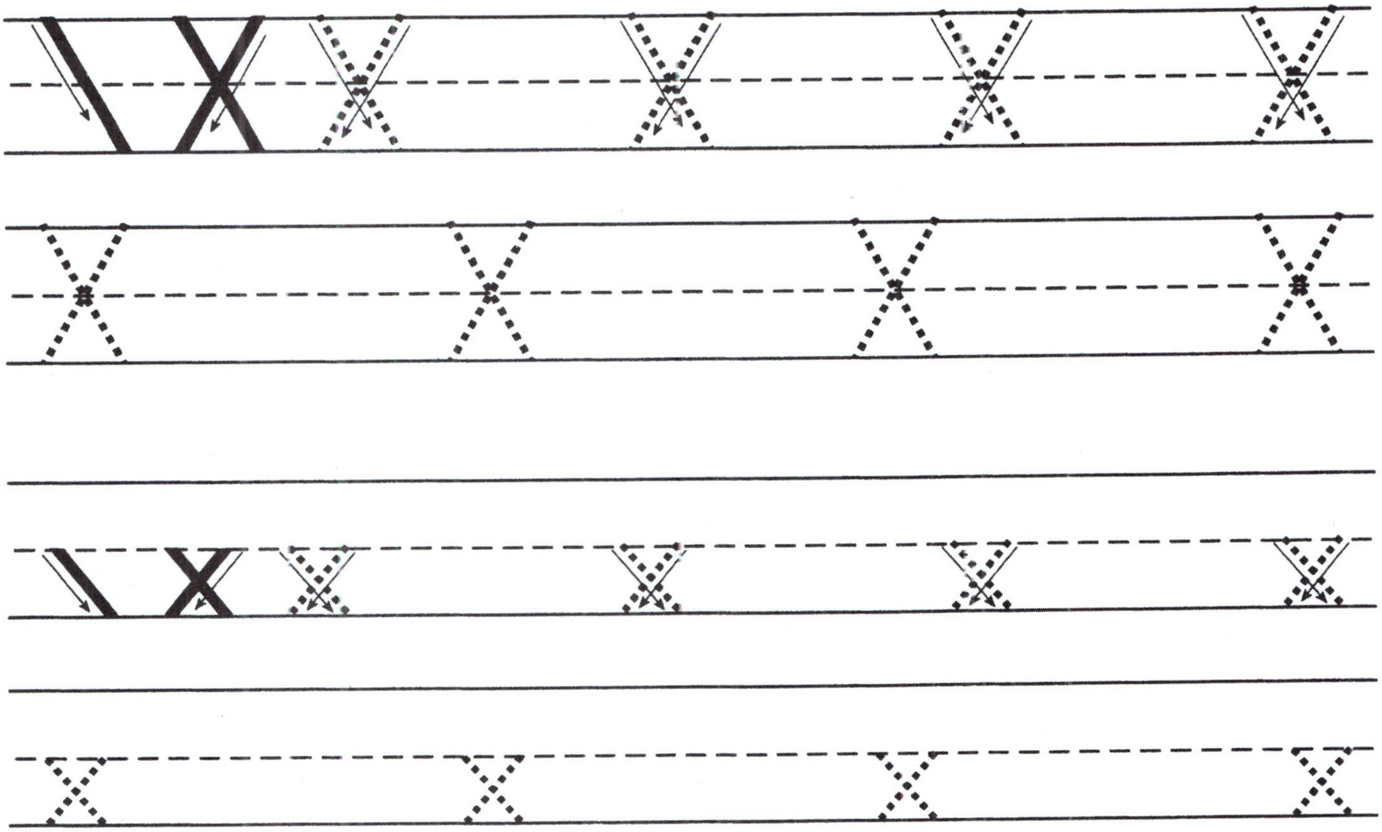

Beginning Writing Skills

Trace each letter. Point to something in the picture that begins with Y.

Skills: Fine motor skill development; Eye/hand coordination; Forming upper/lowercase letters

Beginning Writing Skills

Trace each letter. Point to something in the picture that begins with Z.

Skills: Fine motor skill development; Eye/hand coordination; Forming upper/lowercase letters

A a

Follow the direction of each arrow. Practice writing and saying each letter. Then point to something in the picture that begins with the letter A.

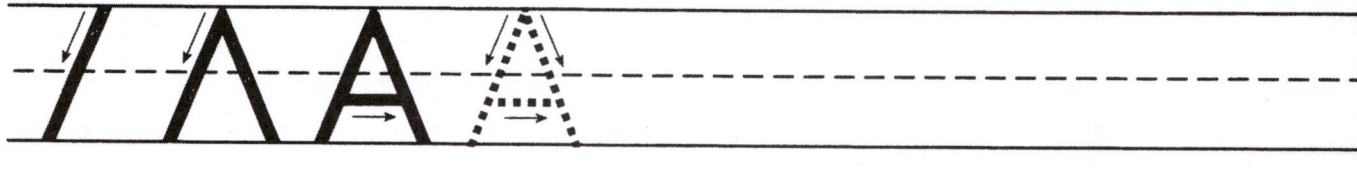

Skills: Forming upper/lowercase "a"; Writing left to right; Saying letter sounds

Beginning Writing Skills

Bb

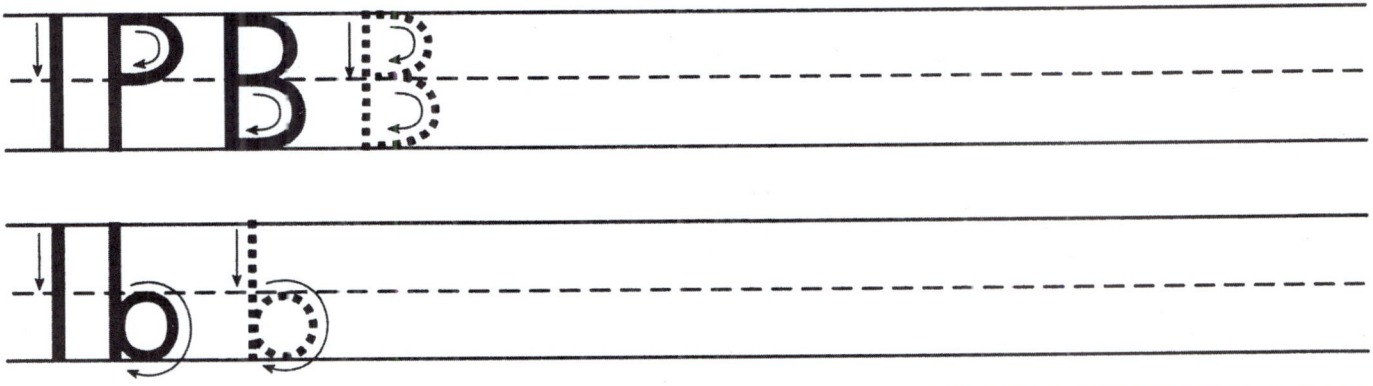

Follow the direction of each arrow. Practice writing and saying each letter. Then point to something in the picture that begins with the letter B.

Skills: Forming upper/lowercase "b"; Writing left to right; Saying letter sounds

Beginning Writing Skills

C c

Follow the direction of each arrow. Practice writing and saying each letter. Then point to something in the picture that begins with the letter C.

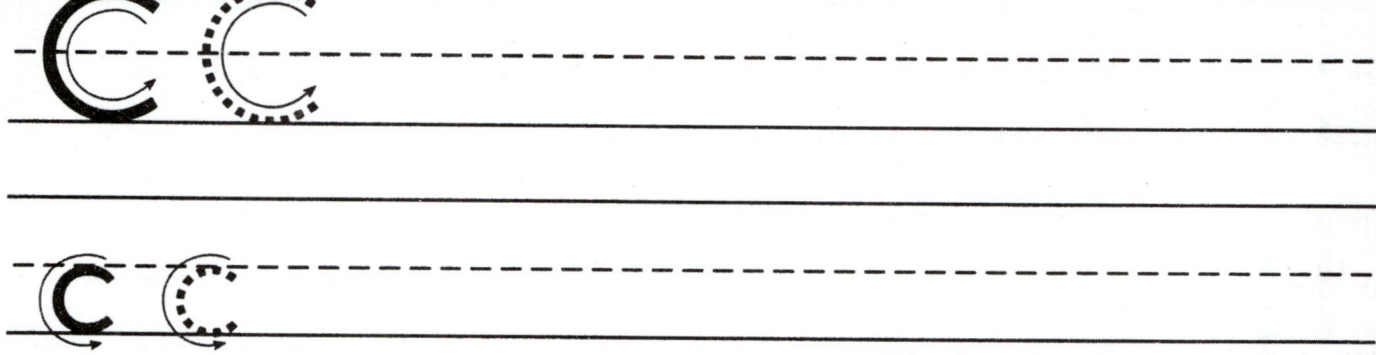

Skills: Forming upper/lowercase "c"; Writing left to right; Saying letter sounds

Beginning Writing Skills

D d

Follow the direction of each arrow. Practice writing and saying each letter. Then point to something in the picture that begins with the letter D.

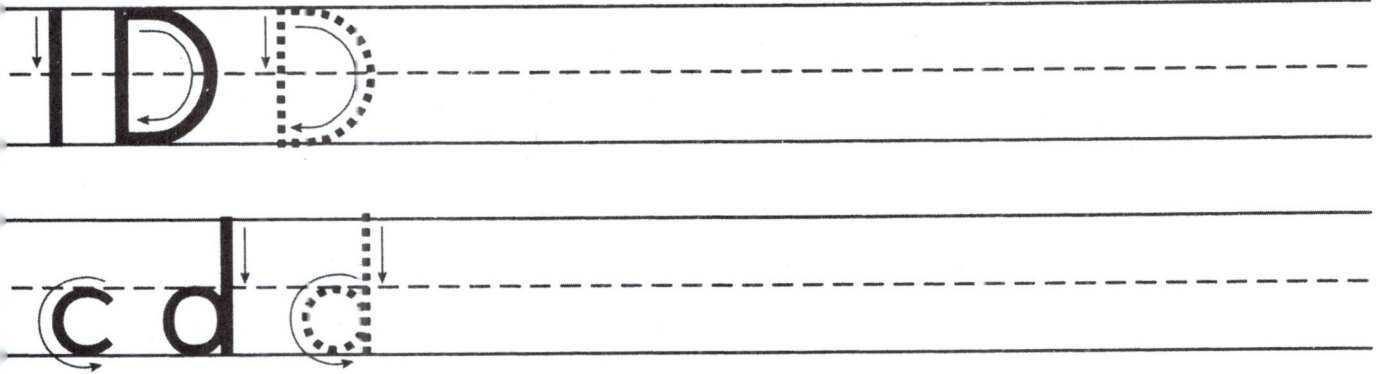

Skills: Forming upper/lowercase "d"; Writing left to right; Saying letter sounds

Beginning Writing Skills

Ee

Follow the direction of each arrow. Practice writing and saying each letter. Then point to something in the picture that begins with the letter E.

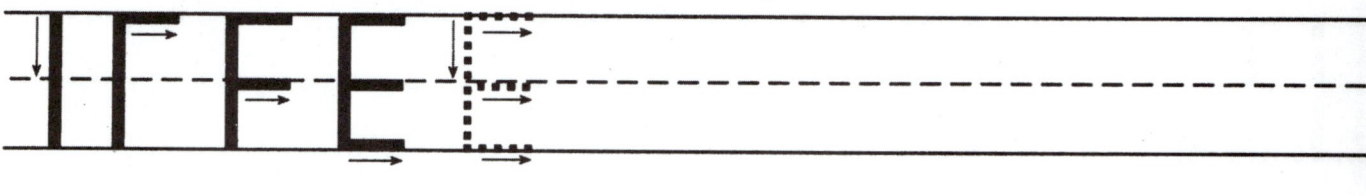

Skills: Forming upper/lowercase "e"; Writing left to right; Saying letter sounds

Beginning Writing Skills

F f

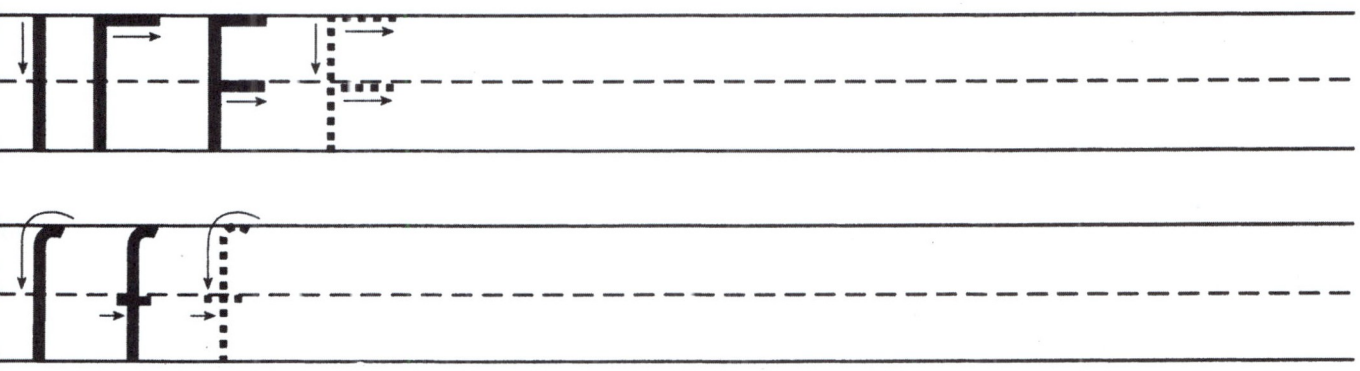

Follow the direction of each arrow. Practice writing and saying each letter. Then point to something in the picture that begins with the letter F.

Skills: Forming upper/lowercase "f"; Writing left to right; Saying letter sounds

Beginning Writing Skills

Gg

Follow the direction of each arrow. Practice writing and saying each letter. Then point to something in the picture that begins with the letter G.

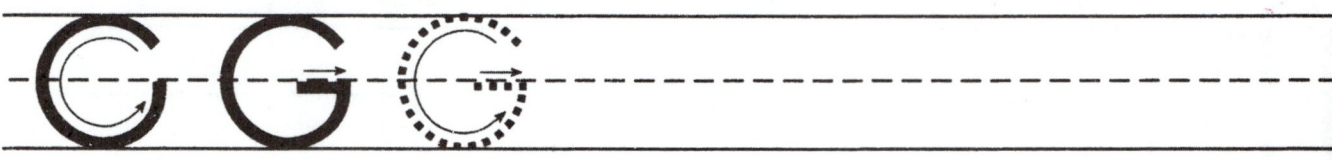

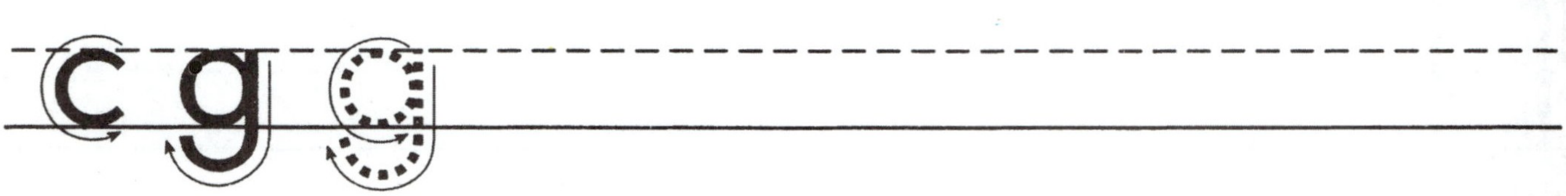

Skills: Forming upper/lowercase "g"; Writing left to right; Saying letter sounds

Beginning Writing Skills

H h

Follow the direction of each arrow. Practice writing and saying each letter. Then point to something in the picture that begins with the letter H.

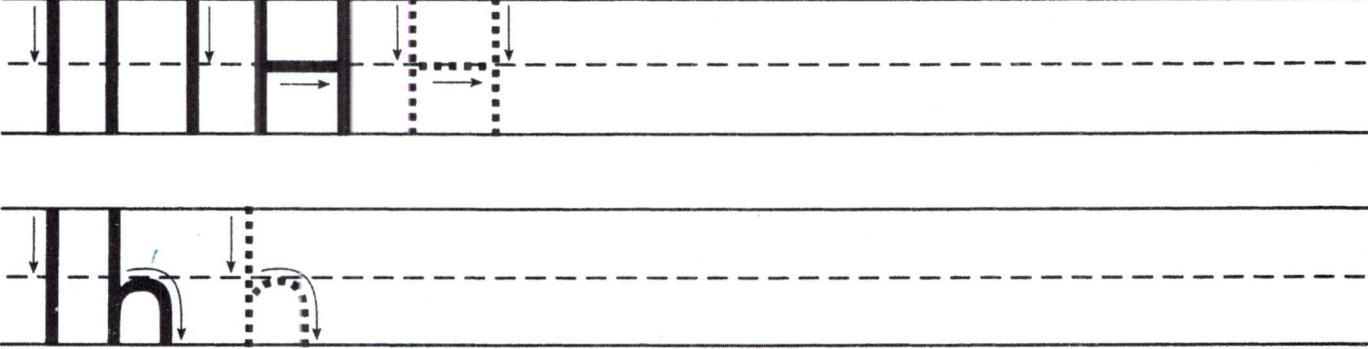

Skills: Forming upper/lowercase "h"; Writing left to right; Saying letter sounds

Beginning Writing Skills

I i

Follow the direction of each arrow. Practice writing and saying each letter. Then point to something in the picture that begins with the letter I.

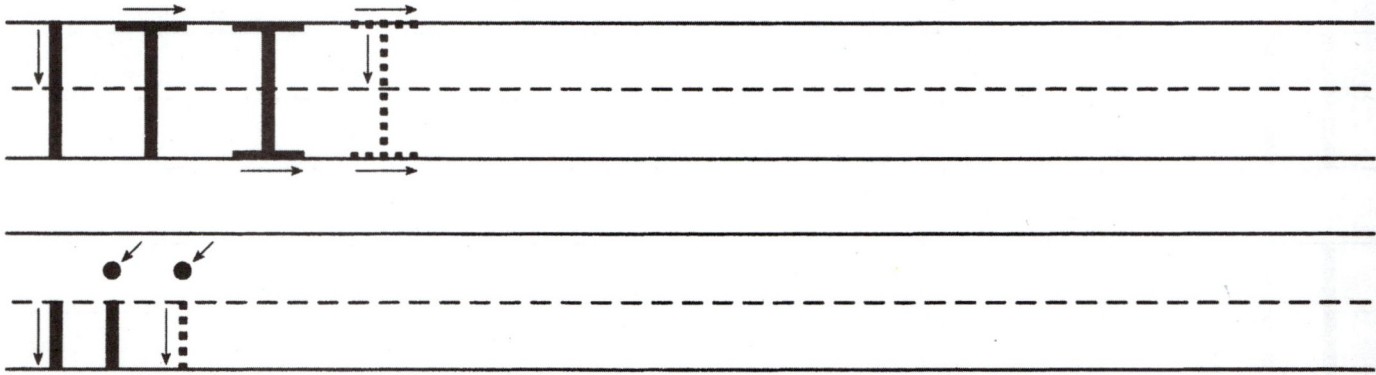

Skills: Forming upper/lowercase "i"; Writing left to right; Saying letter sounds

Beginning Writing Skills

J j

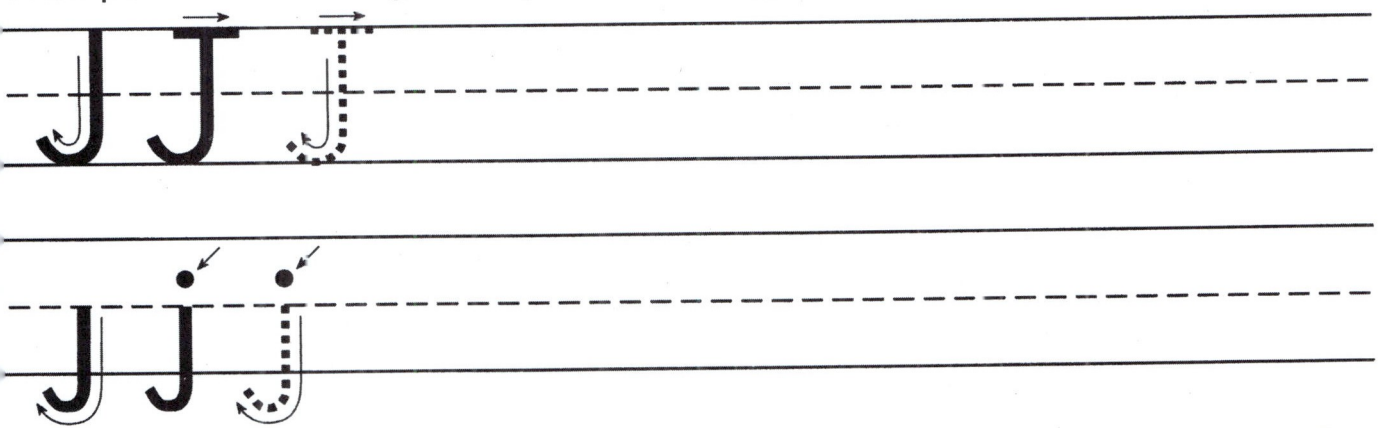

Follow the direction of each arrow. Practice writing and saying each letter. Then point to something in the picture that begins with the letter J.

Skills: Forming upper/lowercase "j"; Writing left to right; Saying letter sounds

 **Beginning Writing Skills**

Kk

Follow the direction of each arrow. Practice writing and saying each letter. Then point to something in the picture that begins with the letter K.

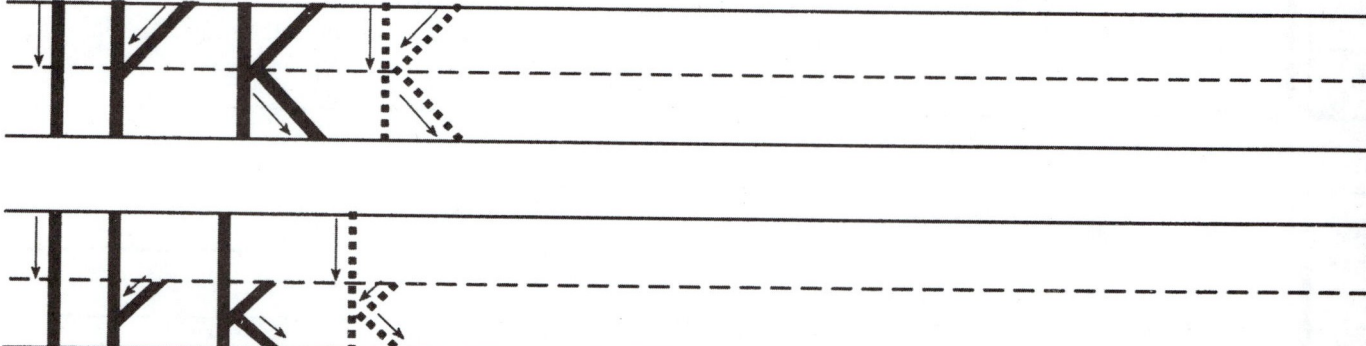

Skills: Forming upper/lowercase "k"; Writing left to right; Saying letter sounds

Beginning Writing Skills

L l

Follow the direction of each arrow. Practice writing and saying each letter. Then point to something in the picture that begins with the letter L.

Skills: Forming upper/lowercase "l"; Writing left to right; Saying letter sounds

Beginning Writing Skills

Mm

Follow the direction of each arrow. Practice writing and saying each letter. Then point to something in the picture that begins with the letter M.

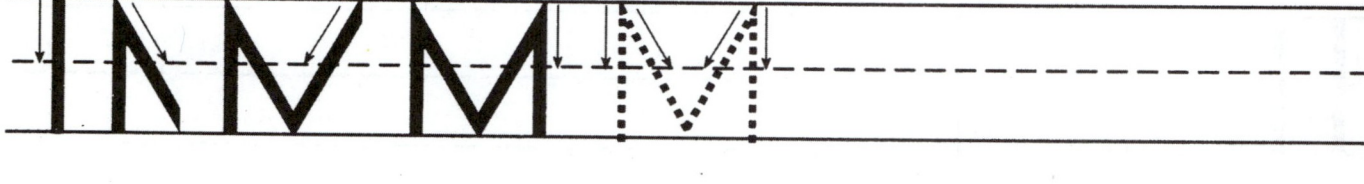

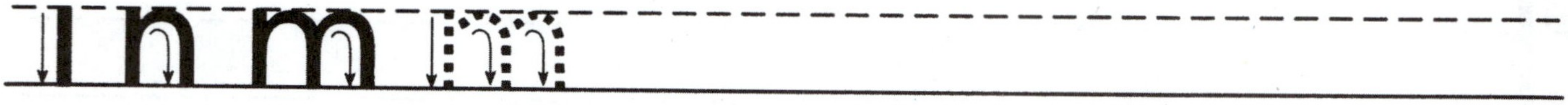

Skills: Forming upper/lowercase "m"; Writing left to right; Saying letter sounds

Beginning Writing Skills

N n

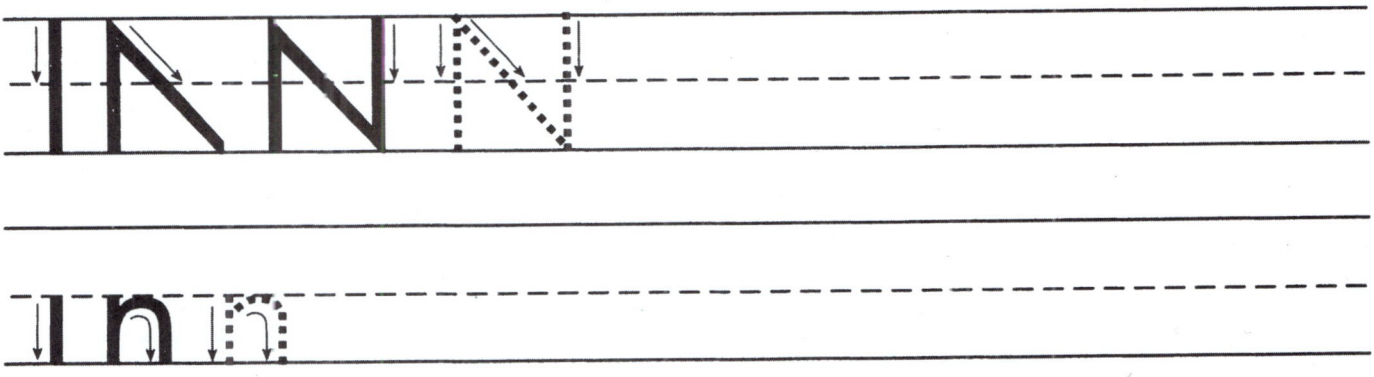

Follow the direction of each arrow. Practice writing and saying each letter. Then point to something in the picture that begins with the letter N.

Skills: Forming upper/lowercase "n"; Writing left to right; Saying letter sounds

Beginning Writing Skills

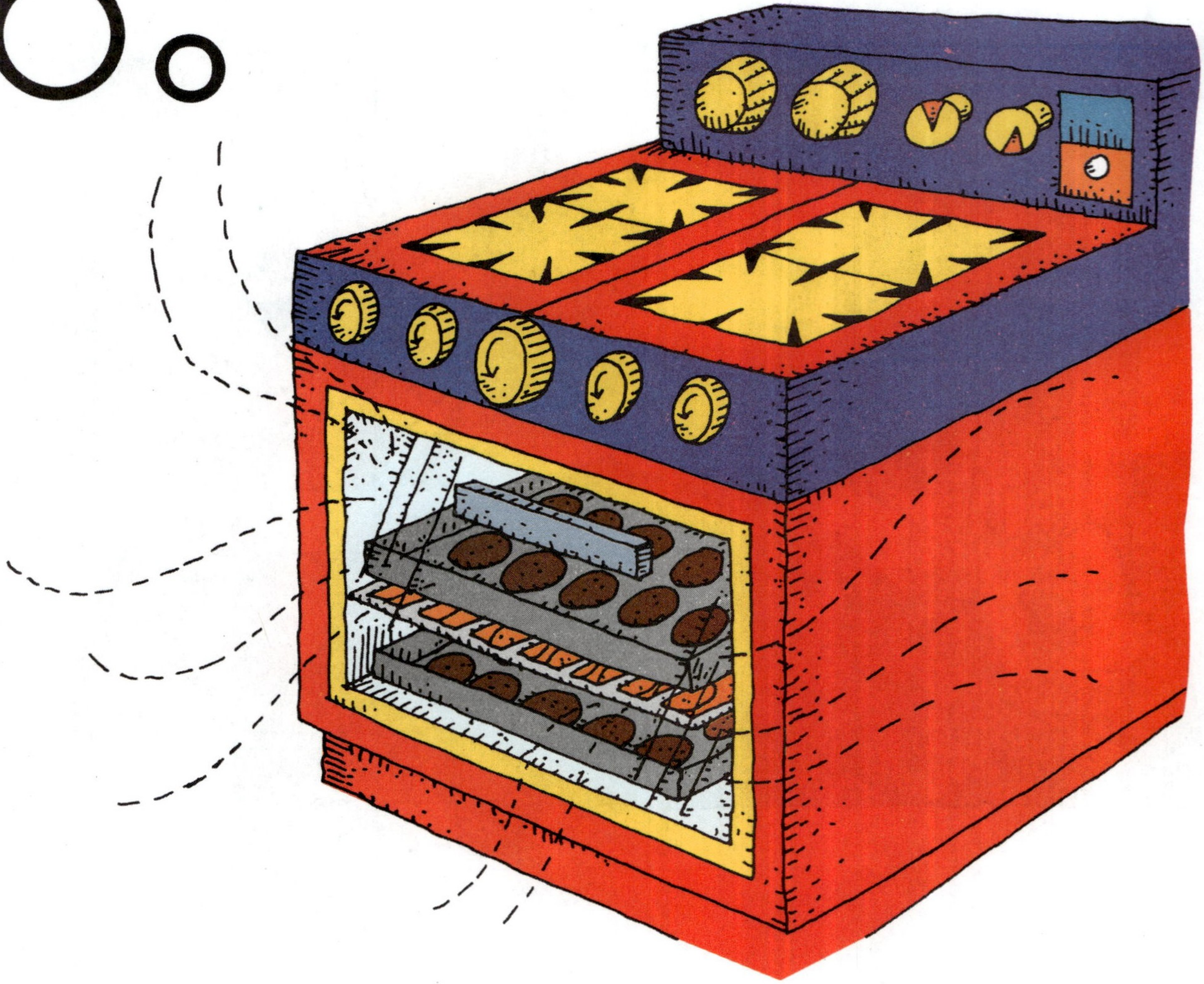

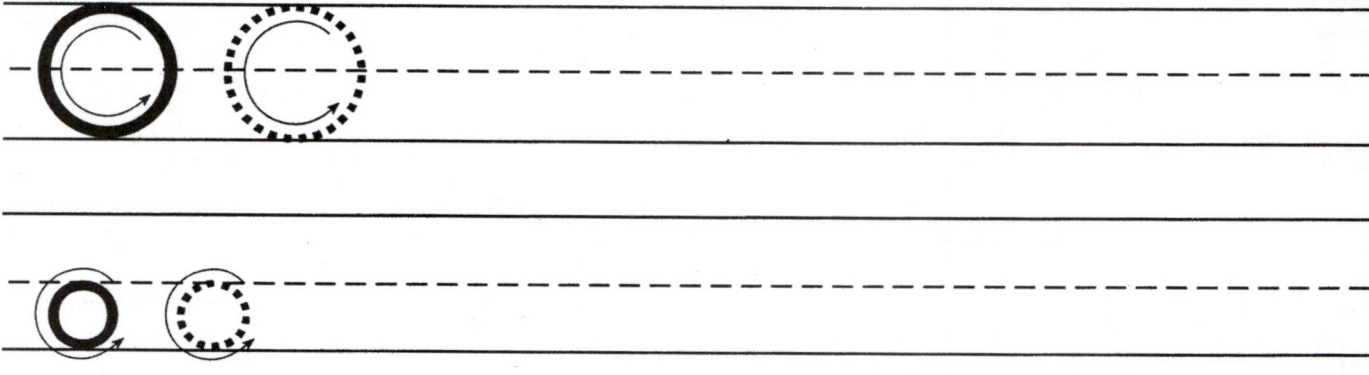

Follow the direction of each arrow. Practice writing and saying each letter. Then point to something in the picture that begins with the letter O.

Skills: Forming upper/lowercase "o"; Writing left to right; Saying letter sounds

Beginning Writing Skills

P p

Follow the direction of each arrow. Practice writing and saying each letter. Then point to something in the picture that begins with the letter P.

Skills: Forming upper/lowercase "p"; Writing left to right; Saying letter sounds

Beginning Writing Skills

Q q

Follow the direction of each arrow. Practice writing and saying each letter. Then point to something in the picture that begins with the letter Q.

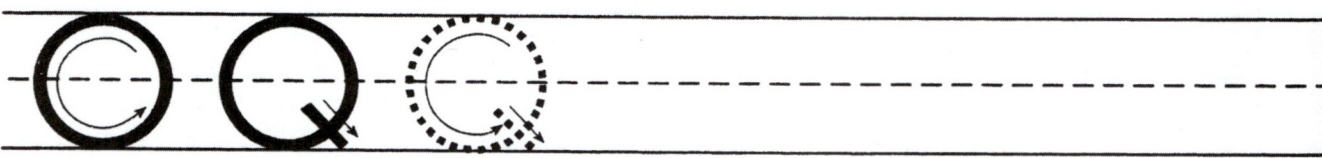

Skills: Forming upper/lowercase "q"; Writing left to right; Saying letter sounds

Beginning Writing Skills

R r

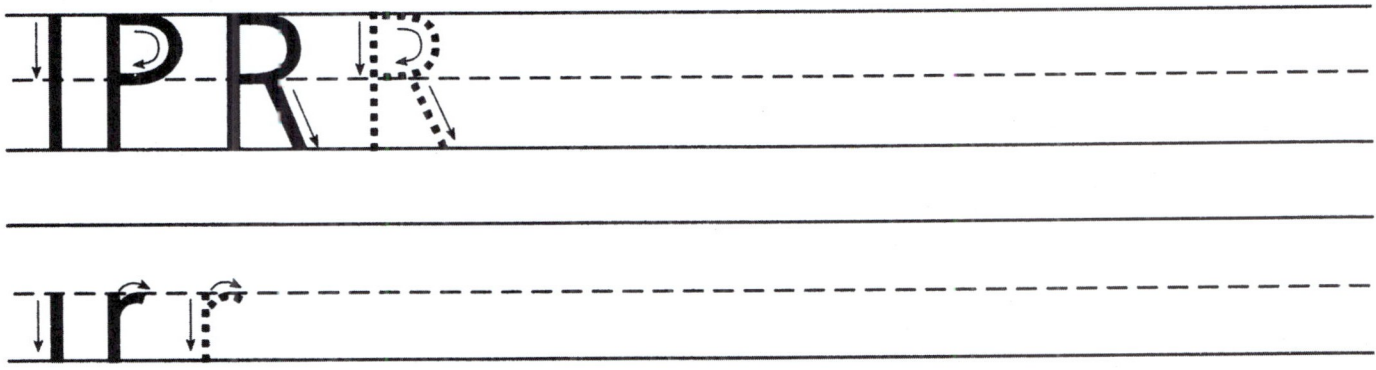

Follow the direction of each arrow. Practice writing and saying each letter. Then point to something in the picture that begins with the letter R.

Skills: Forming upper/lowercase "r"; Writing left to right; Saying letter sounds

Beginning Writing Skills

S s

Follow the direction of each arrow. Practice writing and saying each letter. Then point to something in the picture that begins with the letter S.

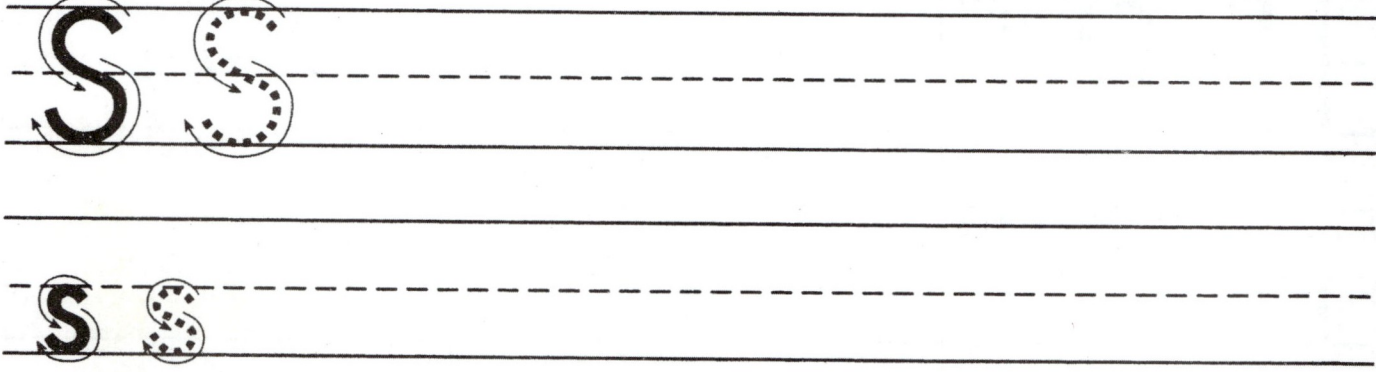

Skills: Forming upper/lowercase "s"; Writing left to right; Saying letter sounds

Beginning Writing Skills

T t

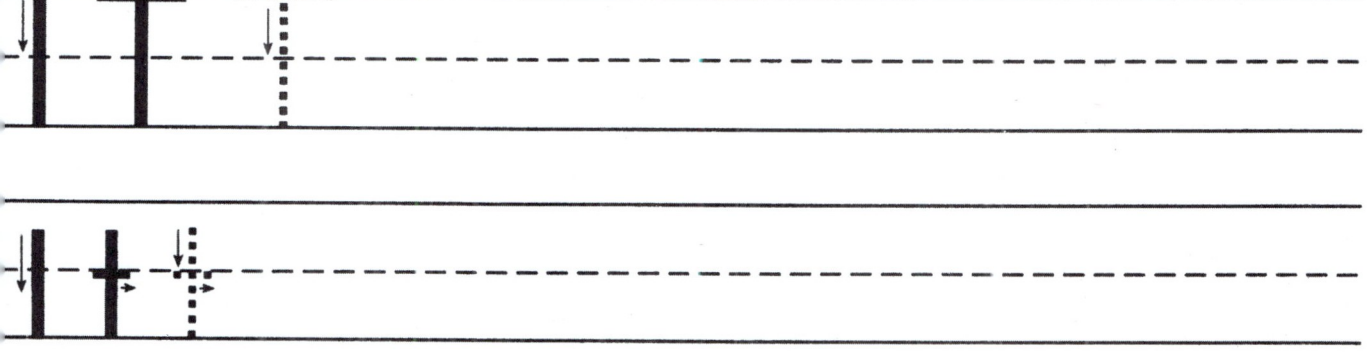

Follow the direction of each arrow. Practice writing and saying each letter. Then point to something in the picture that begins with the letter T.

Skills: Forming upper/lowercase "t"; Writing left to right; Saying letter sounds

Beginning Writing Skills

U u

Follow the direction of each arrow. Practice writing and saying each letter. Then point to something in the picture that begins with the letter U.

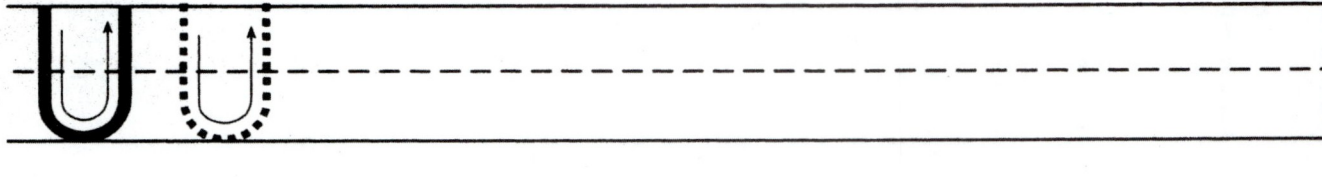

Skills: Forming upper/lowercase "u"; Writing left to right; Saying letter sounds

Beginning Writing Skills

V v

Follow the direction of each arrow. Practice writing and saying each letter. Then point to something in the picture that begins with the letter V.

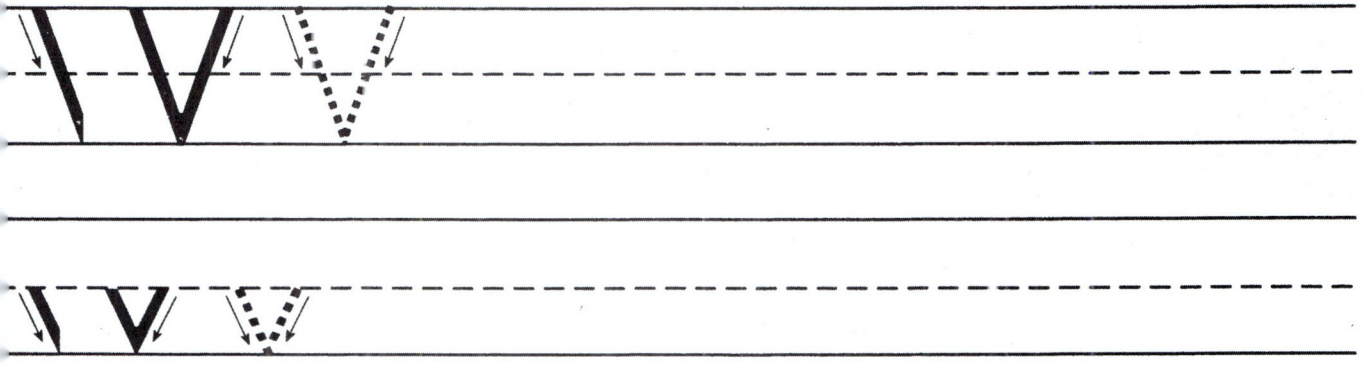

Skills: Forming upper/lowercase "v"; Writing left to right; Saying letter sounds

Beginning Writing Skills

W w

Follow the direction of each arrow. Practice writing and saying each letter. Then point to something in the picture that begins with the letter W.

Skills: Forming upper/lowercase "w"; Writing left to right; Saying letter sounds

Beginning Writing Skills

X x

Follow the direction of each arrow. Practice writing and saying each letter. Then point to something in the picture that begins with the letter X.

Skills: Forming upper/lowercase "x"; Writing left to right; Saying letter sounds

Beginning Writing Skills

Y y

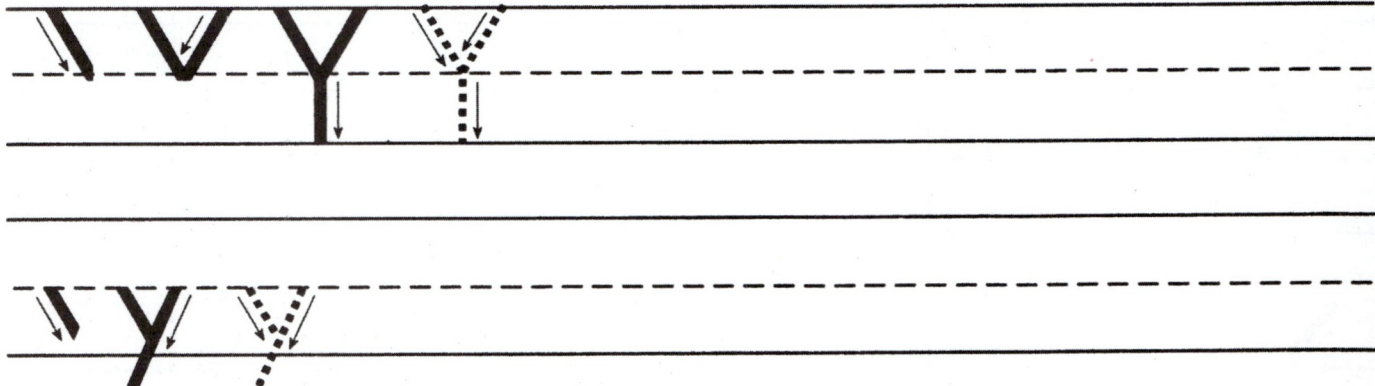

Follow the direction of each arrow. Practice writing and saying each letter. Then point to something in the picture that begins with the letter Y.

Skills: Forming upper/lowercase "y"; Writing left to right; Saying letter sounds

Beginning Writing Skills

Zz

Follow the direction of each arrow. Practice writing and saying each letter. Then point to something in the picture that begins with the letter Z.

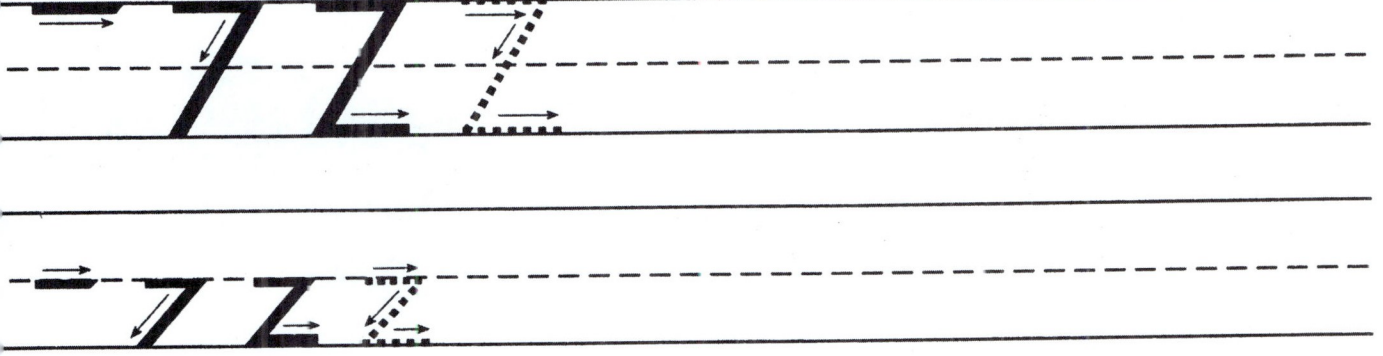

Skills: Forming upper/lowercase "z"; Writing left to right; Saying letter sounds

Beginning Writing Skills

Start at the dot. Trace the broken lines.

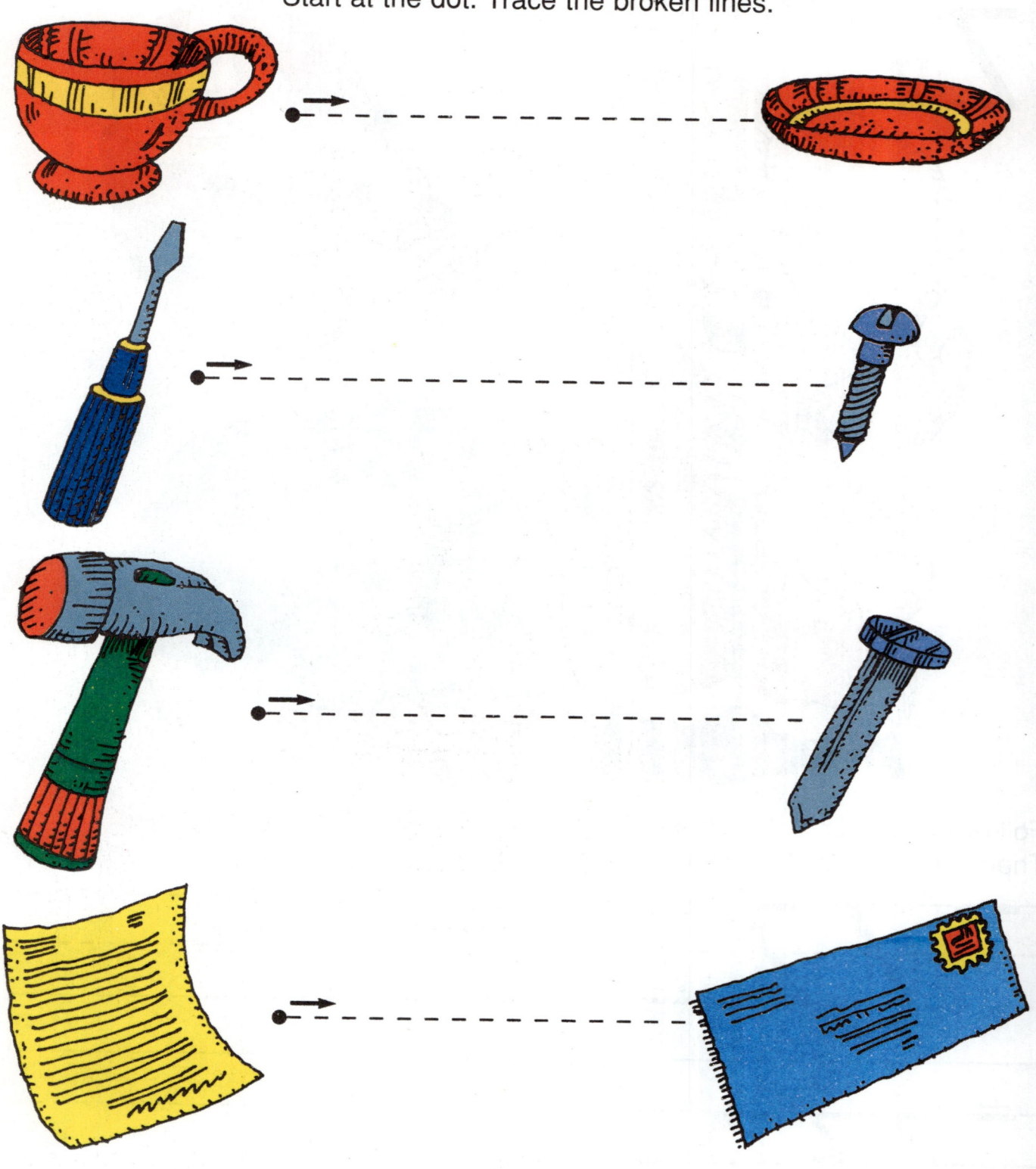

Skills: Writing from left to right; Association; Fine motor skill development

Beginning Writing Skills

Connect the dots from A to Z. Then color the picture.

Skills: Letter order; Recognizing uppercase letters

Beginning Writing Skills

Connect the dots from a to z. Then color the picture.

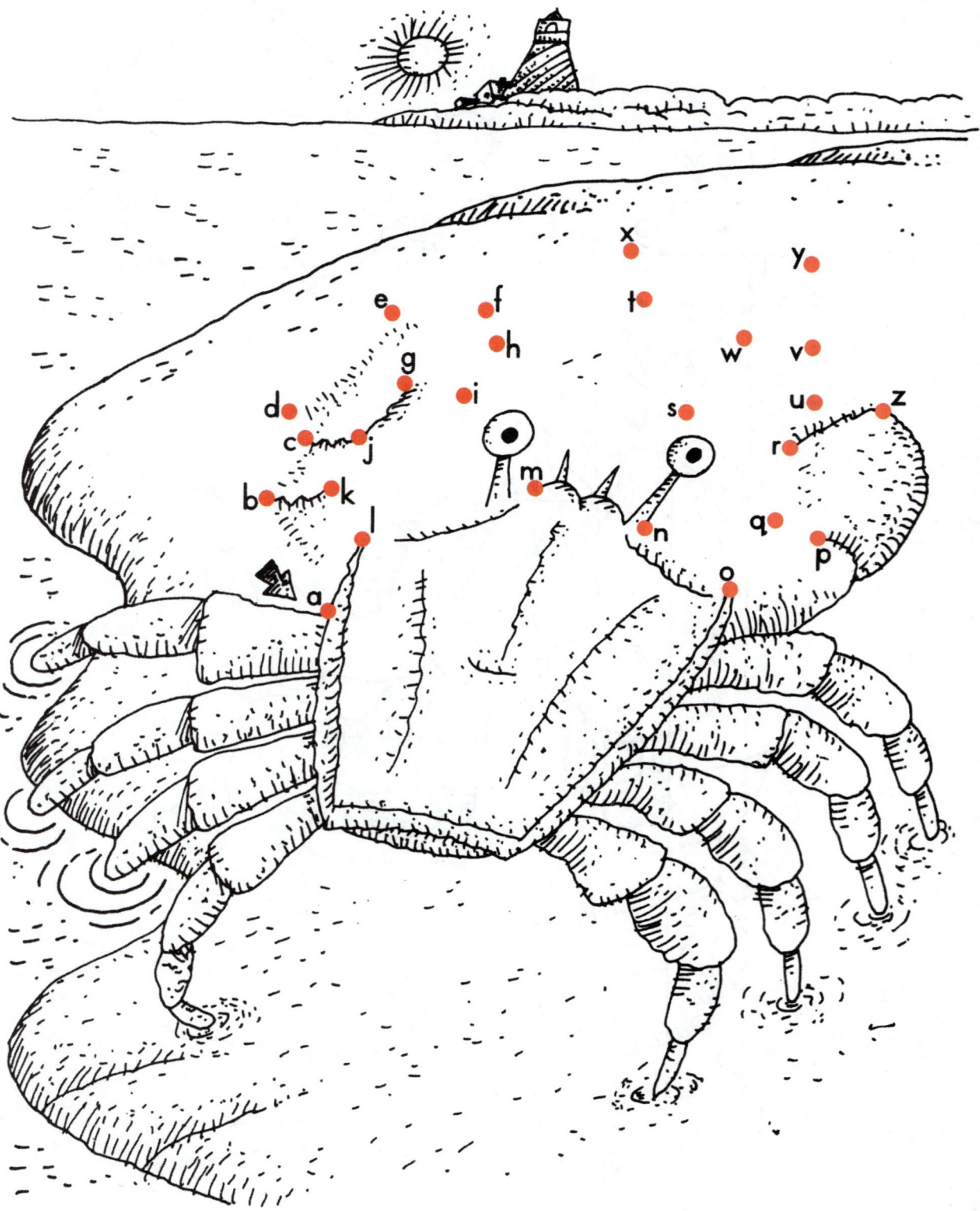

Skills: Letter order; Recognizing lowercase letters

Practice Page

Use these pages to practice writing letters.

Practice Page

Excellent!

Give yourself a star!

Colors and Shapes

Colors and Shapes

Trace each ◯. Color each ◯.

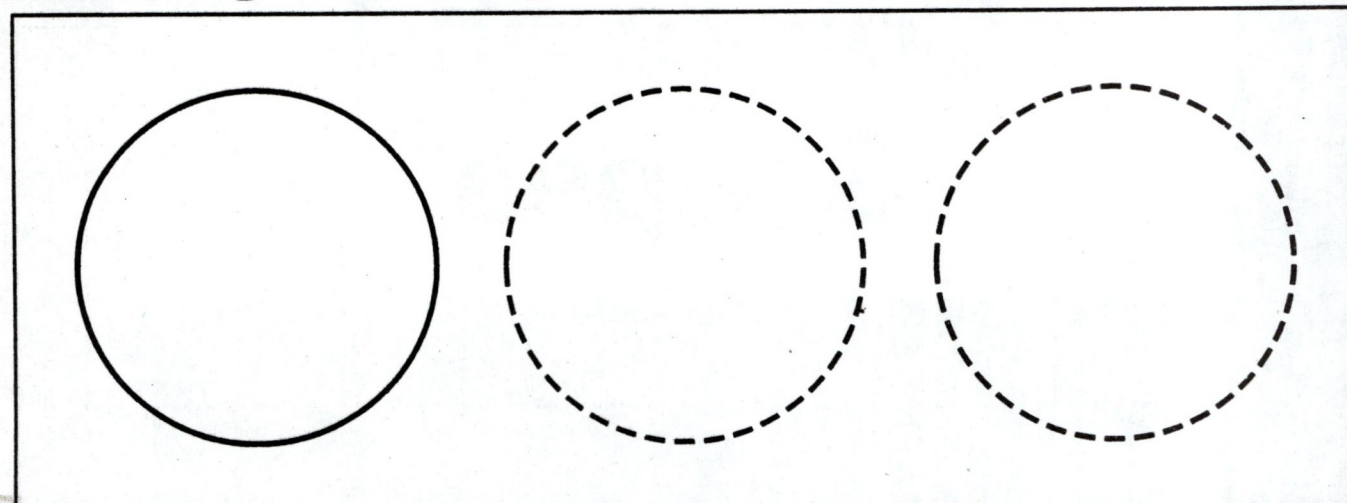

Skills: Fine motor skill development; Shape recognition

Colors and Shapes

Trace each ☐. Color each ☐.

Colors and Shapes

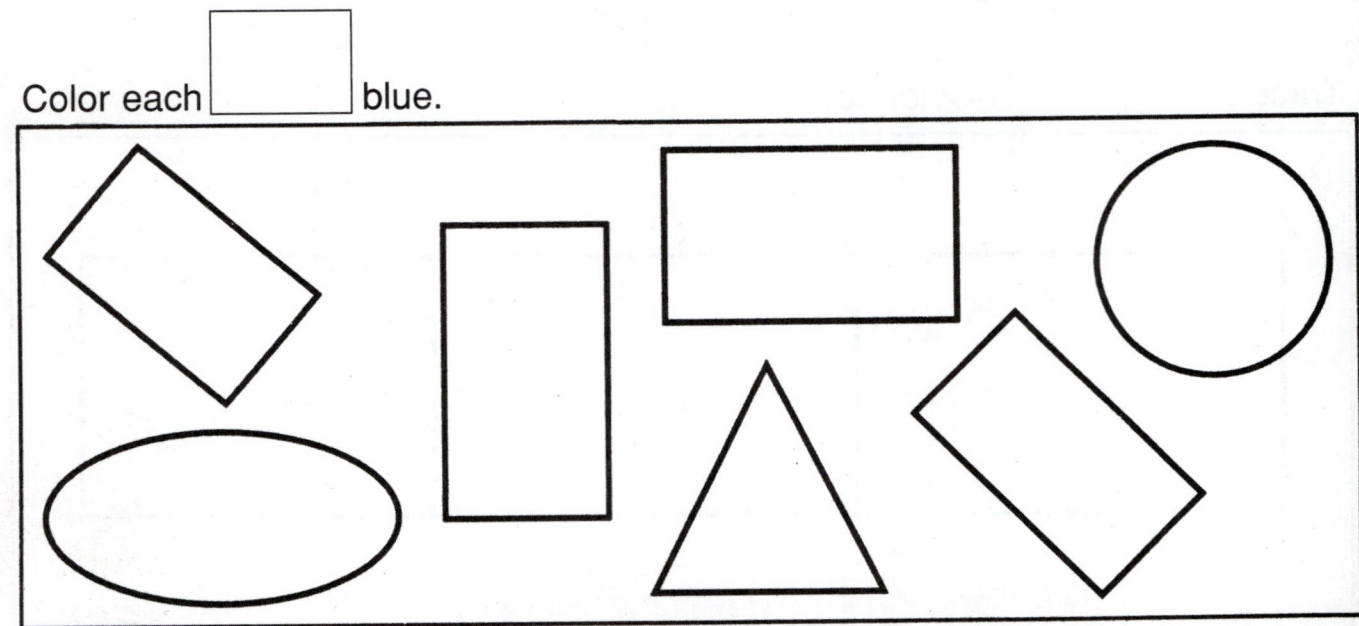

Color each 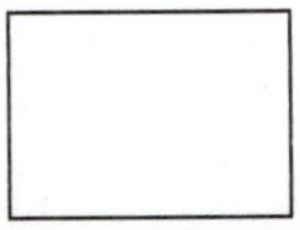 ▢ blue.

Skills: Shape recognition; Color recognition

Colors and Shapes

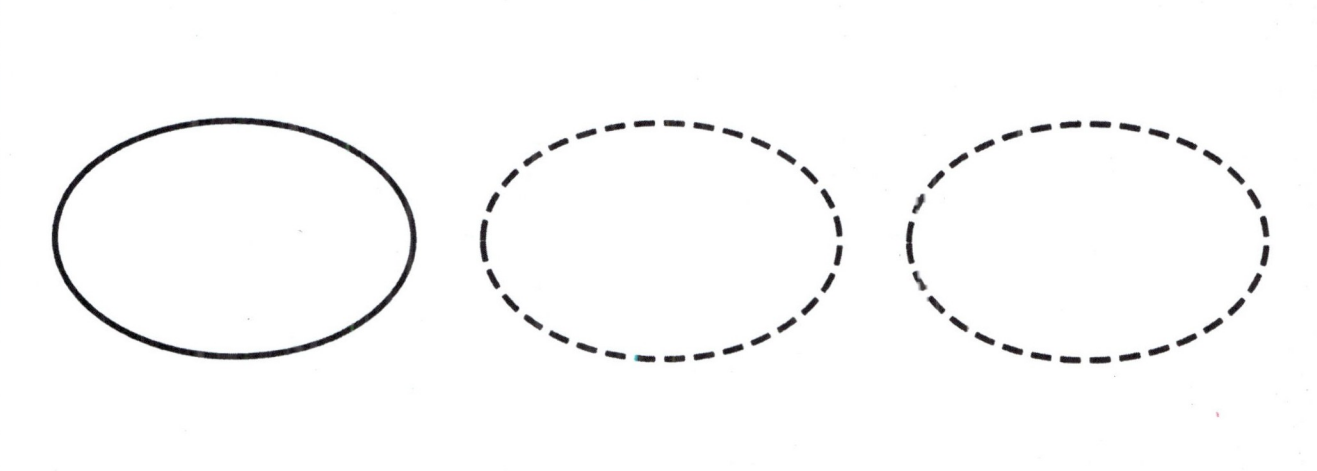

Trace each 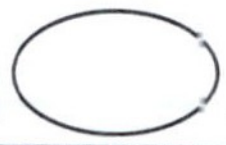 ◯. Color each ◯.

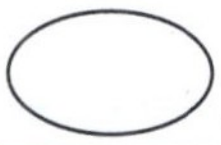

Skills: Fine motor skill development; Shape recognition

# Colors and Shapes

Color each 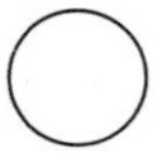 ◯ green.

Skills: Shape recognition; Color recognition

Colors and Shapes

Trace each △. Color each △.

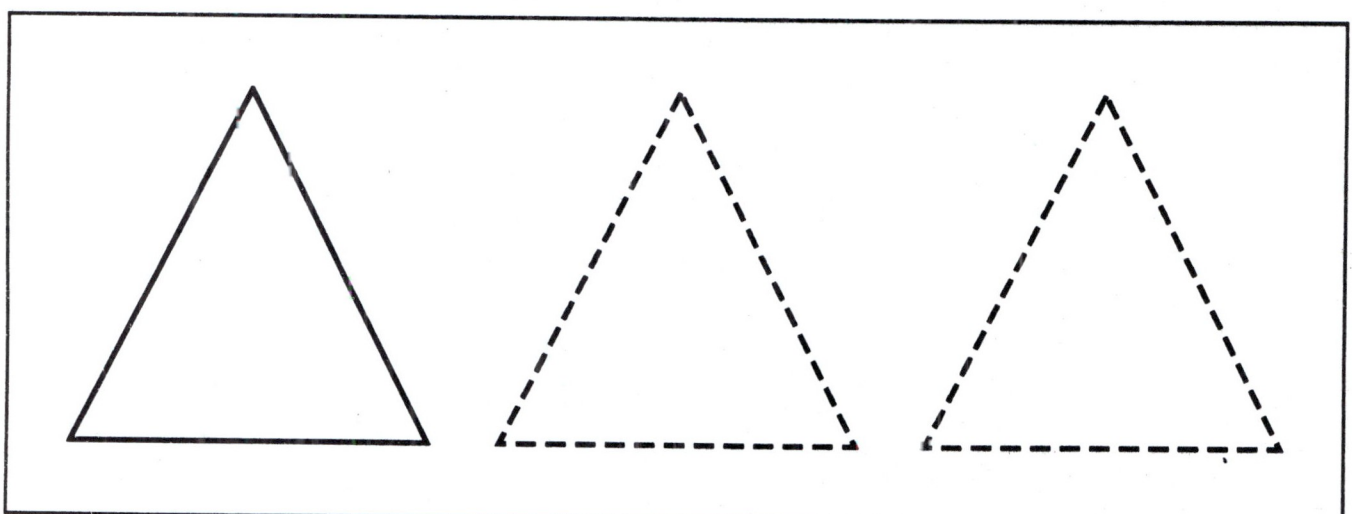

Skills: Fine motor skill development; Shape recognition

Colors and Shapes

Color each △ yellow.

Skills: Shape recognition; Color recognition

Colors and Shapes

Color each 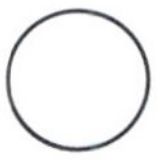 ◯ red. Color each △ green.

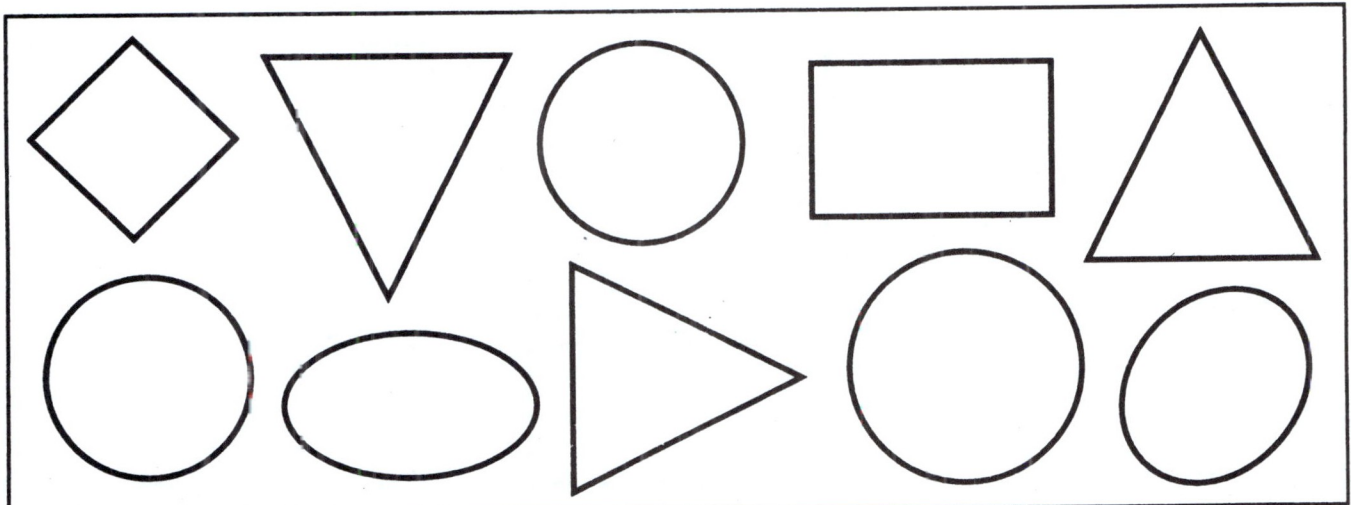

Skills: Shape recognition; Color recognition

# Colors and Shapes

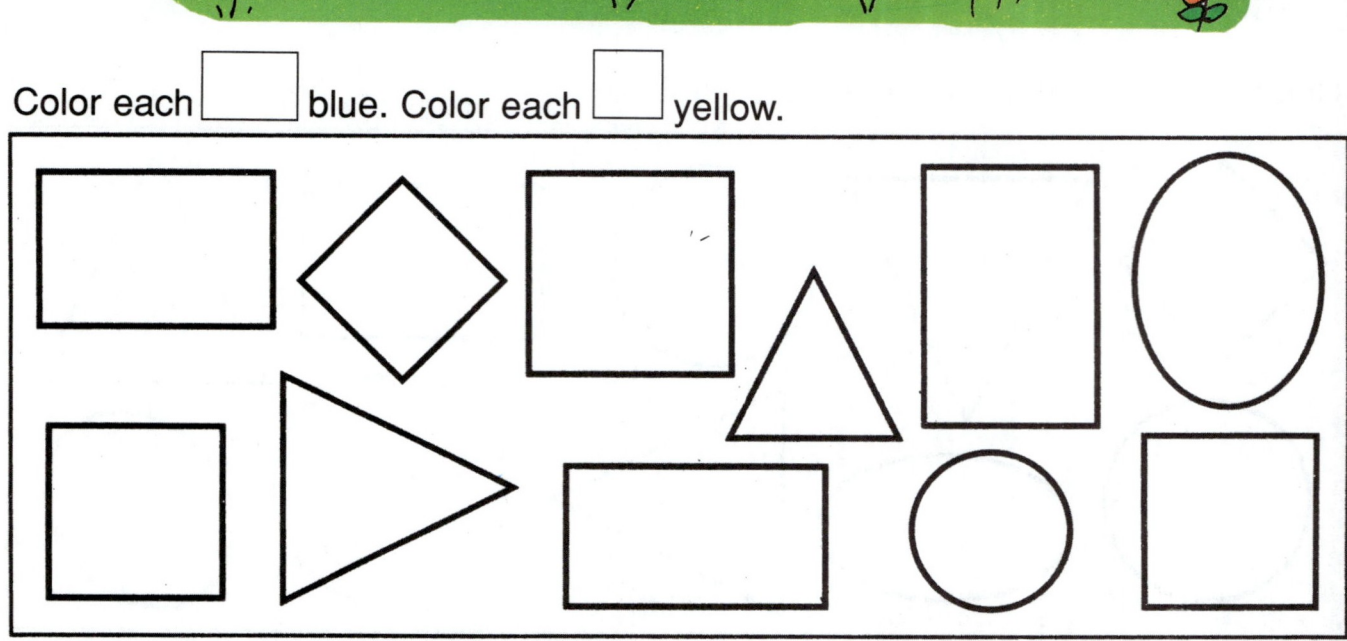

Color each ☐ blue. Color each ☐ yellow.

Skills: Shape recognition; Color recognition

Colors and Shapes

Color each ◯ green.

Skills: Shape recognition; Color recognition

Colors and Shapes

Trace each  ⌒. Color each ⌒.

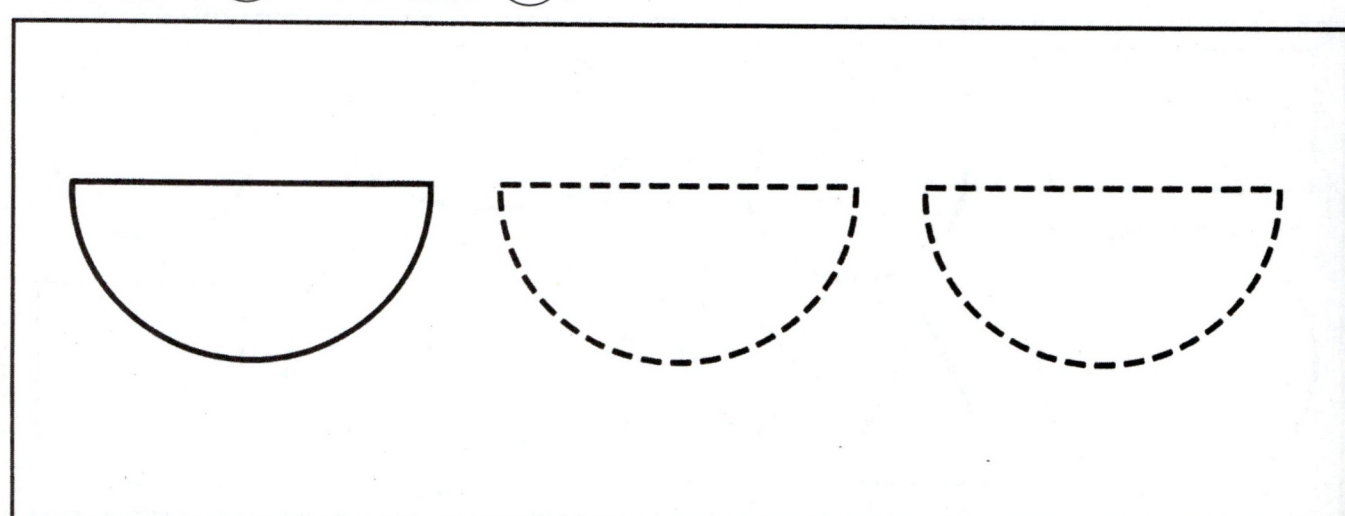

Skills: Fine motor skill development; Shape recognition

Colors and Shapes

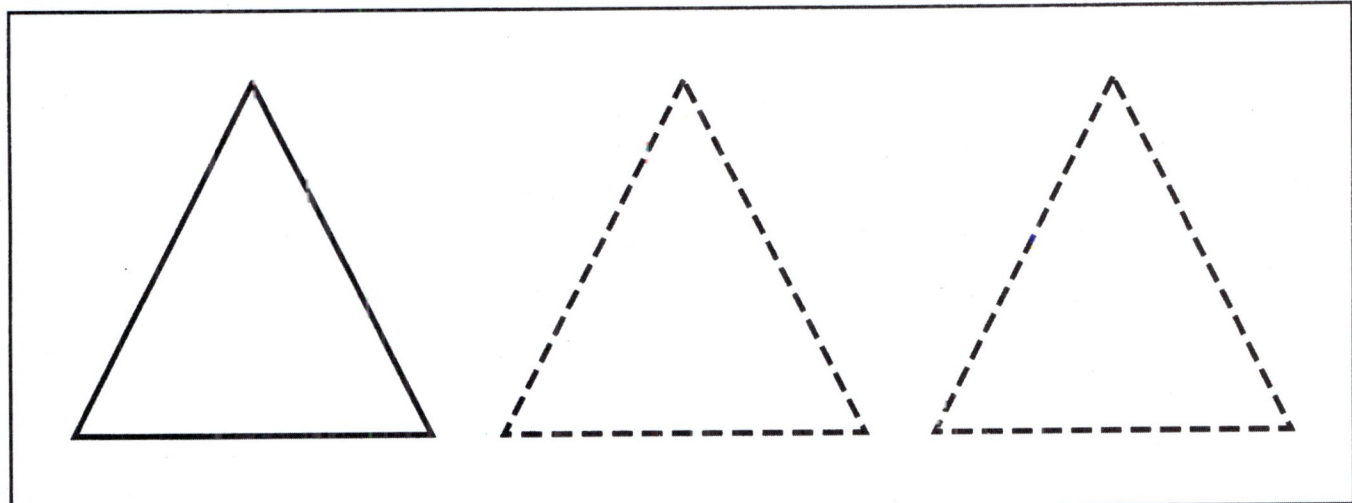

Trace each △. Color each △.

Skills: Fine motor skill development; Shape recognition

Colors and Shapes

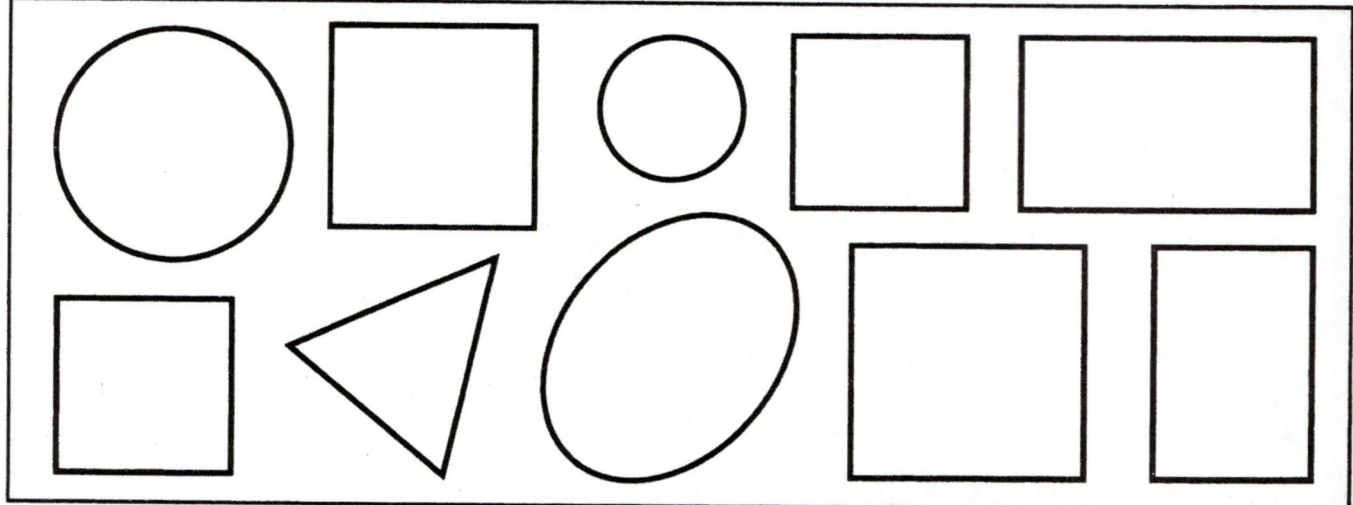

Color each ☐ yellow.

Skills: Shape recognition; Color recognition

Colors and Shapes

Trace each ☐. Color each ☐.

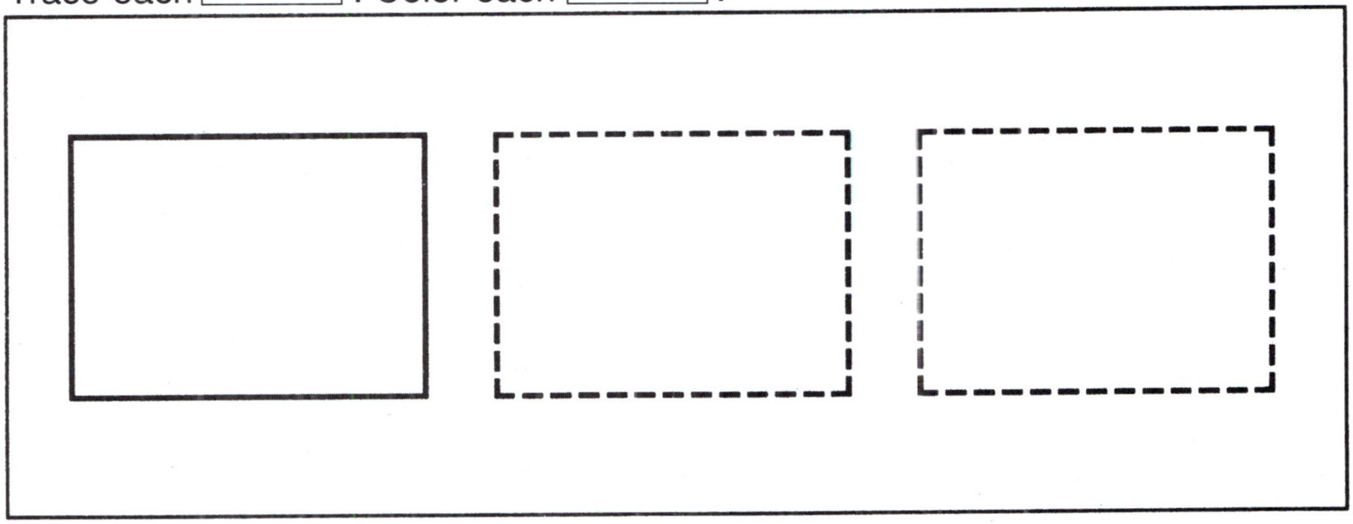

Skills: Fine motor skill development; Shape recognition

Colors and Shapes

Color each ◯ yellow.

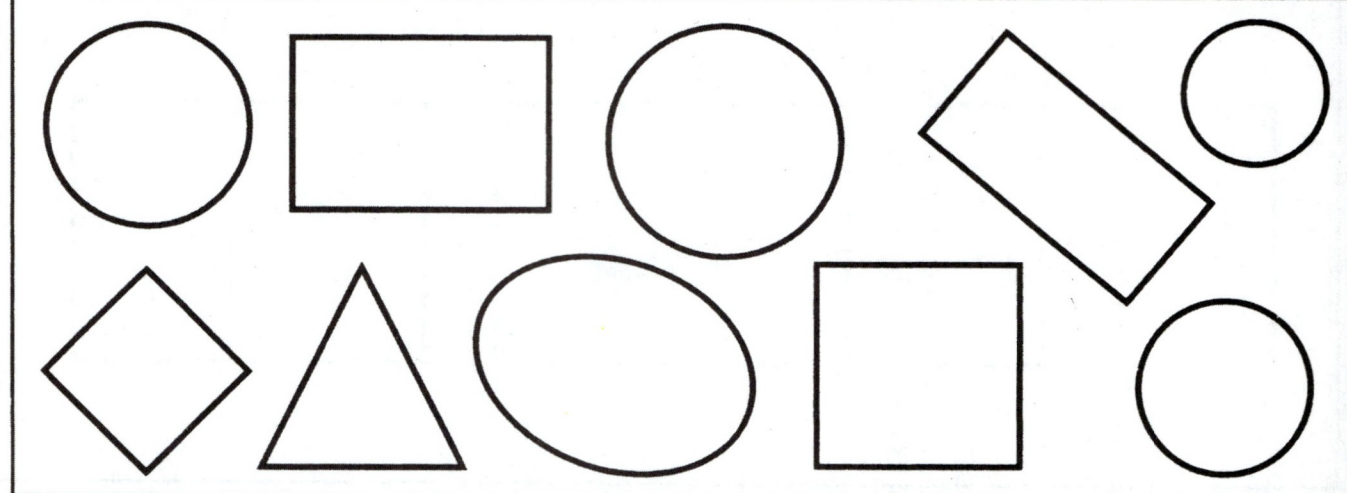

Skills: Shape recognition; Color recognition

Colors and Shapes

Color each ☐ black.

Skills: Shape recognition; Color recognition

Colors and Shapes

Trace each 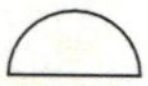 ⌒. Color each ⌒.

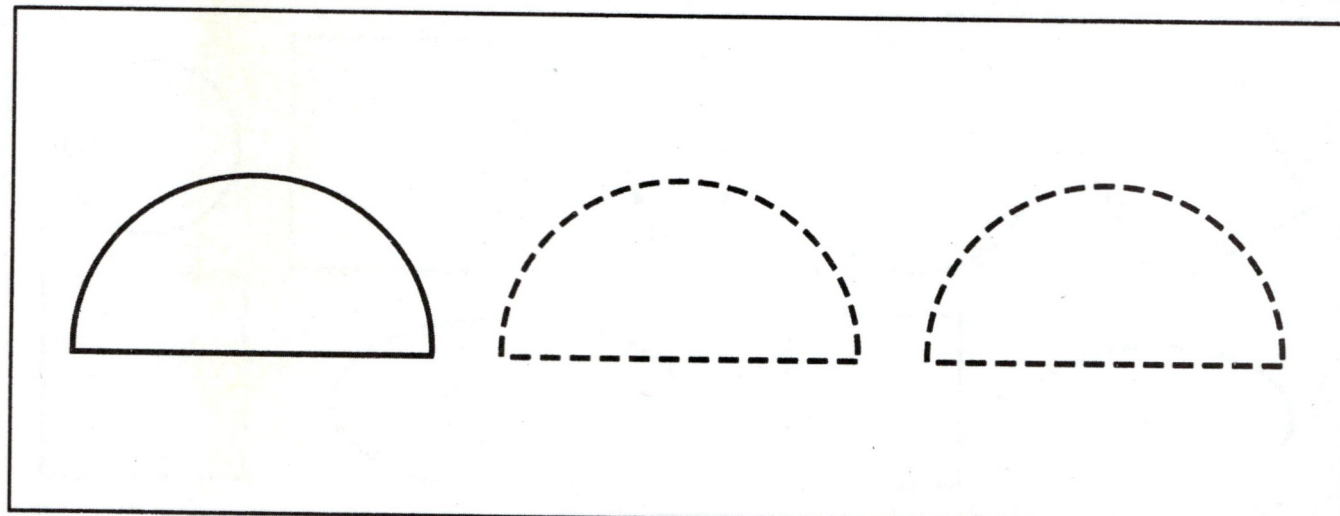

Skills: Fine motor skill development; Shape recognition

Colors and Shapes

Color each  ☐ green.

Skills: Shape recognition; Color recognition

 Colors and Shapes

Trace each ◯. Color each ◯.

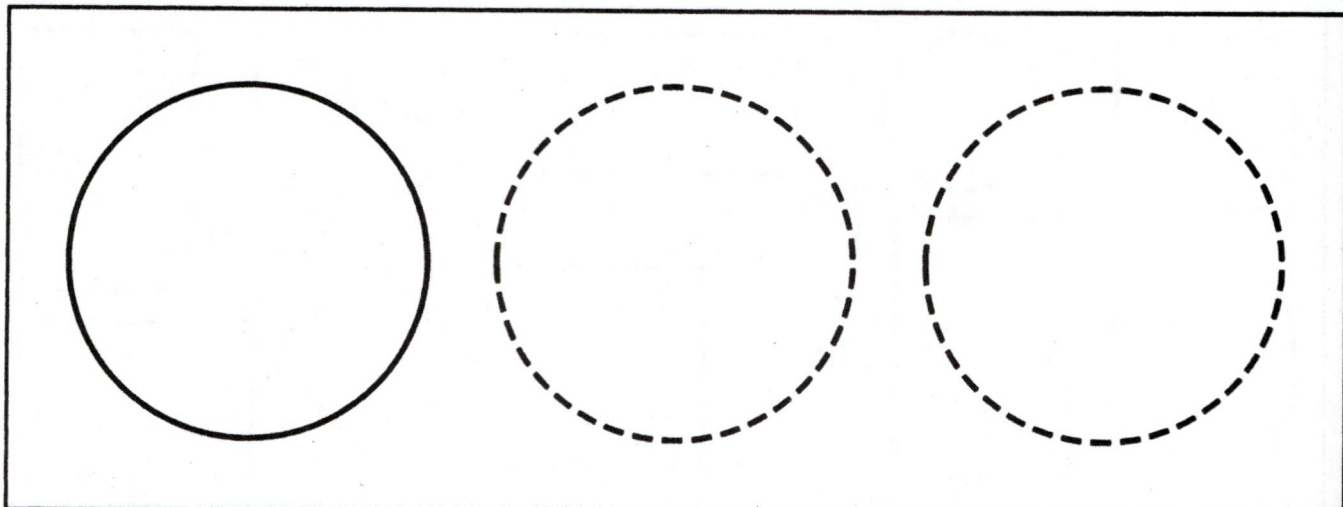

Skills: Fine motor skill development; Shape recognition

Colors and Shapes

Color each △ black. Leave each ▢ white.

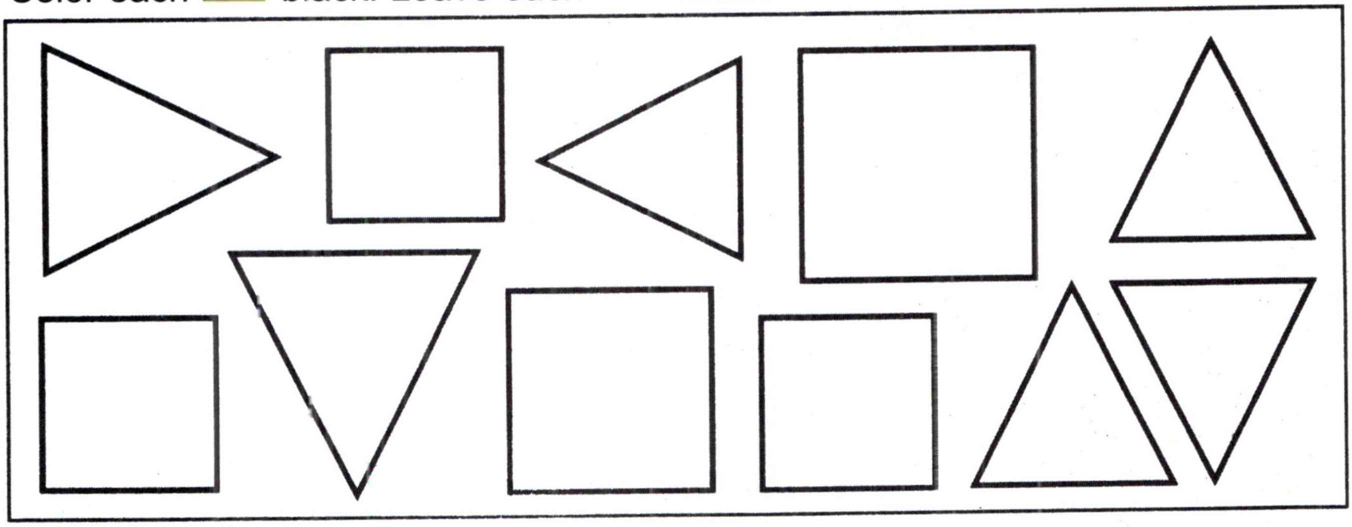

Skills: Shape recognition; Color recognition

Colors and Shapes

red

Color these things that are red.

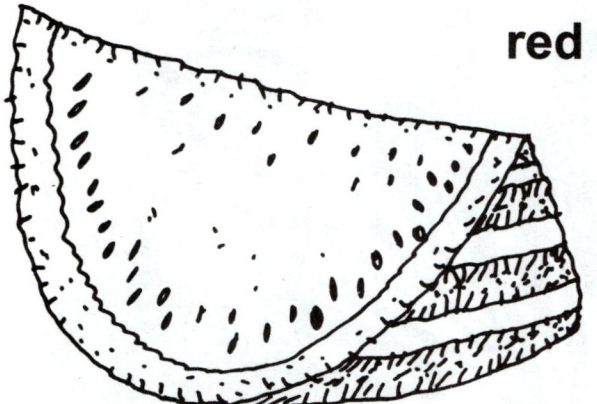

watermelon

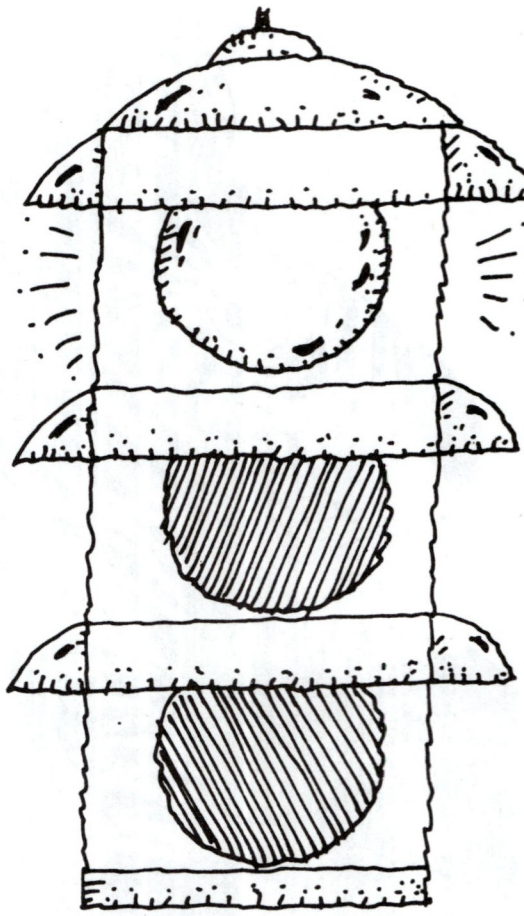

red light

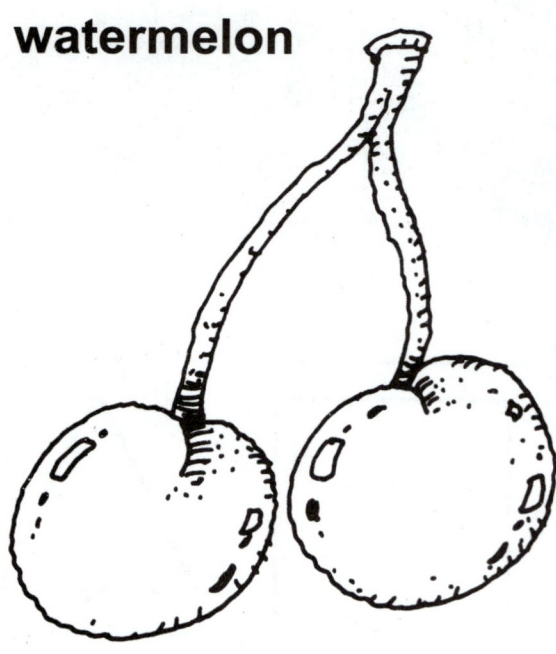

cherries

heart

Skills: Distinguishing color; Classification; Word recognition

Colors and Shapes

yellow

Color these things that are yellow.

sun

corn

banana

lemon

Skills: Distinguishing color; Classification; Word recognition

Colors and Shapes

blue

Color these things that are blue.

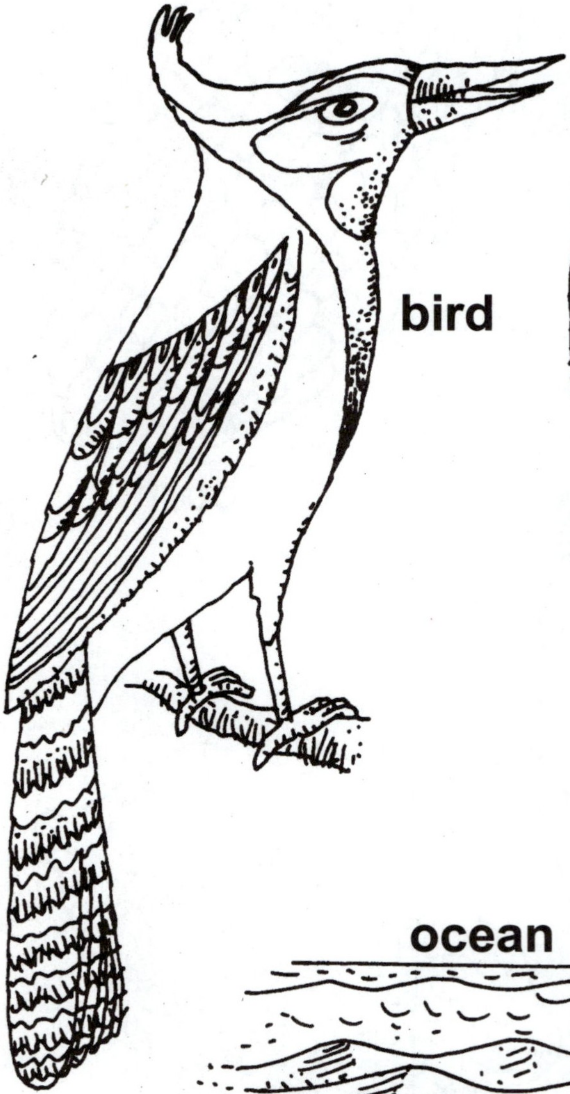

bird

blueberries

ocean

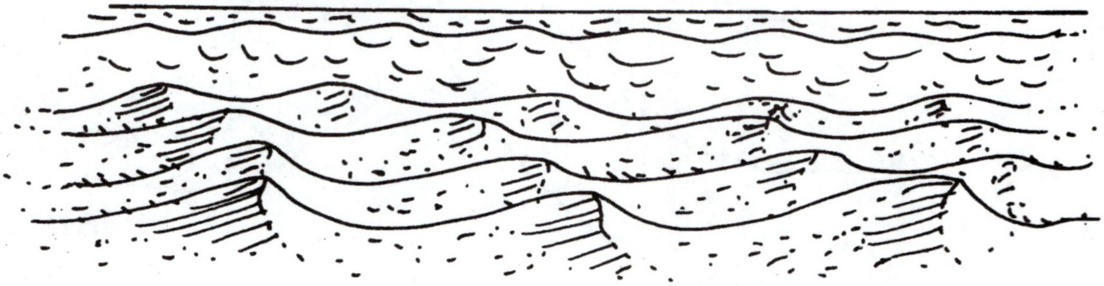

Skills: Distinguishing color; Classification; Word recognition

Colors and Shapes

orange

Color these things that are orange.

orange

pumpkin

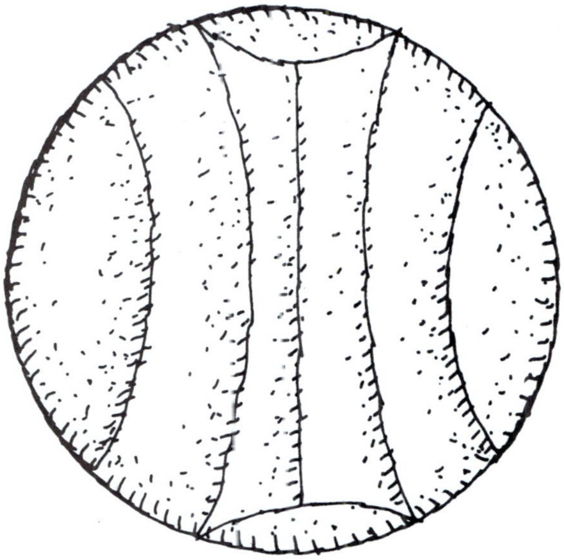

basketball

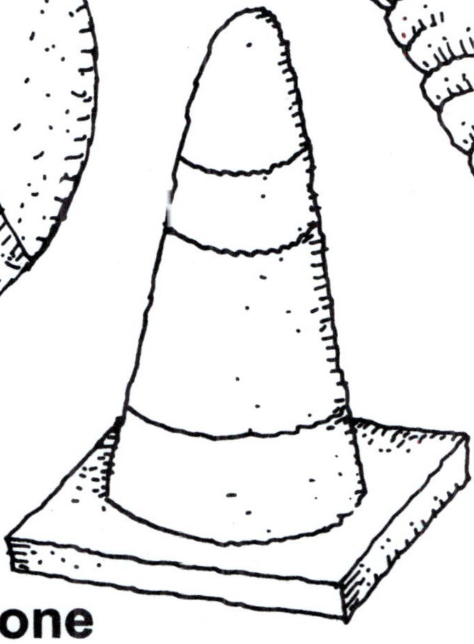

cone

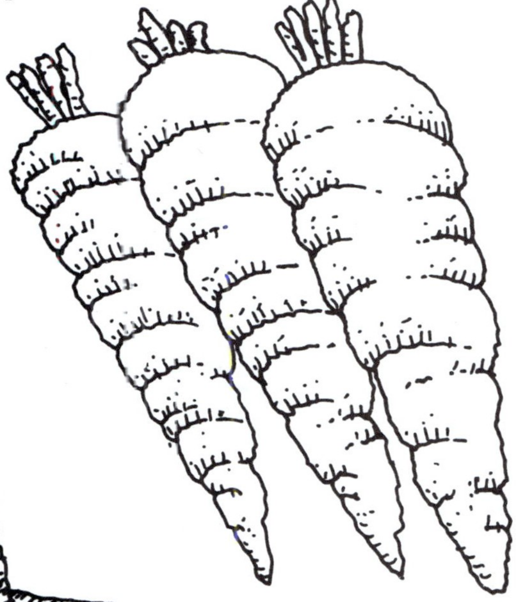

carrots

Skills: Distinguishing color; Classification; Word recognition

Colors and Shapes

purple

Color these things that are purple.

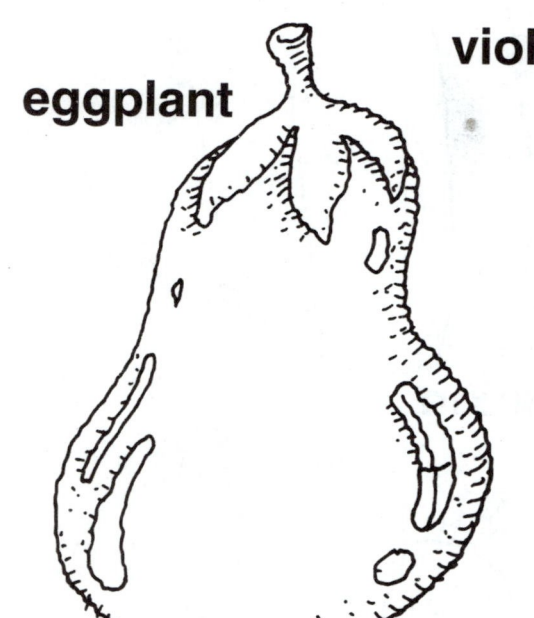
eggplant

violets

grape jelly

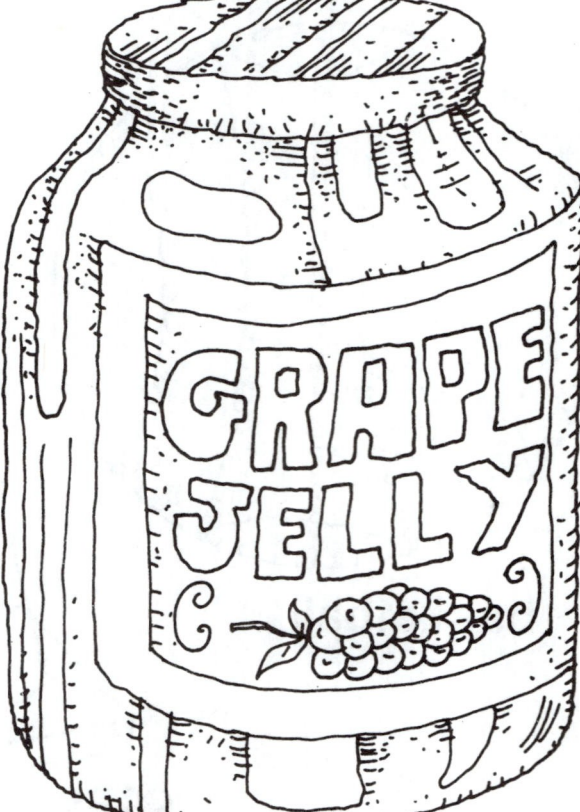

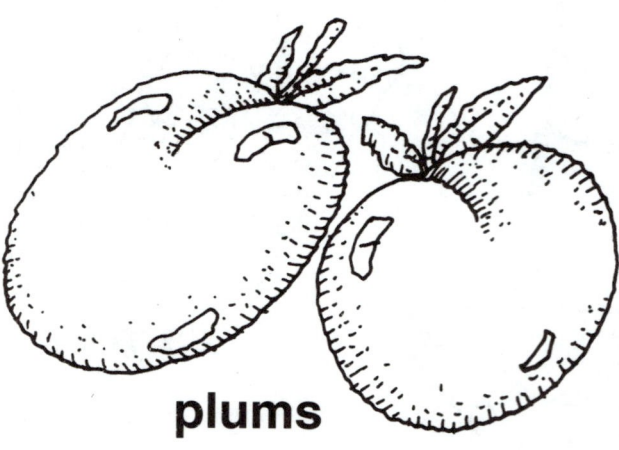
plums

Skills: Distinguishing color; Classification; Word recognition

Colors and Shapes

green

Color these things that are green.

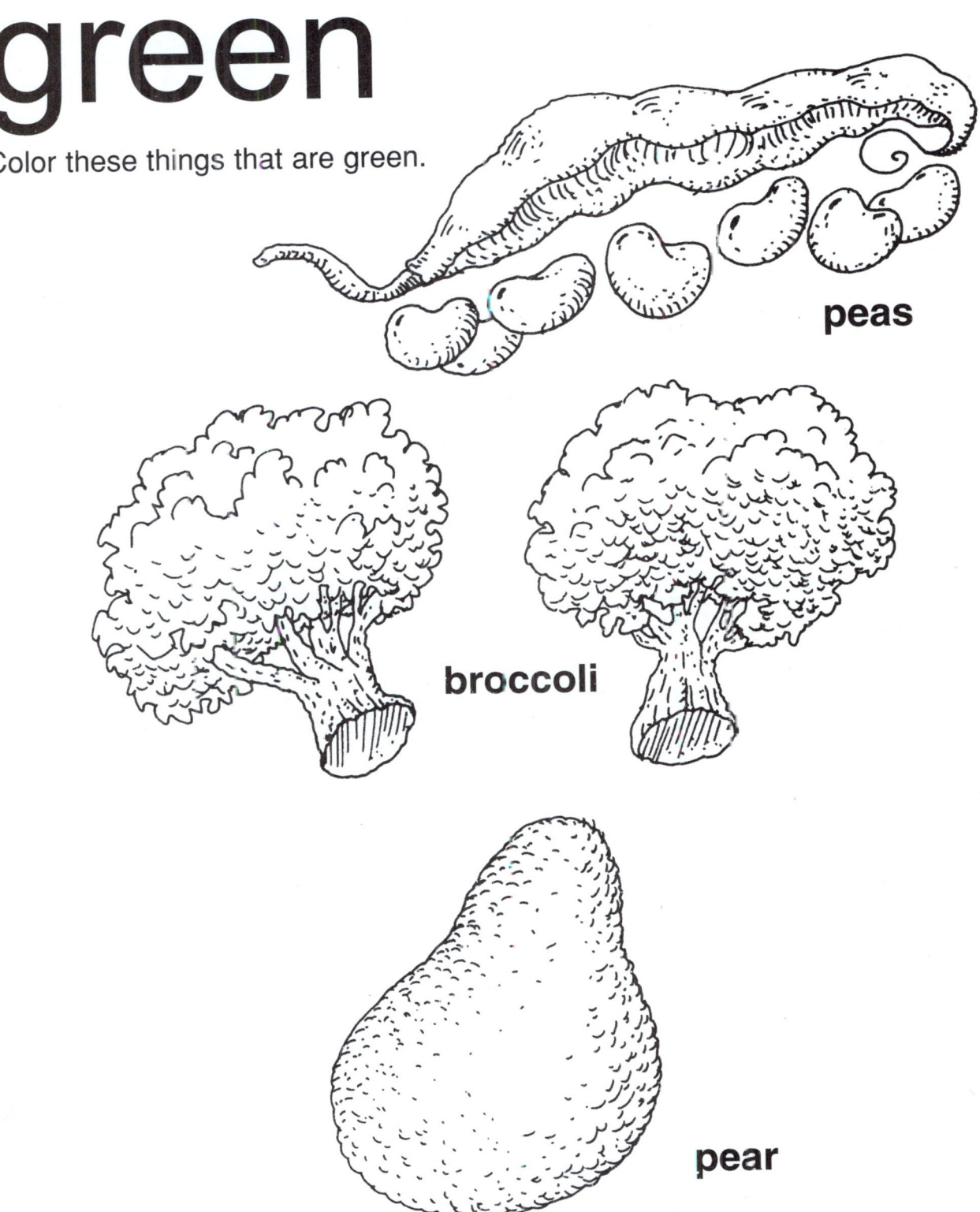

peas

broccoli

pear

Skills: Distinguishing color; Classification; Word recognition

Colors and Shapes

black

Color these things that are black.

hat

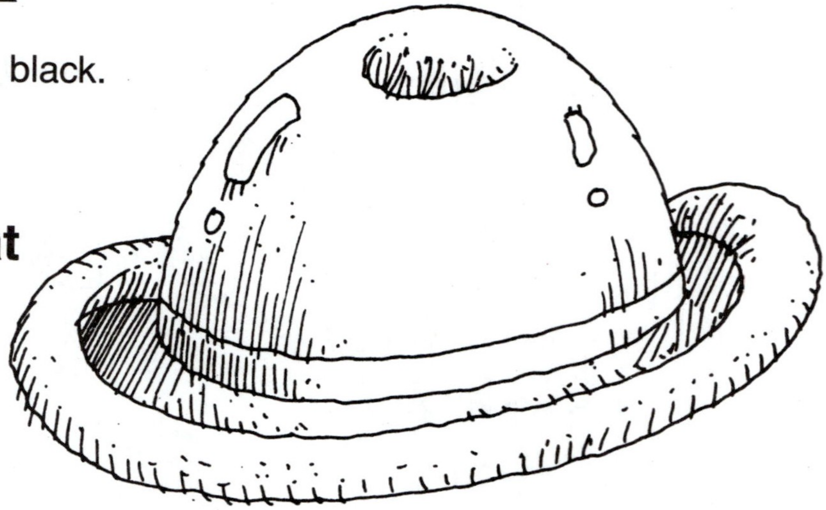

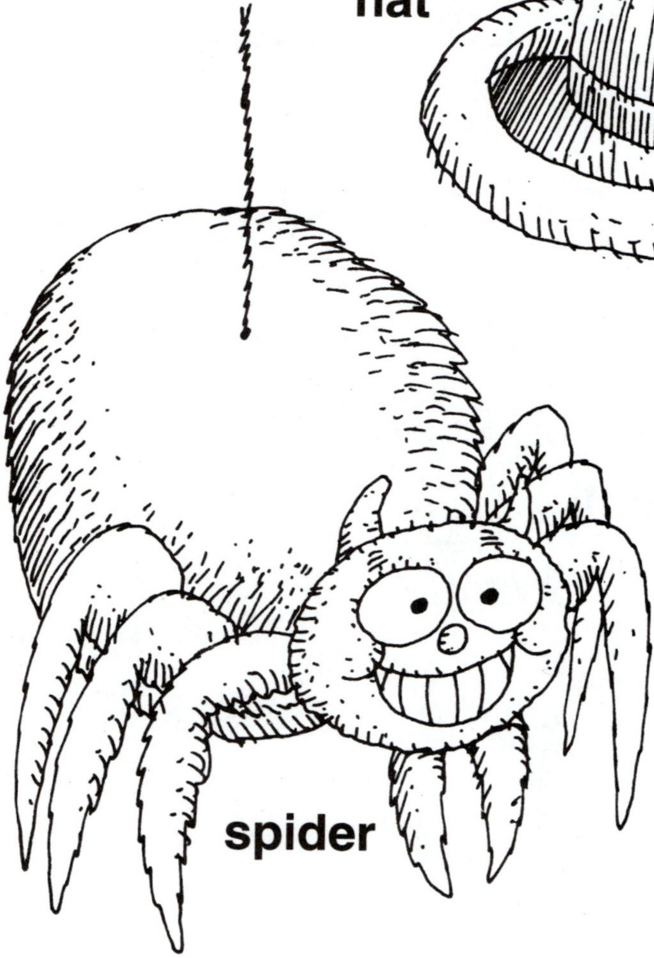

spider

witch's hat

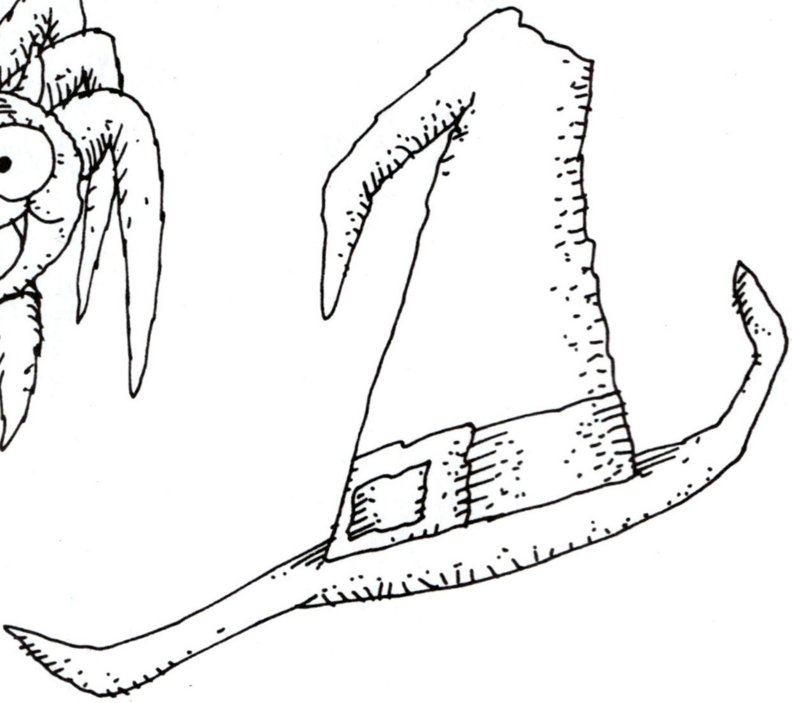

Colors and Shapes

brown

Color these things that are brown.

chocolate bar

fudge pop

log

chocolate ice cream

Skills: Distinguishing color; Classification; Word recognition

Colors and Shapes

Color this set of paints.

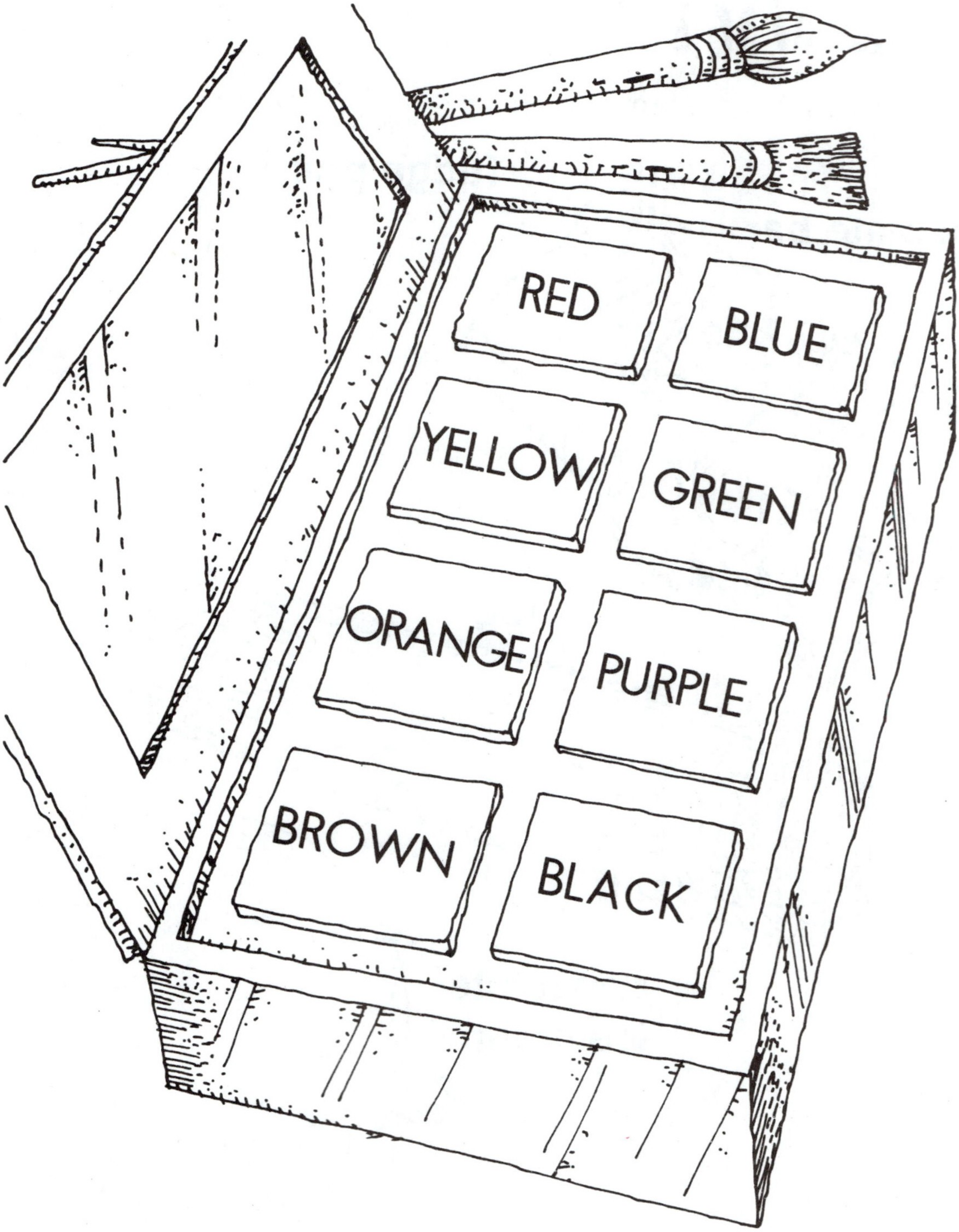

Colors and Shapes

Look at this circle: ◯.

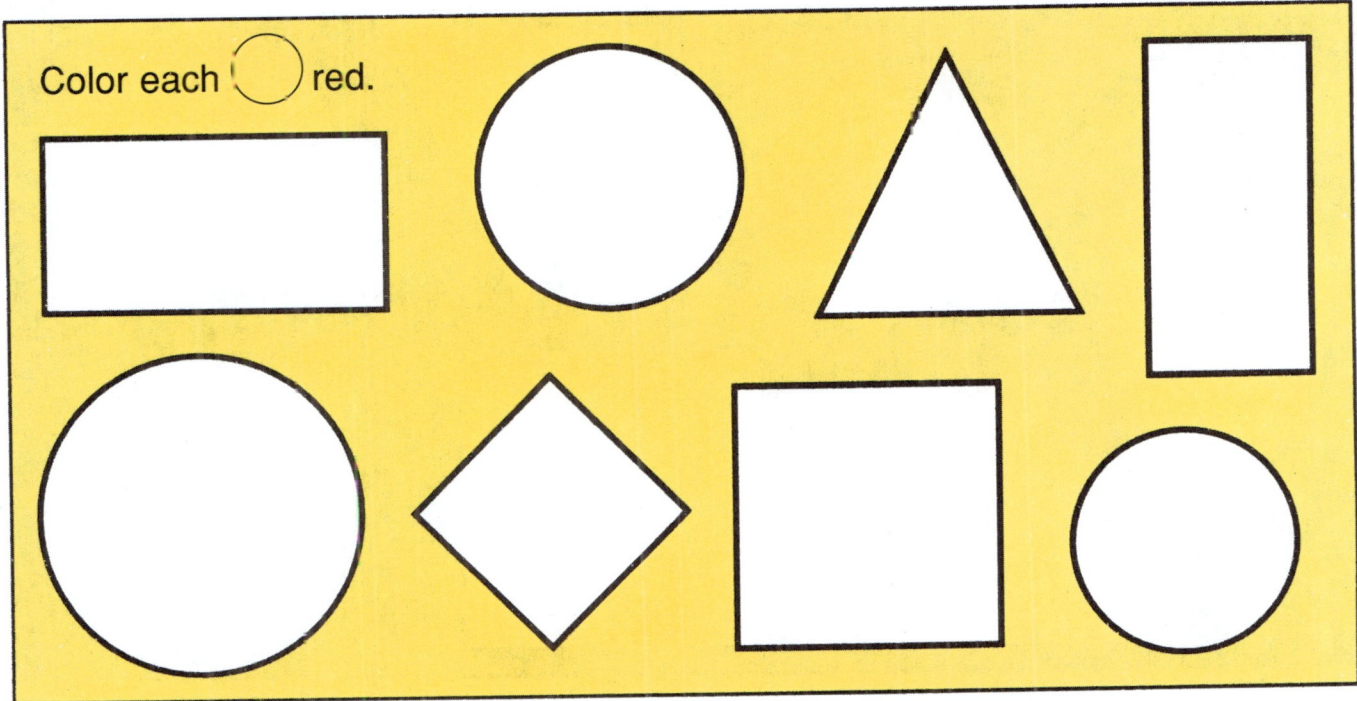

Look at this square: ☐.

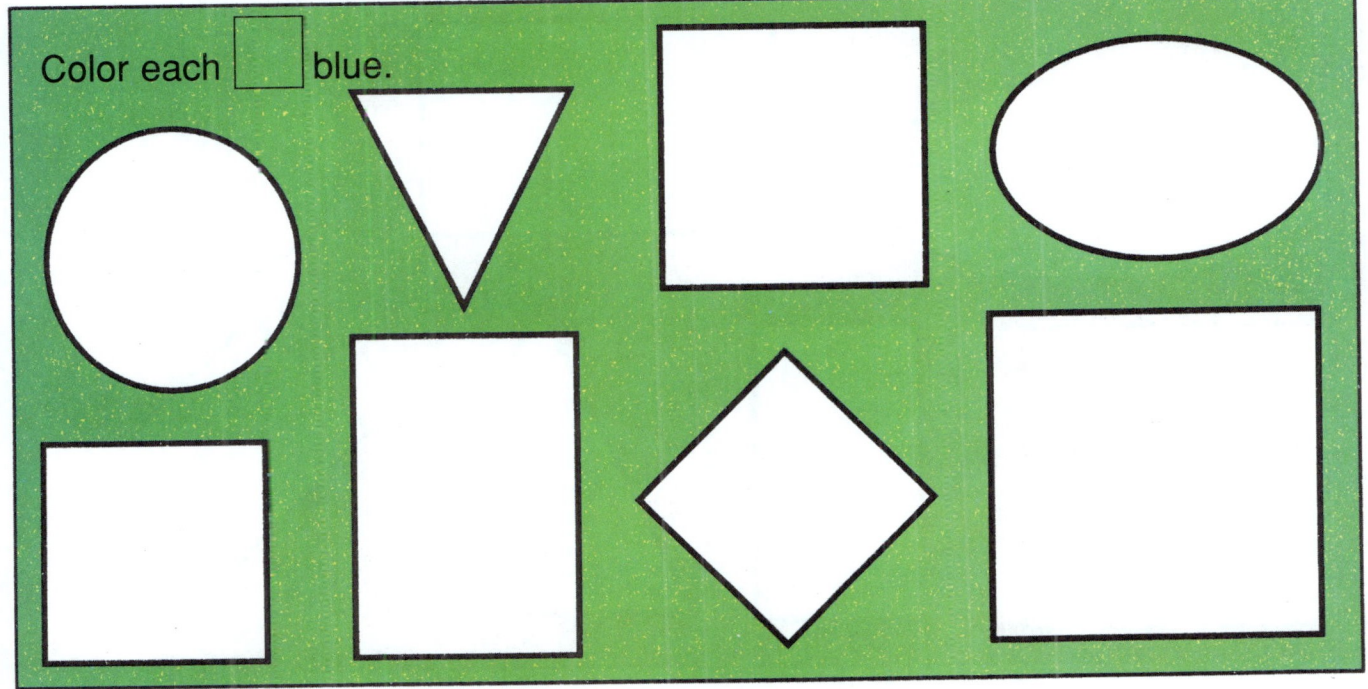

Skills: Shape recognition; Visual discrimination; Color recognition

Colors and Shapes

Look at this triangle: △ .

Color each △ green.

Look at this rectangle: ▭ .

Color each ▭ yellow.

Skills: Shape recognition; Visual discrimination; Color recognition

Colors and Shapes

Look at the first shape in each row.
Look at the other shapes. Color the shape that matches the first shape.

Skills: Shape recognition; Visual discrimination

Colors and Shapes

Color each ◯ red. Color each △ blue. Color each ▭ yellow.

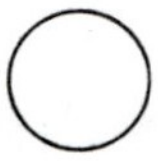

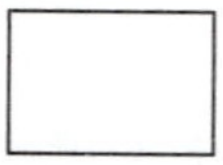

Skills: Color matching; Shape recognition; Following directions

Well Done!

Give yourself a star!

Reading Readiness

Reading Readiness

Look at the pictures. Draw a line to match the pictures that look the same.

Skills: Visual discrimination; Matching like figures; Following directions

Reading Readiness

Color the pictures in each row that are the same.

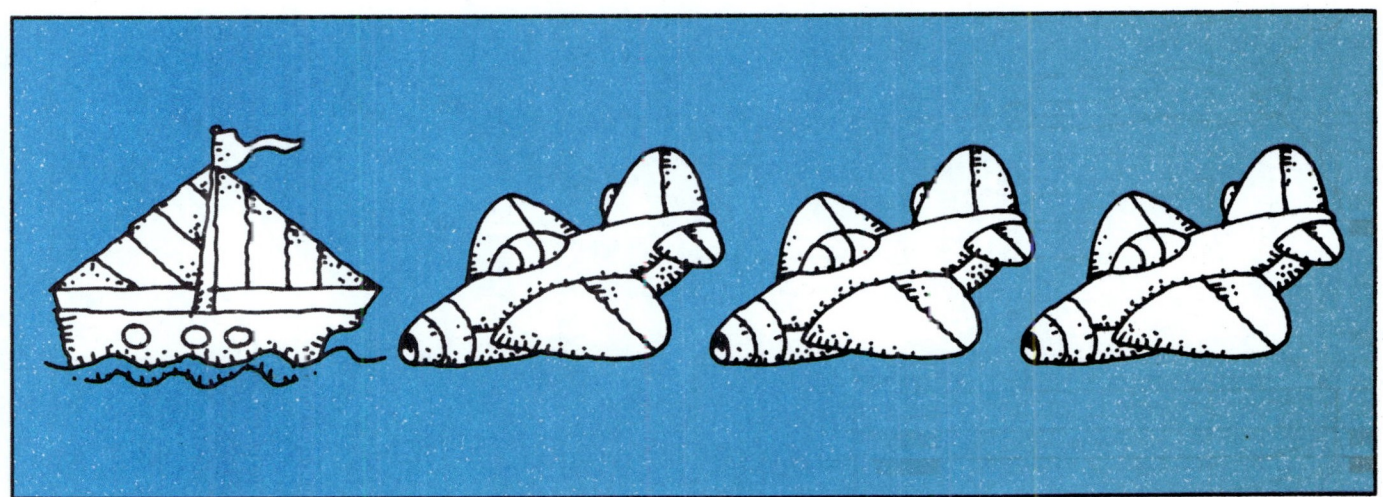

Skills: Visual discrimination; Matching like figures; Following directions

Reading Readiness

Color the pictures in each row that belong together.

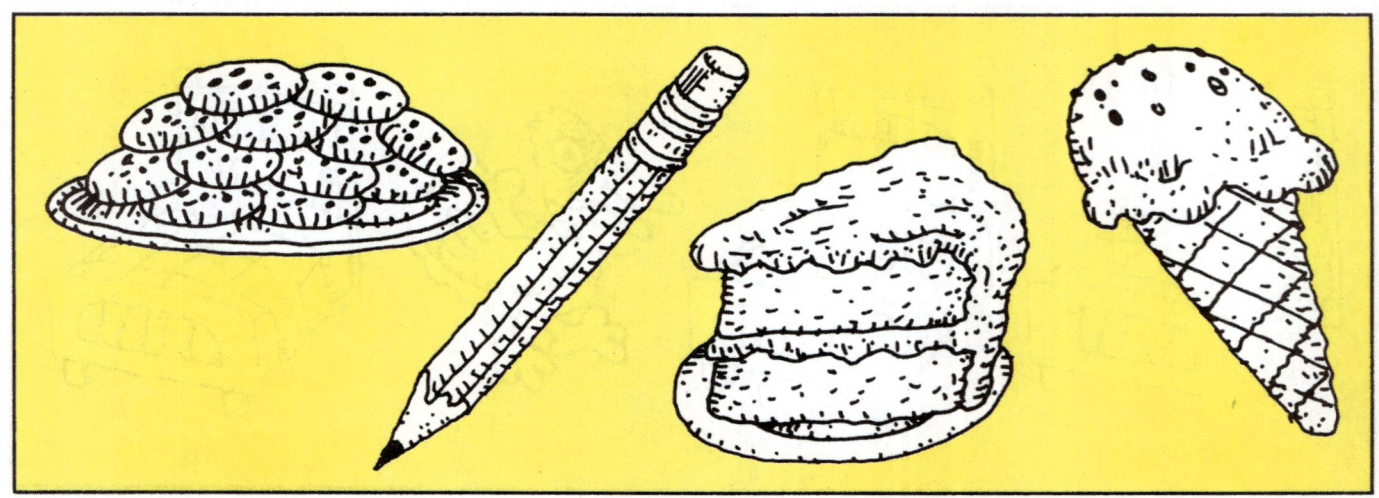
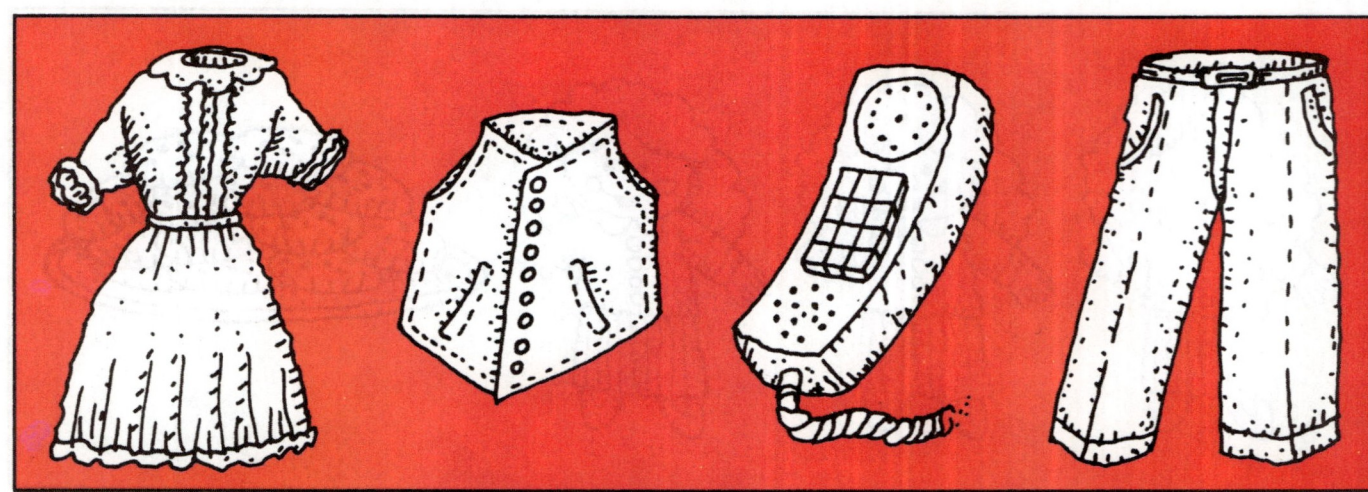

Skills: Association; Classification; Logical reasoning

Reading Readiness

Color the two pictures in each box that go together.

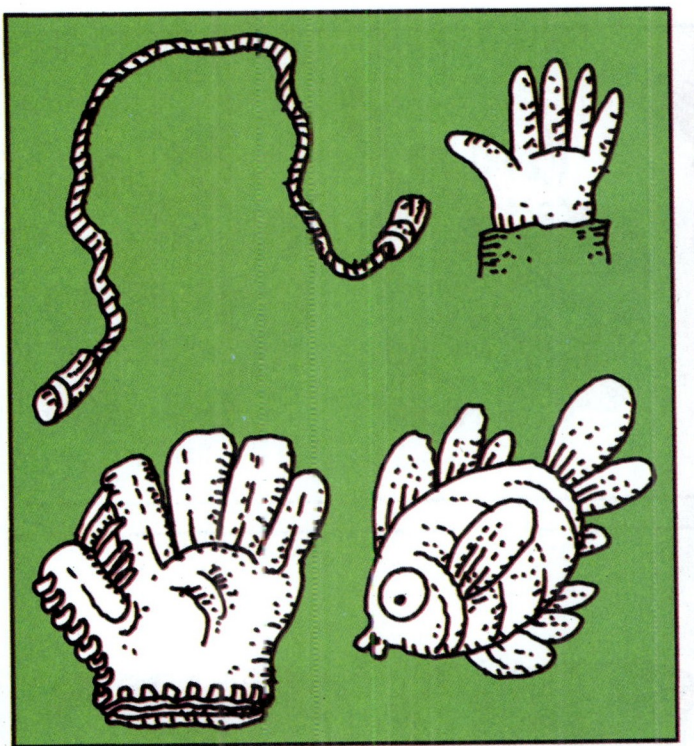

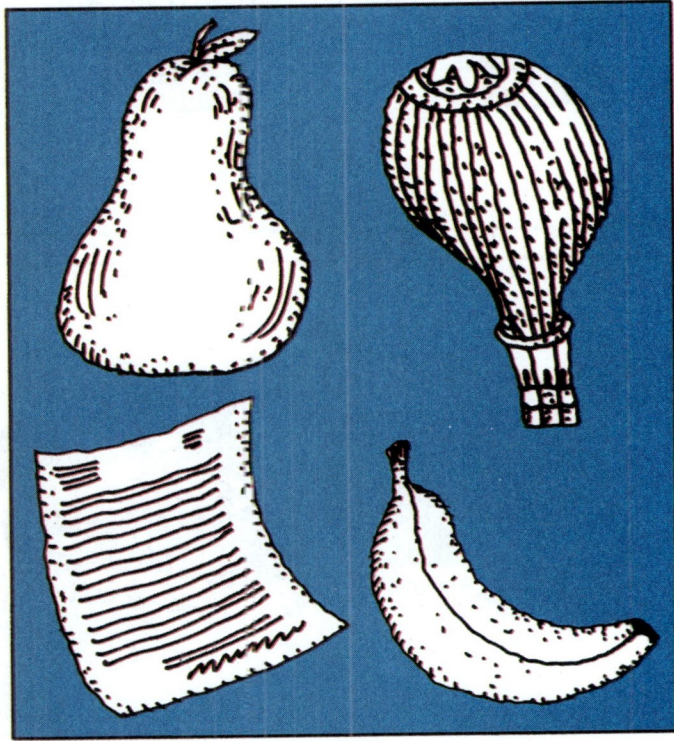

Skills: Association; Classification; Logical reasoning

Reading Readiness

Look at the pictures.
Circle the picture in each row that is different from the others.

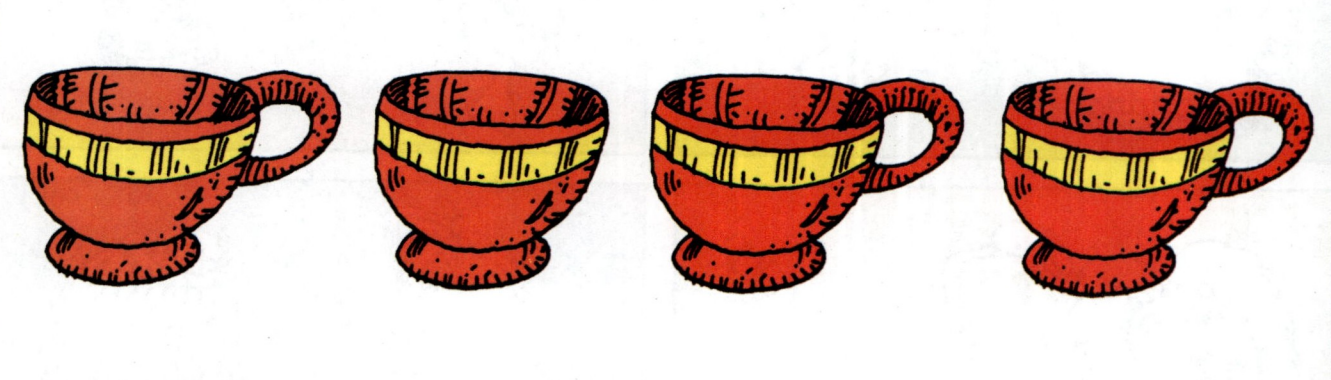

Skills: Visual discrimination; Noticing details; Following directions

Reading Readiness

Look at the pictures in each row.
Cross out the one that is different. Color the others.

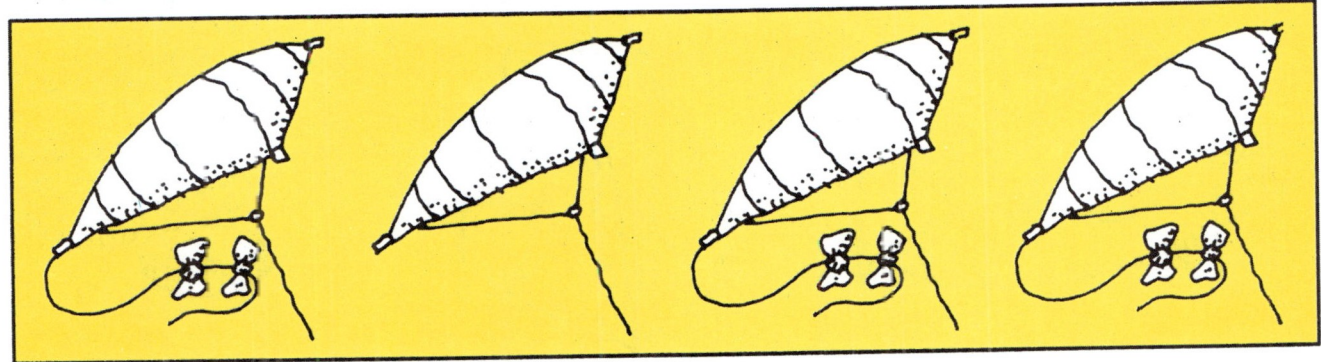

Skills: Visual discrimination; Noticing details; Following directions

Reading Readiness

Look at each picture. Which ones could you eat? Circle them. Then color all of the pictures.

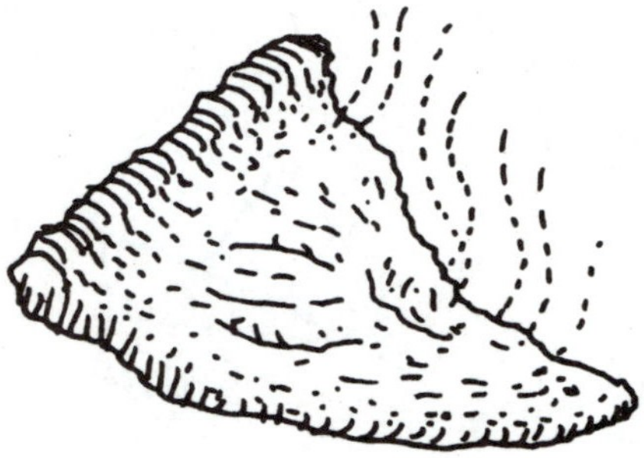

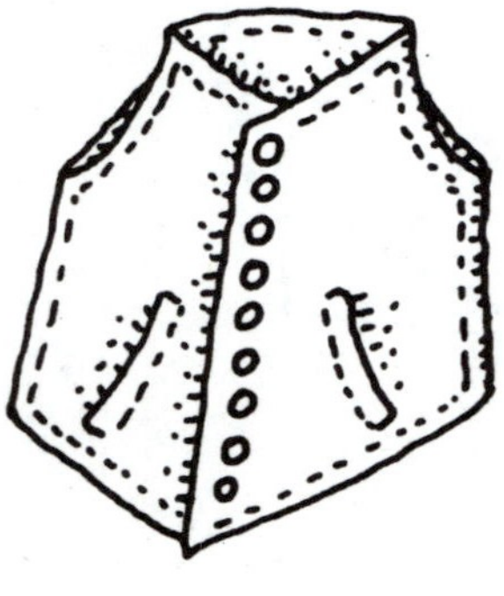

Skills: Association; Classification; Logical reasoning

Reading Readiness

Color the things that go in the air red.
Color the things that go in the water yellow.
Color the things that go on the land blue.

Skills: Classification; Sorting; Logical reasoning

Reading Readiness

Cross out the picture in each box that does not go with the others.
Color the other pictures.

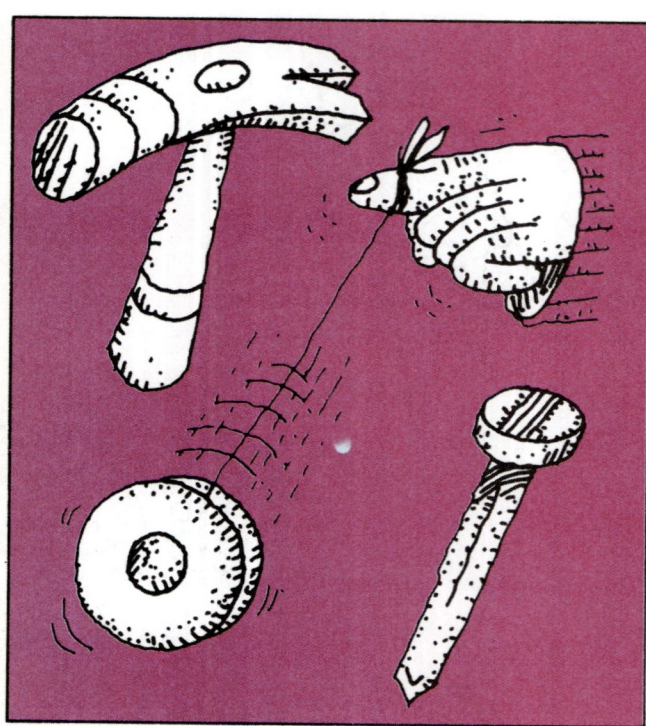

Skills: Association; Classification; Logical reasoning

Reading Readiness

Match the picture of each mother to her baby.

Skills: Association; Matching; Fine motor skill development

Reading Readiness

Where do you see these animals?
Circle the ones that you see on the land.
Draw a line under the ones that you see in the water.
Draw a line above the ones that you see in the air.

Skills: Classification; Association; Logical reasoning

Reading Readiness

Look at the pictures in each row.
Circle the picture that goes in a different direction from the others.
Then color the pictures.

Skills: Visual discrimination; Understanding directionality; Following directions

Reading Readiness

Look at the pictures in each row.
Circle the picture that goes in a different direction from the others.
Then color the pictures.

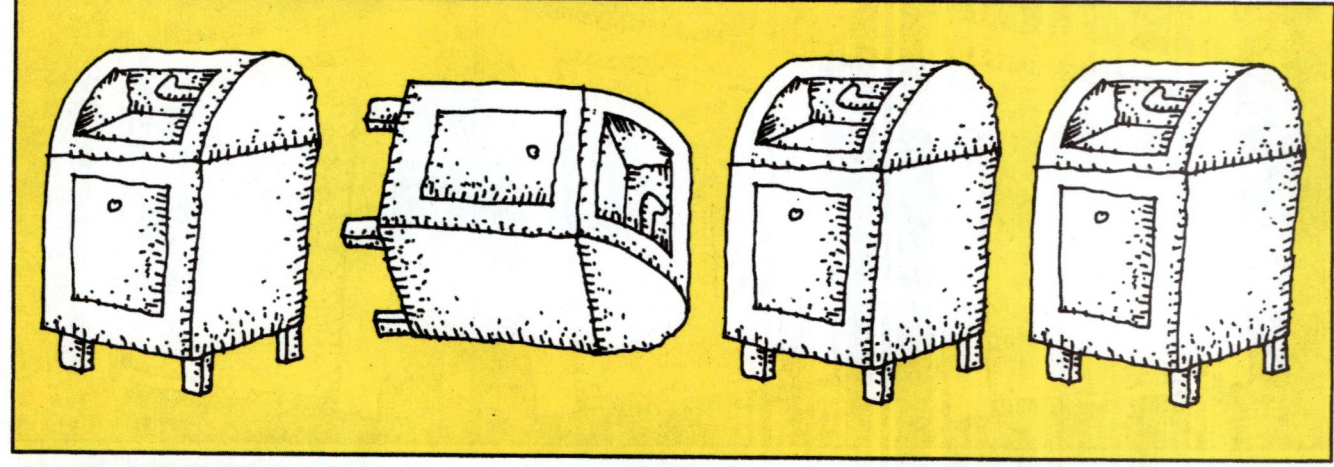

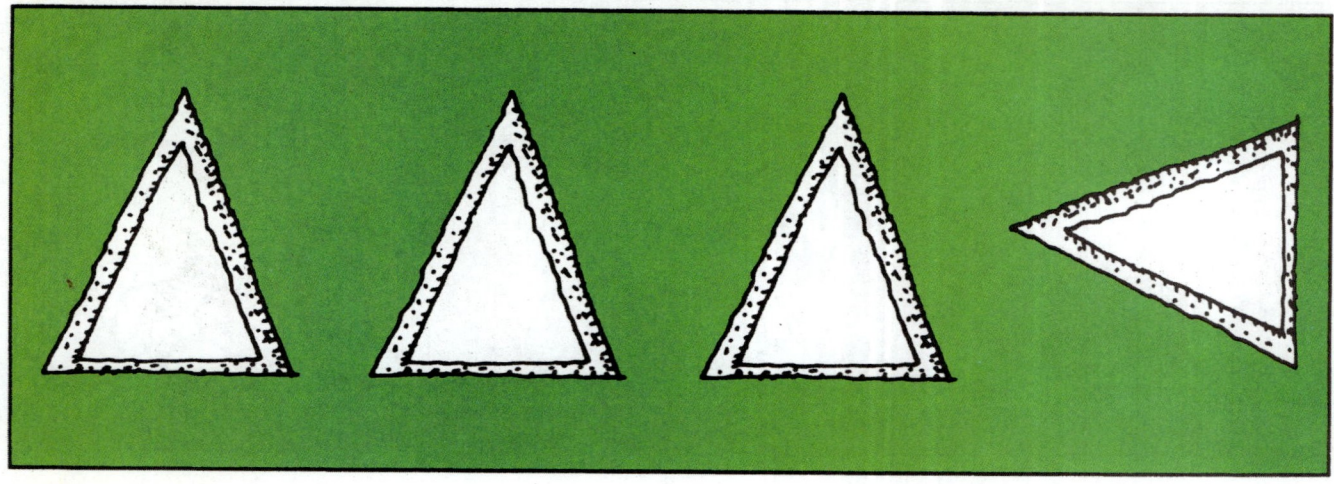

Skills: Visual discrimination; Understanding directionality; Following directions

Reading Readiness

Here are some animals you might see at a zoo.
Look carefully at each animal.
When you are ready, turn the page to play a memory game.

Skills: Visual memory; Association; Following directions

Reading Readiness

Look at the pictures on this page.
Which ones do you remember from the previous page?
Circle the ones you remember. Then color all the pictures.

Skills: Visual memory; Association; Following directions

Reading Readiness

Look at the picture of the cat in the center.
Say the name of each animal around the cat.
Draw a line from the cat to the pictures whose names rhyme with the word cat.

Skills: Auditory discrimination; Reproducing sounds

141

Reading Readiness

Look at the first picture in each row and say its name.
Circle the picture in the same row whose name rhymes with it.

Skills: Auditory discrimination; Reproducing sounds

Reading Readiness

Look at each picture and say its name.
Draw lines to match the rhyming pictures.

Skills: Auditory discrimination; Reproducing sounds

Reading Readiness

Look at each row of pictures.
Something is missing from one picture. Circle that picture.

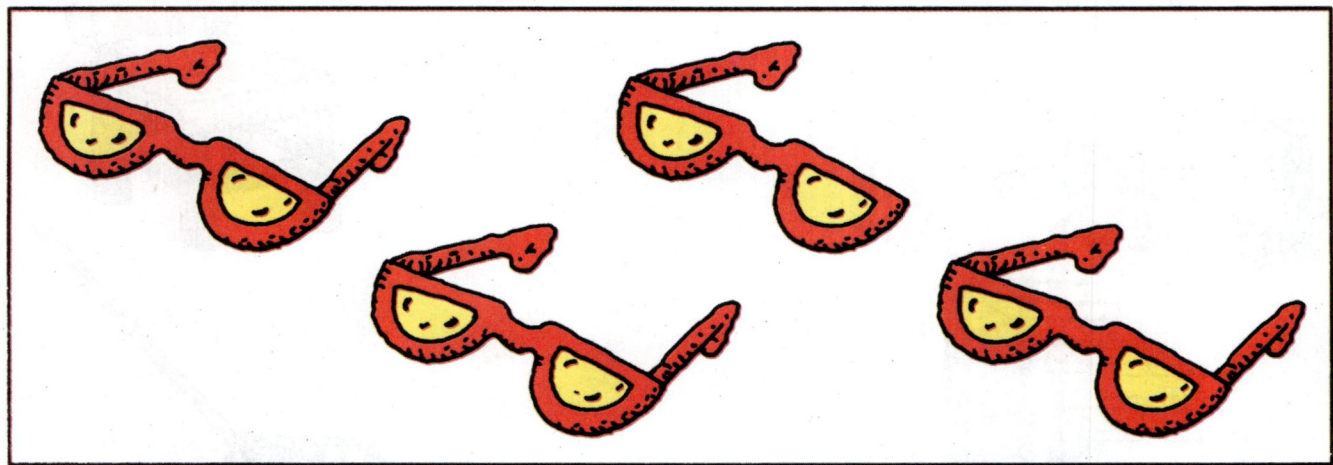

Skills: Visual discrimination; Noticing details

Reading Readiness

Look at the pictures in each row.
Circle the picture that is facing right.

Skills: Visual discrimination; Spacial orientation

Reading Readiness

Circle the pictures in each row that are the same.

Skills: Visual discrimination; Matching

146

Reading Readiness

Circle the pictures in each row that belong together.

Skills: Association; Classification; Logical reasoning

Reading Readiness

It's fun to play at a farm.
Draw a line to connect each mother with her baby.

Skills: Association; Classification

Reading Readiness

Look at the shapes.
Draw a line to connect each pair.

Skills: Understanding pairs; Matching

Reading Readiness

Color the A spaces red.
Color the B spaces blue.
Color the C spaces white.

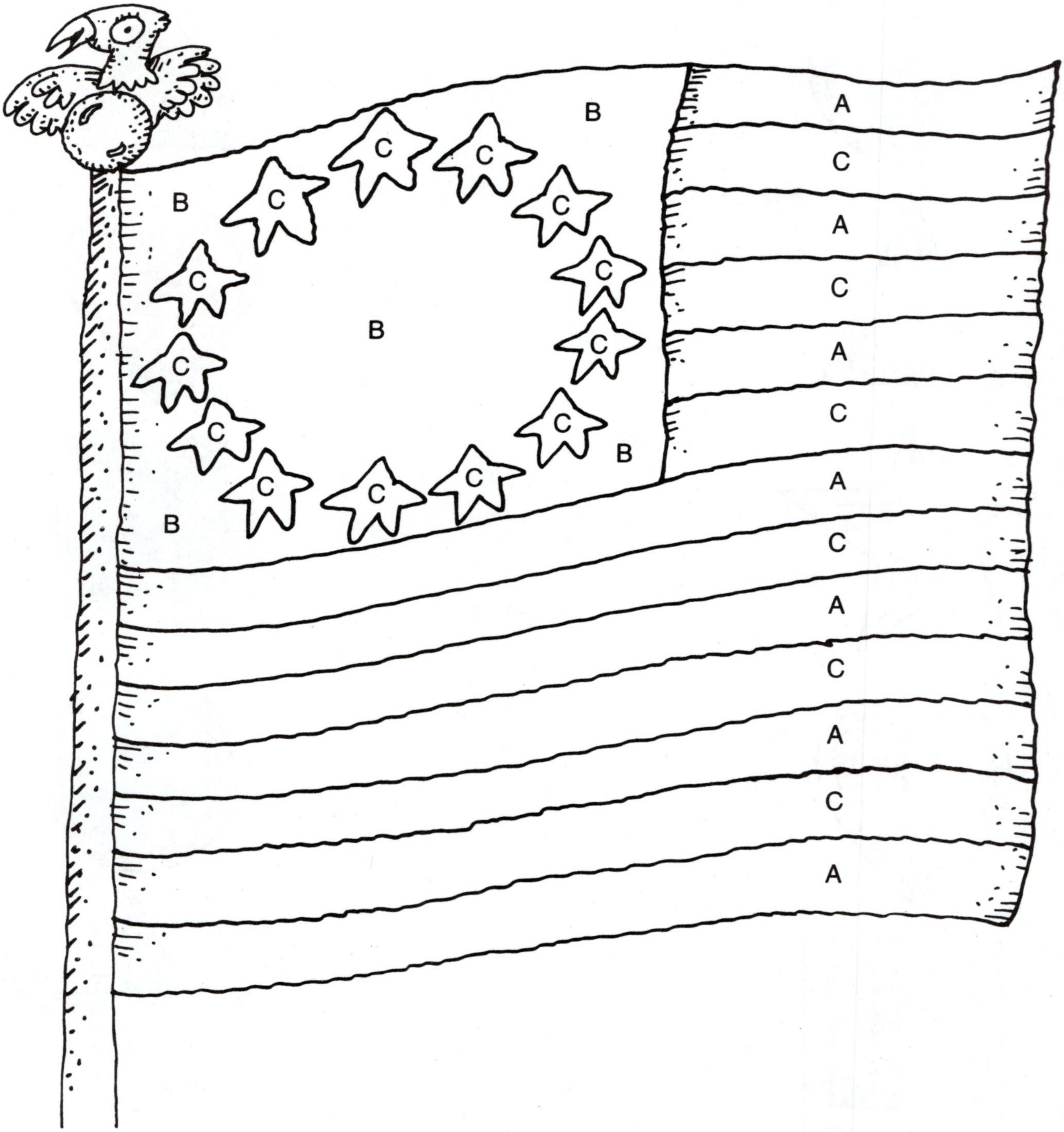

Skills: Distinguishing color; Matching letters to color codes

Reading Readiness

The pirates are looking for buried treasure.
Find a path through the maze to help them find their way.

Start

Finish

Skills: Visual perception; Fine motor skill development

Reading Readiness

Help the lion tamer get to the circus.
Find a path through the maze to help him find his way.

Start

Finish

Skills: Visual perception; Fine motor skill development

Reading Readiness

Look at the pattern in each row.
Draw a circle around a picture at the end of the row that continues the pattern.

Skills: Observing and continuing patterns; Visual discrimination

Reading Readiness

Look at the pattern in each row.
Draw a circle around a picture at the end of the row that continues the pattern.

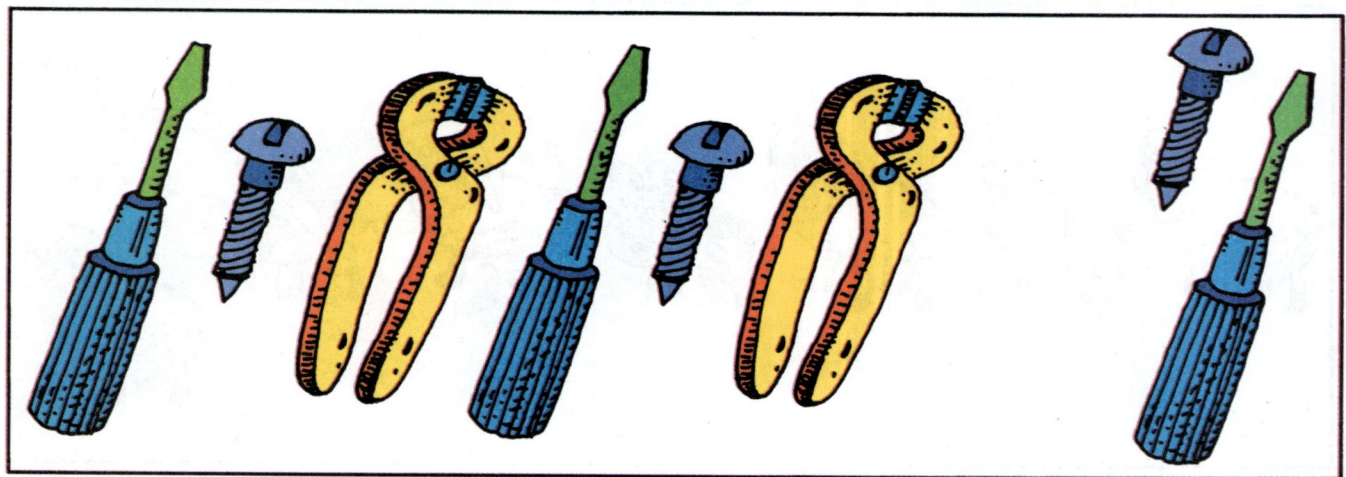

Skills: Observing and continuing patterns; Visual discrimination

Reading Readiness

Look at the pattern in each row.
Draw a circle around a picture at the end of the row that continues the pattern.

Skills: Observing and continuing patterns; Visual discrimination

 **Reading Readiness**

Trace the broken lines to complete the animals.
Then color the picture.

Skills: Fine motor skill development; Eye/hand coordination

Reading Readiness

Trace the dots to complete the pictures.
Then color the pictures.

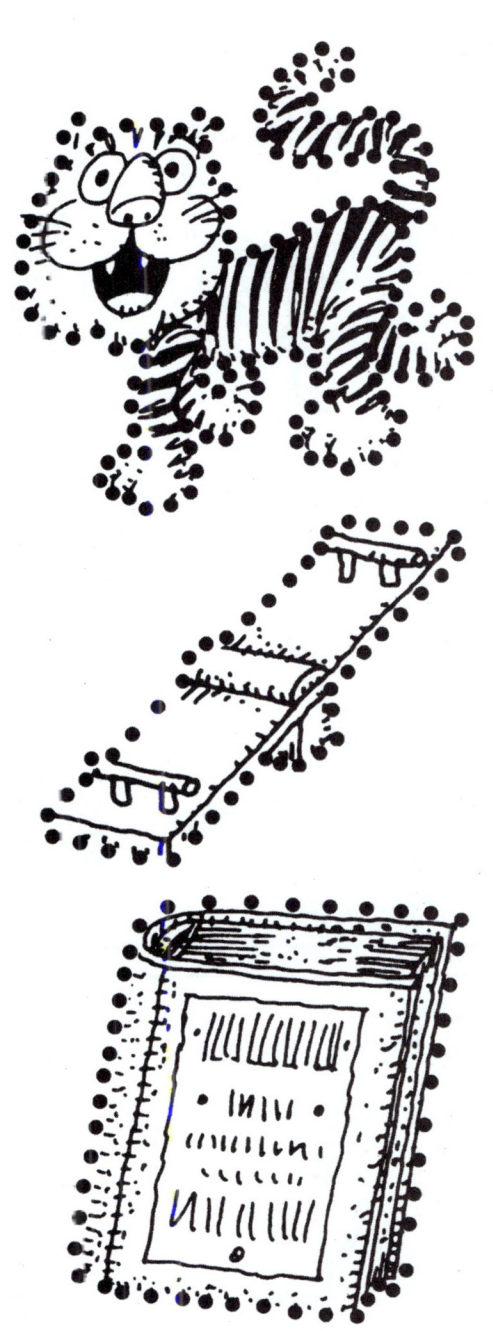

Skills: Fine motor skill development; Eye/hand coordination

Reading Readiness

Look closely at each row of pictures.
One of the pictures is in a different position. Circle that picture.

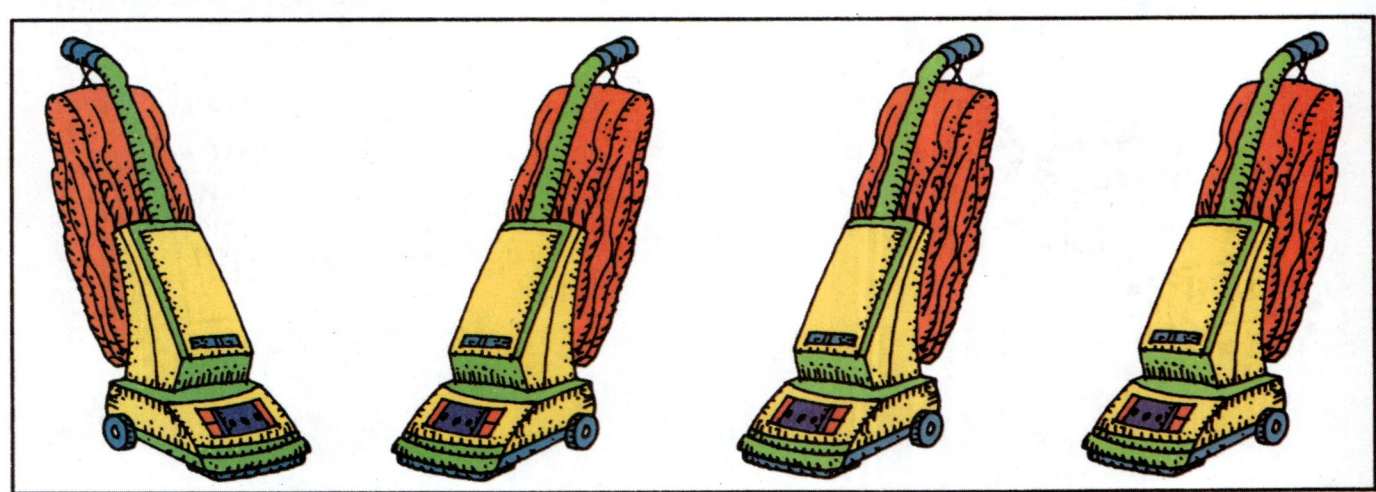

Skills: Visual discrimination; Spatial orientation; Following directions

Reading Readiness

Look closely at each row of pictures.
One of the pictures is in a different position. Put an X on that picture.

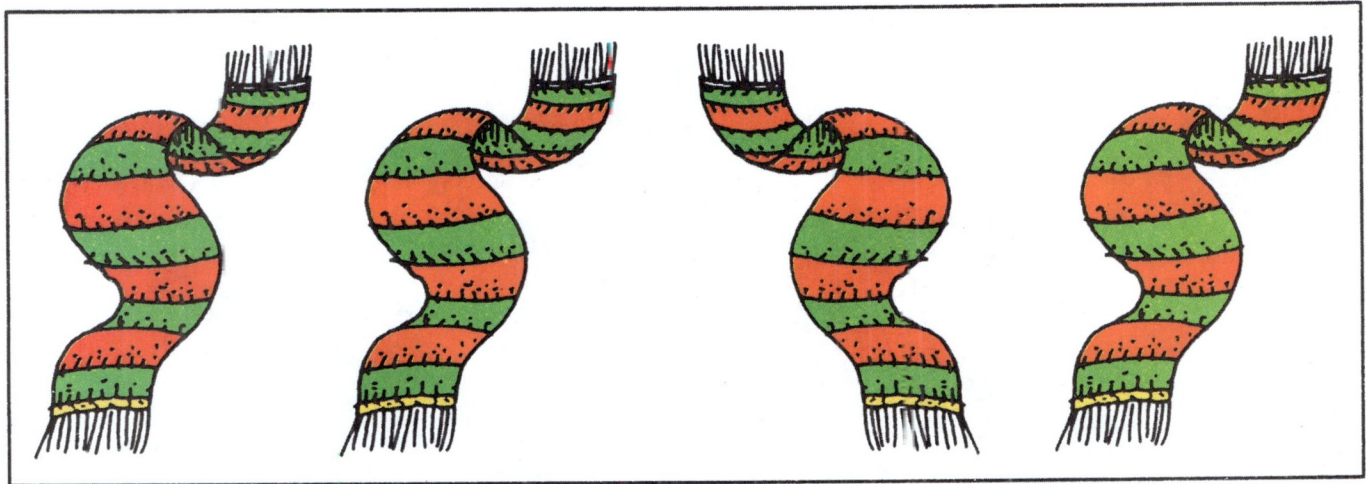

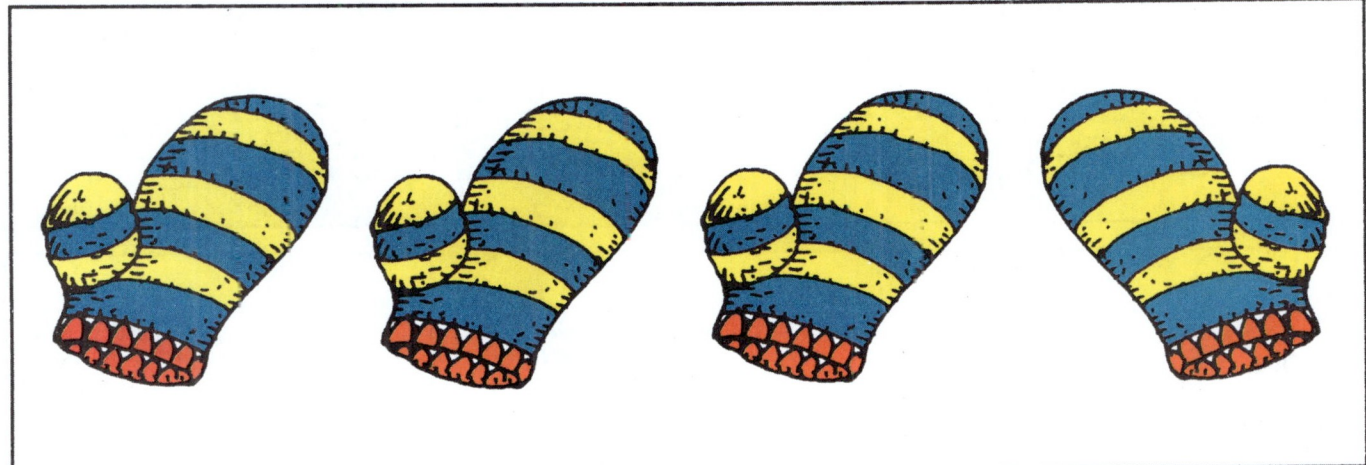

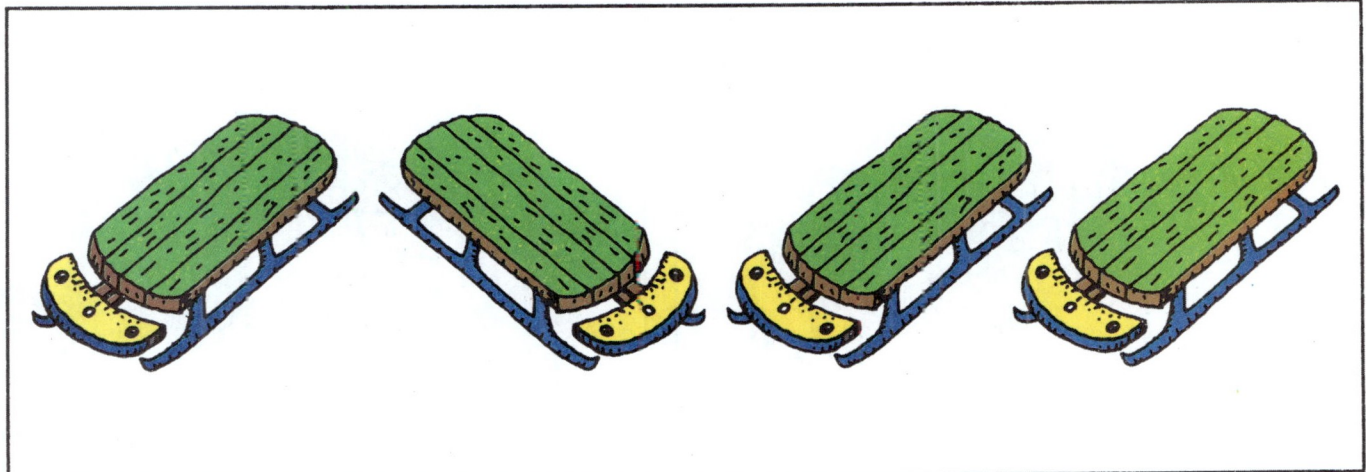

Skills: Visual discrimination; Spacial orientation; Following directions

Reading Readiness

Look at the large pictures. Then look at the detail in each small box. Find that detail in each large picture and circle it.

Skills: Visual discrimination; Noticing details

Reading Readiness

Look at the large pictures. Then look at the detail in each small box. Find that detail in each large picture and circle it.

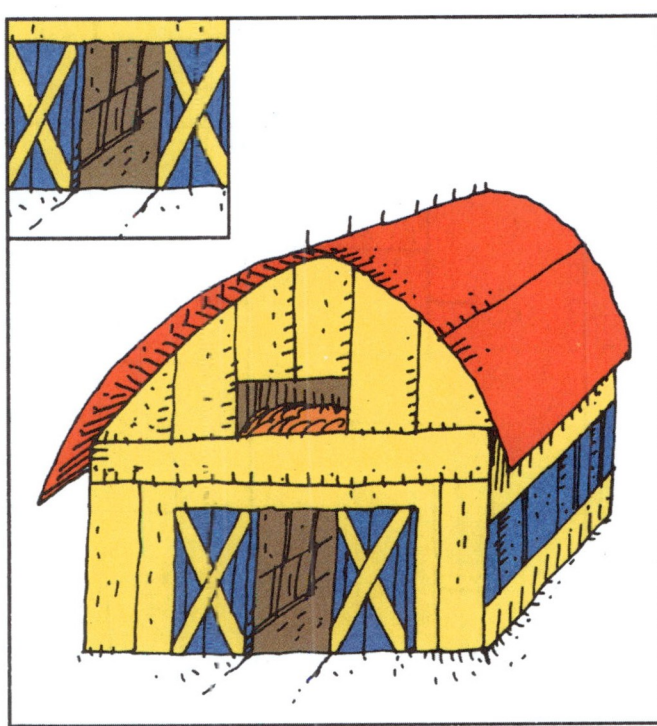

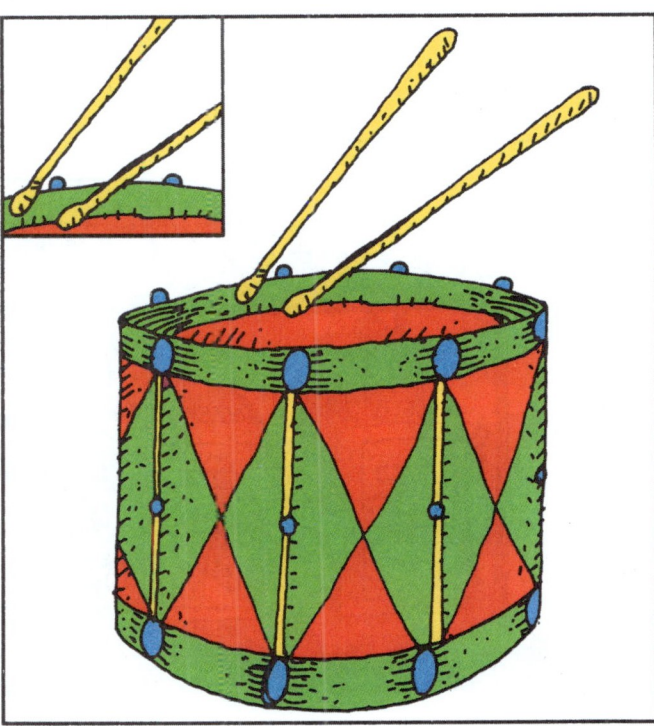

Skills: Visual discrimination; Noticing details

Reading Readiness

The car needs gas. Help it get to the gas station.
Find a path through the maze.

Start

Finish

Skills: Visual perception; Fine motor skill development

Reading Readiness

Help the ducks find their way to the pond.
Find a path through the maze.

Reading Readiness

Cluck, cluck, cluck, I sit on my nest. Laying eggs is what I do best. Connect the dots from A to Z to find out what lays eggs. Then color the picture.

Skills: Letter order; Recognition of uppercase letters

Reading Readiness

Connect the dots from a to z to find out what is walking slowly to the lily pads. Then color the picture.

Skills: Letter order; Recognition of lowercase letters

Reading Readiness

Look closely at the picture.
Find and circle the letters C, A, T, M, O, U, S, E hidden in the picture.

Skills: Recognizing letters of the alphabet

Good Job!

Give yourself a star!

Picture Dictionary

Picture Dictionary

Aa

airplane An airplane is a flying machine that has engines and wings.

apple An apple is a fruit that grows on trees.

anchor An anchor is a heavy piece of metal used for keeping a boat in one place.

astronaut An astronaut explores outer space.

ant An ant is a tiny insect.

What other word begins with **a**? Write the word below. Then draw and tell about it.

Skills: Building vocabulary

Picture Dictionary

Bb

baby A baby is a very young child.

bear A bear is a large furry animal.

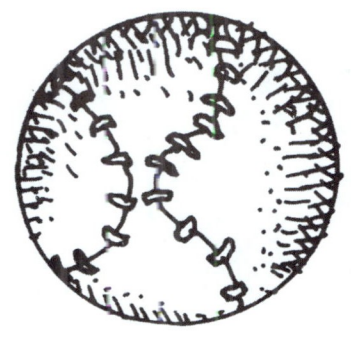

ball A ball is a round toy used for sports.

bib A bib is something you wear to keep your clothes clean while you eat.

banana A banana is a yellow fruit that has a long, curved shape.

bird A bird is an animal with feathers and wings.

Skills: Building vocabulary

Picture Dictionary

boat A boat is a floating vehicle for sailing on the water.

boy A boy is a male child.

book A book has pages with words to read and pictures to look at.

butterfly A butterfly is an insect with big, delicate wings.

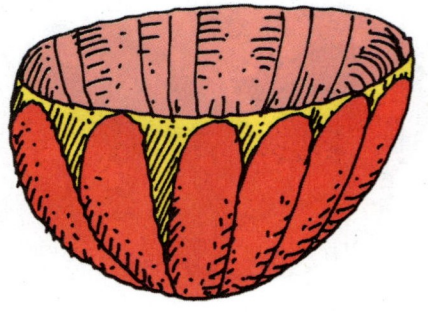

bowl A bowl is a round container for foods like cereal or soup.

What other word begins with **b**? Write the word below. Then draw and tell about it.

BAT

Skills: Building vocabulary

Picture Dictionary

cake A cake is a dessert usually made using flour, sugar, and eggs.

clock A clock is an instrument used for telling time.

castle A castle is a large stone fortress where kings, queens, and knights lived hundreds of years ago.

corn Corn is a vegetable that grows on a tall stalk.

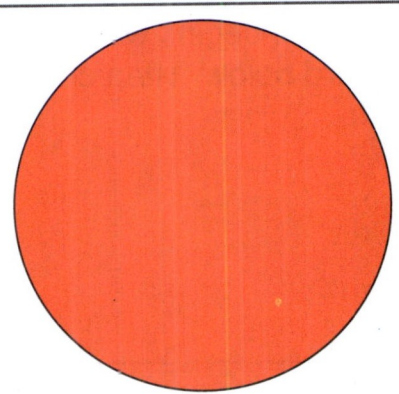

circle A circle is a round shape.

What other word begins with **c**? Write the word below. Then draw and tell about it.

CAT

Skills: Building vocabulary

Picture Dictionary

deer A deer is a brown furry animal that lives in the forest.

doctor A doctor is a person who takes care of people who are ill.

desk A desk is a piece of furniture that people sit at to write.

duck A duck is a bird that flies in the air and swims in the water.

dinosaur A dinosaur is a huge prehistoric animal that lived millions of years ago.

What other word begins with **d**? Write the word below. Then draw and tell about it.

_____

- - - - - - - - - - - - - - - - - - -

_____

Skills: Building vocabulary

Picture Dictionary

Ee

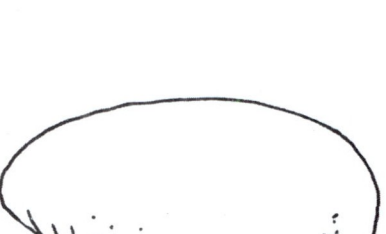

egg An egg is what a baby bird hatches from. It has a hard shell.

elephant An elephant is a very large gray animal with a trunk.

eight Eight is a number that is one more than seven.

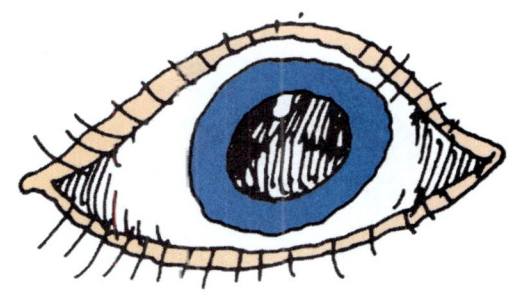

eye An eye is a body part that helps you to see. People have two eyes.

elbow An elbow is the joint that allows your arm to bend.

What other word begins with **e**? Write the word below. Then draw and tell about it.

_____

Skills: Building vocabulary

Picture Dictionary

farmer A farmer is a person who grows things on a farm.

flag A flag is a piece of colored fabric attached to a pole, often symbolizing a country.

feather A feather is the soft outer covering on a bird.

fruit A fruit is a part of a plant that has seeds or a pit. You can eat many kinds of fruit.

fish A fish is an animal that lives in the water and breathes through gills.

What other word begins with **f**? Write the word below. Then draw and tell about it.

_____

- - - - - - - - - - - - - - - - - - -

_____

Skills: Building vocabulary

Picture Dictionary

garage A garage is a building where cars are kept.

giant A giant is a very big and strong person in fairy tales.

garden A garden is a plot of land that is used to grow flowers or vegetables.

gift A gift is something given from one person to another.

gate A gate is a door in a fence or a wall.

giraffe A giraffe is a tall animal with a long neck.

Skills: Building vocabulary

Picture Dictionary

girl A girl is a female child.

grandparents Grandparents are the parents of your mother or father.

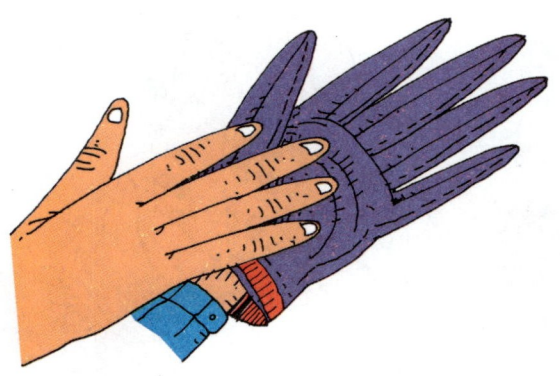

glove A glove is a covering with separate fingers to keep the hands warm.

grass Grass is a plant with thin green leaves that grows in fields and lawns.

goat A goat is a four-legged animal with horns.

What other word begins with **g**? Write the word below. Then draw and tell about it.

_____

- - - - - - - - - - - - - - - - - - -

_____

Skills: Building vocabulary

Picture Dictionary

Hh

hammer A hammer is a tool with a long handle and a heavy head for banging things.

horse A horse is a four-legged animal with a long tail and a mane.

harp A harp is a musical instrument with a large frame and strings.

hug A hug is putting your arms tightly around another person in a loving way.

helicopter A helicopter is a flying machine that has a propeller on top instead of wings.

What other word begins with **h**?
Write the word below. Then draw and tell about it.

Skills: Building vocabulary

Picture Dictionary

I i

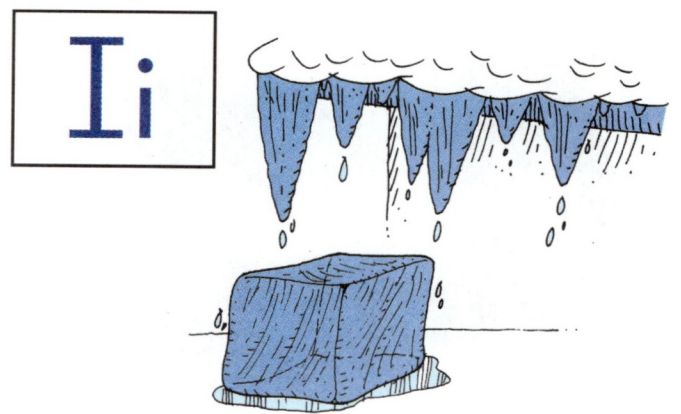

ice Ice is frozen water.

iron An iron is a tool that is heated up and used to take the wrinkles out of clothes.

ice cream Ice cream is a frozen dessert made from cream and sugar.

ivy Ivy is a kind of green plant that often grows on walls and gates.

insect An insect is an invertebrate with a jointed, or segmented, body.

What other word begins with **i**? Write the word below. Then draw and tell about it.

_____

- - - - - - - - - - - - - - - -

_____

Skills: Building vocabulary

Picture Dictionary

Jj

jacket A jacket is a short coat.

juice Juice is a liquid that comes from squeezing fruit.

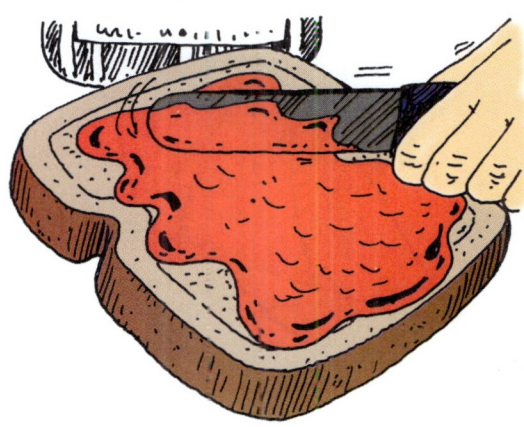

jelly Jelly is a kind of smooth spread made out of fruit.

jungle The jungle is a thick tropical forest.

jet A jet is a very fast airplane.

What other word begins with **j**? Write the word below. Then draw and tell about it.

_____

- - - - - - - - - - - - - - - - - - -

_____

Skills: Building vocabulary

Picture Dictionary

Kk

kangaroo A kangaroo is a large animal that comes from Australia. Female kangaroos carry their babies in pouches.

kitchen A kitchen is a room where food is cooked and stored.

key A key is a flat piece of metal that opens and closes a lock.

kite A kite is a toy that flies in the wind on a string.

king A king is a man who rules his country.

What other word begins with **k**?
Write the word below. Then draw and tell about it.

_____

Skills: Building vocabulary

Picture Dictionary

Ll

ladybug A ladybug is a small beetle that is usually red with black spots.

lemon A lemon is a yellow fruit that has a sour taste.

lamp A lamp is an object that uses flame or electricity to make light.

lion A lion is a large wild cat that lives in the jungle.

leaf A leaf is the thin flat part of a plant.

What other word begins with **l**?
Write the word below. Then draw and tell about it.

_____

- - - - - - - - - - - - - - - - - - -

_____

Skills: Building vocabulary

Picture Dictionary

map A map is a drawing that shows what an area looks like from above.

mouse A mouse is a tiny animal with sharp teeth and a long tail.

milk Milk is a white liquid that comes from female animals. We drink cow's milk.

mug A mug is a heavy cup with a handle.

monkey A monkey is an animal with long arms and a very flexible tail.

What other word begins with **m**? Write the word below. Then draw and tell about it.

Skills: Building vocabulary

Picture Dictionary

Nn

nail A nail is a piece of metal with a sharp end that is hammered into things to hold them together.

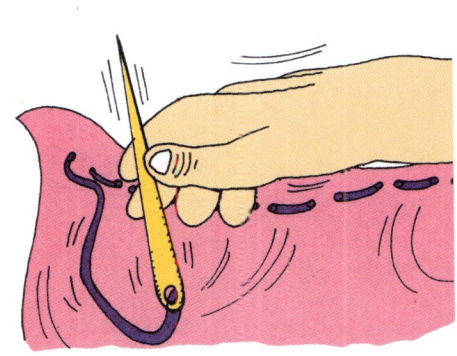

needle A needle is a thin piece of metal used for sewing.

napkin A napkin is a cloth or paper that is used for wiping fingers and mouths.

nest A nest is a home made by birds or other small animals using grass, twigs, and other things.

necklace A necklace is a piece of jewelry worn around the neck.

What other word begins with **n**?
Write the word below. Then draw and tell about it.

_____

Skills: Building vocabulary

Picture Dictionary

Oo

oar An oar is a paddle used for rowing a boat.

onion An onion is a small vegetable with a very strong taste and smell.

octopus An octopus is a sea animal with eight long arms.

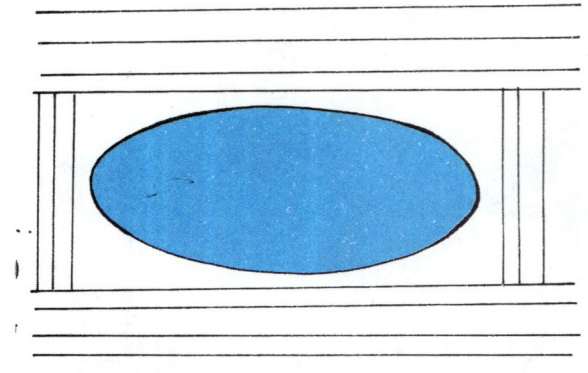

oval An oval is a rounded, oblong shape.

one One is the number before two.

What other word begins with **o**? Write the word below. Then draw and tell about it.

Skills: Building vocabulary

Picture Dictionary

P p

pajamas Pajamas are clothing that people wear while they sleep.

piano A piano is a large keyboard instrument with black and white keys.

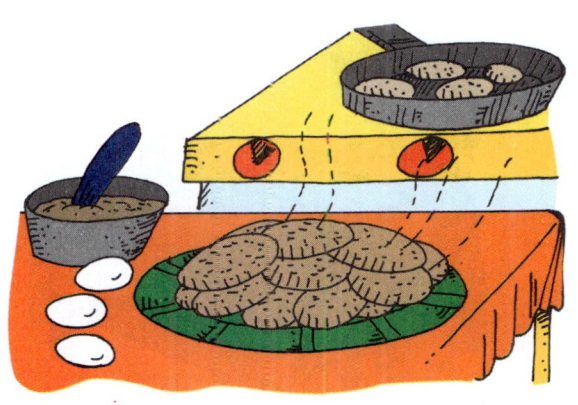

pancake A pancake is a thin, flat breakfast cake made from flour, eggs, and milk.

pot A pot is a deep round pan used for cooking, usually made out of metal.

parrot A parrot is a brightly colored bird with a curved beak. Parrots can be taught to speak.

What other word begins with **p**?
Write the word below. Then draw and tell about it.

Skills: Building vocabulary

Picture Dictionary

quack "Quack" is the sound that a duck makes.

question mark A question mark is a symbol put at the end of a sentence that asks a question.

quarter A quarter is a coin worth 25 cents.

quilt A quilt is a soft, puffy cover for a bed.

queen A queen is a woman who rules a country.

What other word begins with **q**? Write the word below. Then draw and tell about it.

_____

- -

_____

Skills: Building vocabulary

Picture Dictionary

Rr

rabbit A rabbit is a small, furry animal that has long ears and hops.

robot A robot is a machine that is built to do jobs that people do.

rainbow A rainbow is a curve of many-colored light that can be seen in the sky after it rains.

rug A rug is a floor covering made from wool or cloth.

river A river is a wide path of water that flows toward the sea.

What other word begins with **r**?
Write the word below. Then draw and tell about it.

_____

Skills: Building vocabulary

Picture Dictionary

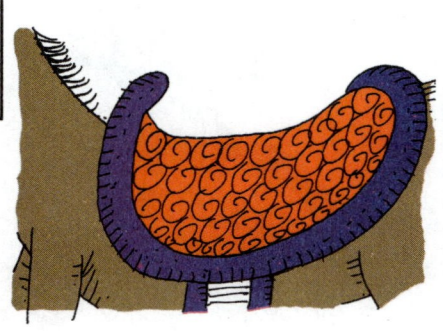

saddle A saddle is a seat for a rider on a horse.

seal A seal is a sea animal that has thick fur and flippers.

saw A saw is a tool used for cutting wood.

ship A ship is a large boat used for carrying people or things.

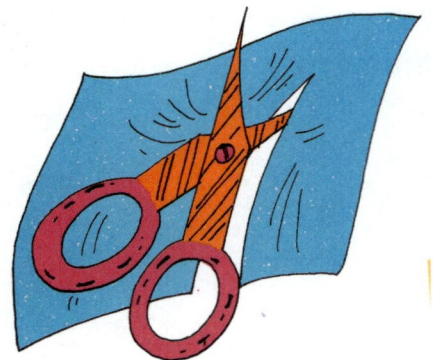

scissors Scissors are sharp tools used for cutting paper or cloth.

What other word begins with **s**? Write the word below. Then draw and tell about it.

_____

Skills: Building vocabulary

Picture Dictionary

table A table is a kind of furniture with a flat top that you can put things on.

T t

tomato A tomato is a type of soft fruit that is red or green.

telephone A telephone is an instrument used for talking to a person in another place.

towel A towel is a large piece of soft material used for drying things.

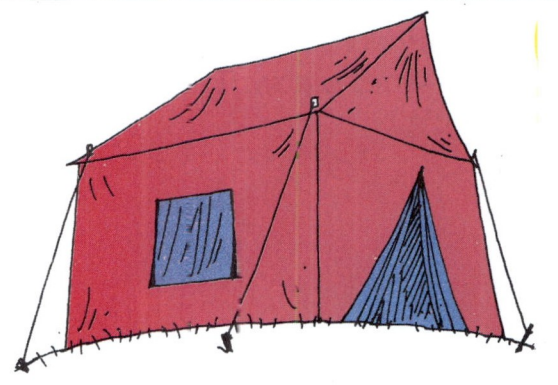

tent A tent is a shelter that is made from poles, rope, and fabric.

What other word begins with **t**? Write the word below. Then draw and tell about it.

Skills: Building vocabulary

Picture Dictionary

umbrella An umbrella is a thing you unfold and hold above your head to keep dry in the rain.

uniform Uniform is a clothing that people wear to show that they belong to a certain group.

umpire An umpire is an official who calls balls, strikes, and outs in a baseball game.

upside-down Upside-down means that the bottom is on the top and the top is on the bottom.

uncle Your uncle is your mother or father's brother.

What other word begins with **u**? Write the word below. Then draw and tell about it.

_____

- -

_____

Skills: Building vocabulary

Picture Dictionary

van A van is a large vehicle with lots of space inside.

violin A violin is a musical instrument with four strings that is played with a bow.

vegetable A vegetable is a part of a plant that people can eat.

voice Your voice is the sound you make when you speak or sing.

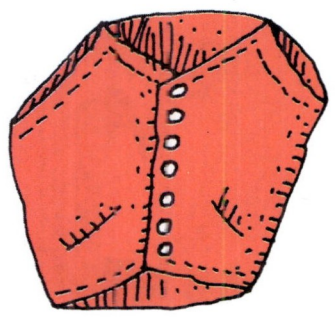

vest A vest is a jacket or sweater without sleeves.

What other word begins with **v**?
Write the word below. Then draw and tell about it.

_____

- -

Skills: Building vocabulary

Picture Dictionary

Ww

wagon A wagon is a cart used to carry people or things.

watch A watch is a small clock that you wear on your wrist.

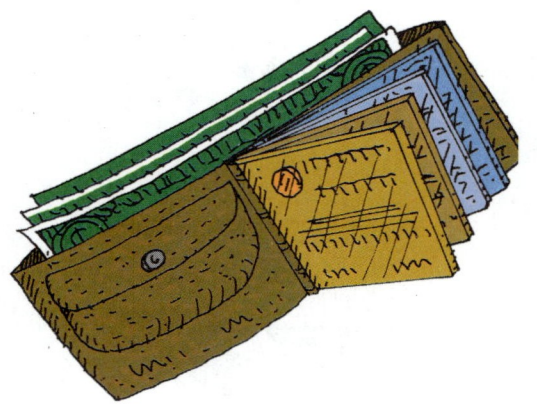

wallet A wallet is a small flat case used for carrying money or cards.

water Water is a clear, flavorless liquid that people drink or wash with.

wand A wand is a magic stick carried by a magician or fairy.

web A web is a net that a spider makes to catch insects.

Skills: Building vocabulary

Picture Dictionary

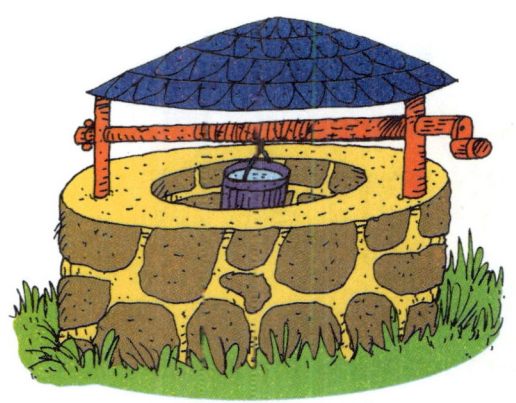

well A well is a deep hole where people lower a bucket to get water.

wolf A wolf is a wild animal that looks like a large dog.

whale A whale is a large mammal that lives in the sea and spouts water.

worm A worm is a small creature with no legs that lives in the dirt.

wheel A wheel is a circular object with flat sides that rolls.

What other word begins with **w**?
Write the word below. Then draw and tell about it.

_____

_____

Skills: Building vocabulary

Picture Dictionary

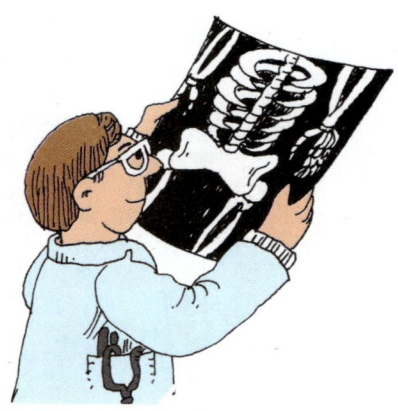

x-ray An x-ray is a picture that shows the inside of the body.

xylophone A xylophone is a musical instrument made of metal or wooden bars that are tapped with a small hammer.

There are not many other words that begin with this letter. But X marks the spot for hidden treasure. There are 7 Xs in this picture, some in words, some not. Can you find and circle all of them?

Skills: Building vocabulary

Picture Dictionary

yak A yak is a wild ox with long hair.

yawn A yawn is when you open your mouth and breathe in. People usually yawn when they are tired.

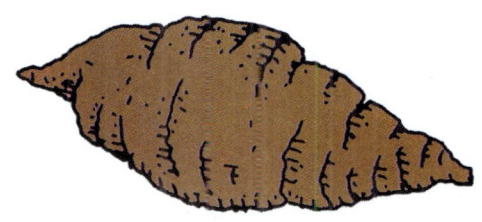

yam Yam is another name for a sweet potato.

yo-yo A yo-yo is a round toy that moves up and down on a string.

yarn Yarn is a kind of string made from wool or cotton, for knitting.

You begins with the letter **y**. Write your name. Then draw a picture of yourself in the frame.

Skills: Building vocabulary

Picture Dictionary

Zz

zebra A zebra is a black and white striped animal that looks like a horse.

zigzag A zigzag is a series of short slanted lines that go back and forth.

zero Zero is a number that equals nothing.

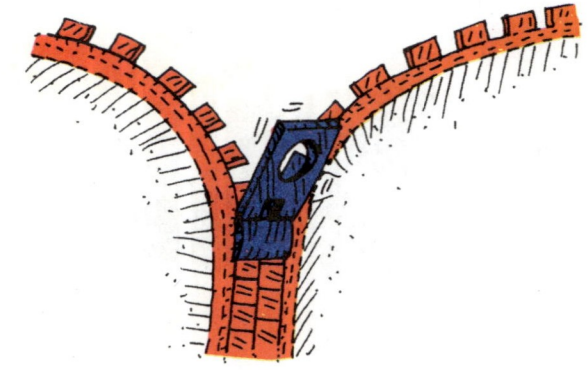

zipper A zipper is used to fasten and unfasten clothing and other things.

zoo A zoo is a place where animals are kept so that people can look at them.

Zoo begins with **z**. Add some animals to this scene at the zoo. Then name the letter at the beginning of each animal's name.

Skills: Building vocabulary

Excellent!

Give yourself a star!

Sounds and Letters

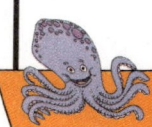

Sounds and Letters

Say the name of each picture. Listen to the first sound.
Then circle the letters with that sound.

Gg Kk Vv 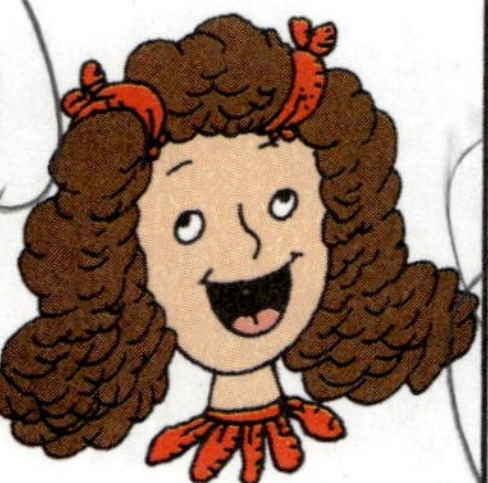	Gg Kk Vv 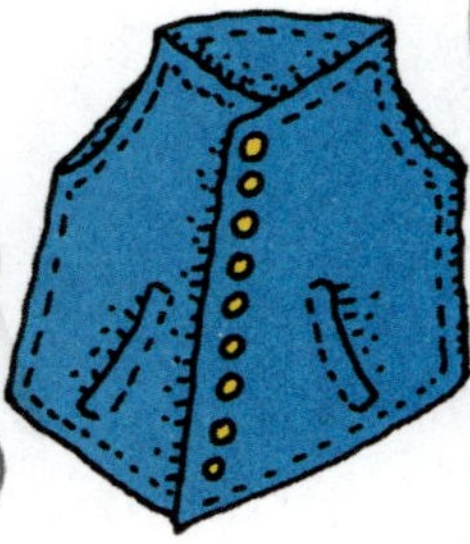	Bb Cc Kk 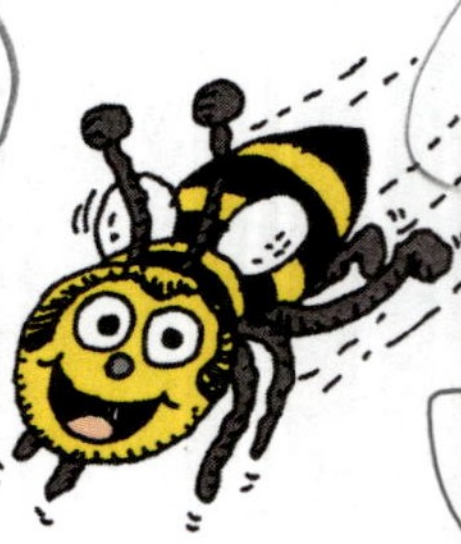	Ff Gg Vv 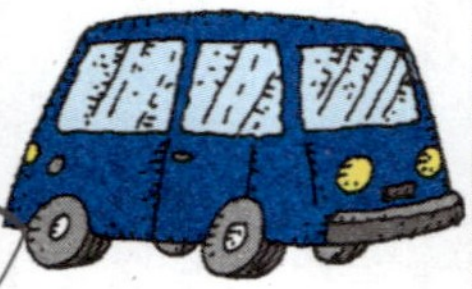
Bb Kk Vv 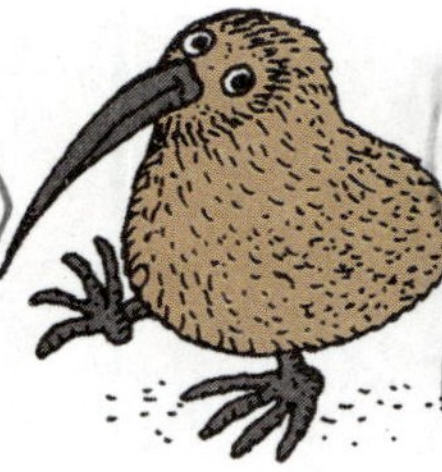	Cc Gg Kk 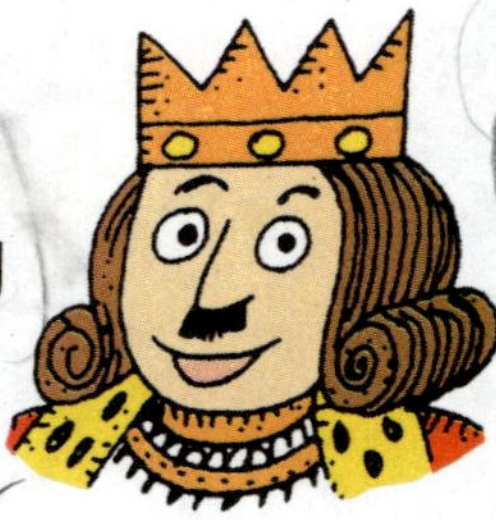	Bb Ff Kk 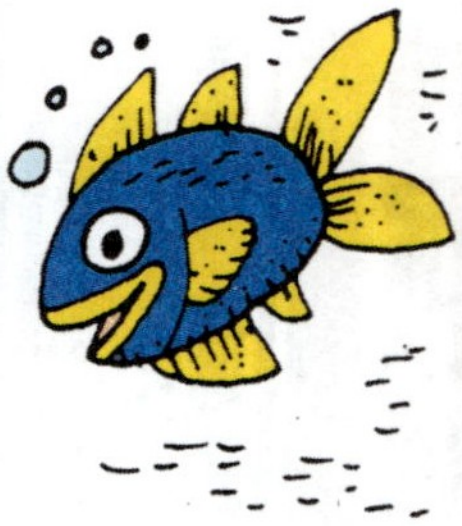	Dd Ff Gg 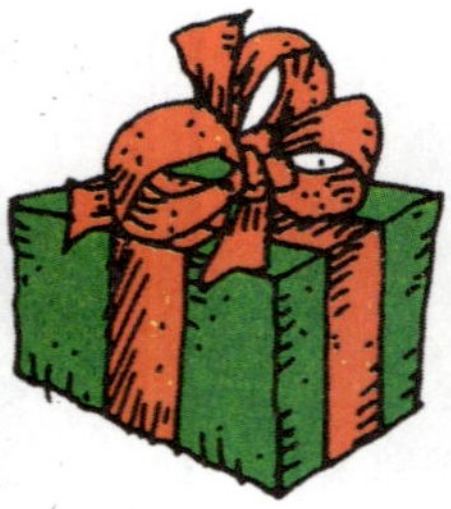
Bb Kk Vv 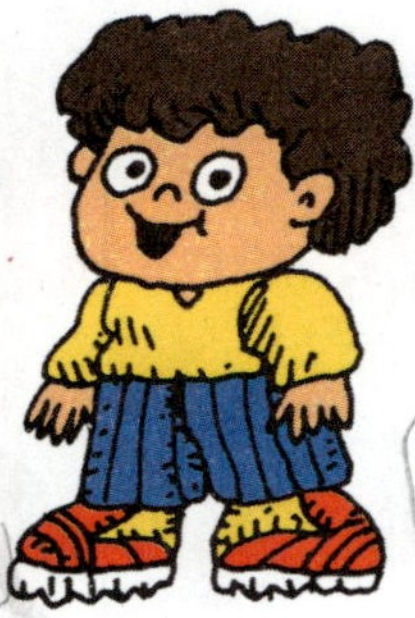	Ff Mm Kk 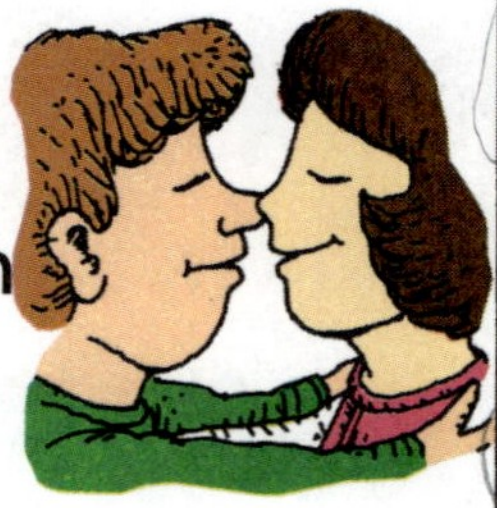	Gg Kk Vv 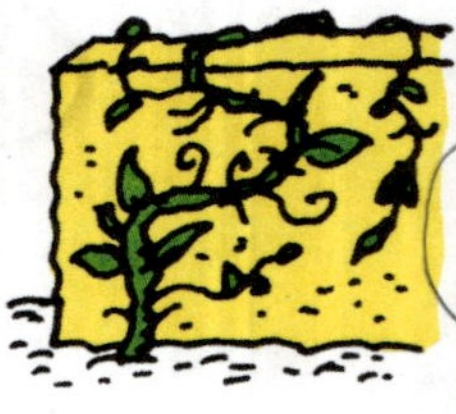	Bb Ff Pp 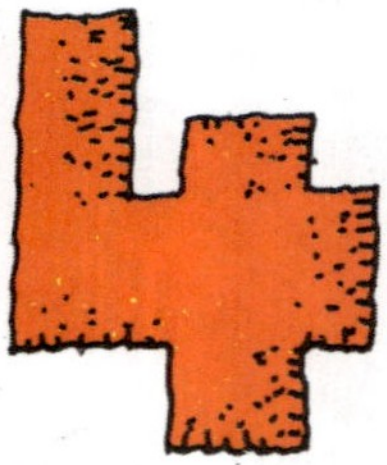
Ff Gg Kk 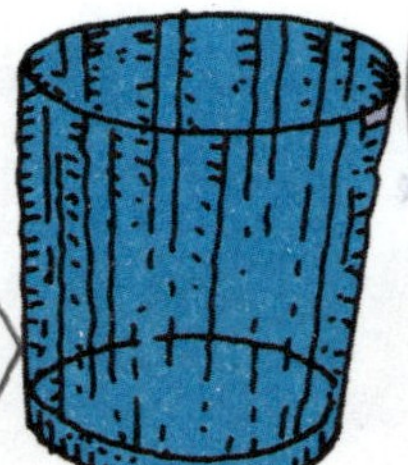	Ff Mm Yy 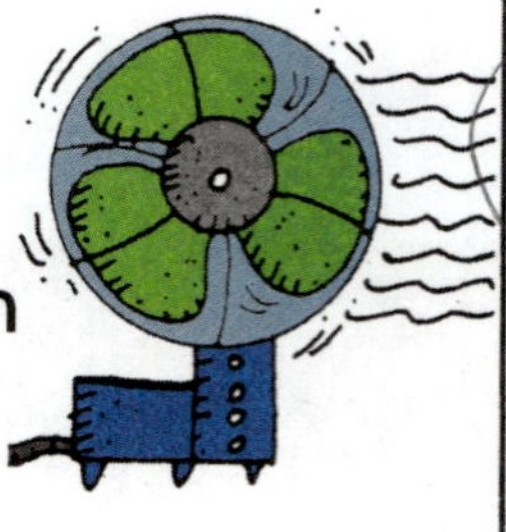	Bb Kk Pp 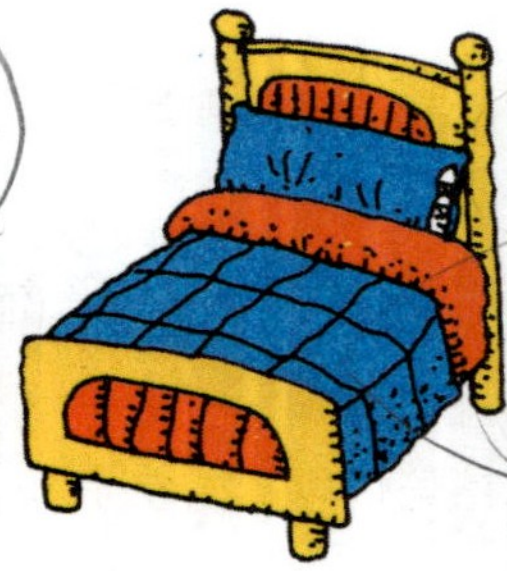	Ff Gg Yy 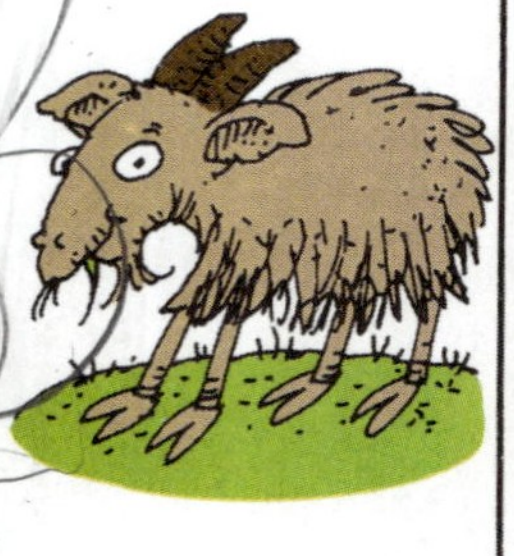

Skills: Auditory and visual discrimination; Recognition of sounds and their symbols

Sounds and Letters

The "b" sound

B b

Which ones begin with b? Color them blue.

Skills: Auditory and visual discrimination; Recognition of the "b" sound; Sound/symbol association

Sounds and Letters

The "c" sound

Cc

Which ones begin with c? Color them blue.

Skills: Auditory and visual discrimination; Recognition of the "c" sound; Sound/symbol association

Sounds and Letters

The "d" sound

Dd

Which ones begin with d? Color them green.

Skills: Auditory and visual discrimination; Recognition of the "d" sound; Sound/symbol association

Sounds and Letters

The "f" sound

Ff

Which ones begin with f? Color them brown.

Skills: Auditory and visual discrimination; Recognition of the "f" sound; Sound/symbol association

Sounds and Letters

The "g" sound

Gg

Which ones begin with g? Color them blue.

Skills: Auditory and visual discrimination; Recognition of the "g" sound; Sound/symbol association

Sounds and Letters

The "h" sound

Hh

Which ones begin with h? Color them red.

Skills: Auditory and visual discrimination; Recognition of the "h" sound; Sound/symbol association

Sounds and Letters

The "j" sound

Jj

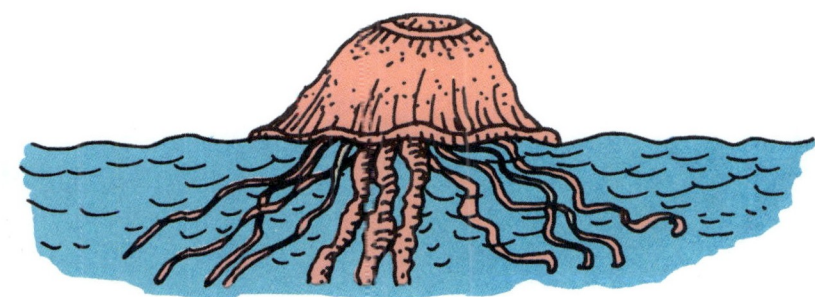

Which ones begin with j? Color them red.

Skills: Auditory and visual discrimination; Recognition of the "j" sound; Sound/symbol association

Sounds and Letters

The "k" sound

Kk

Which ones begin with k? Color them red.

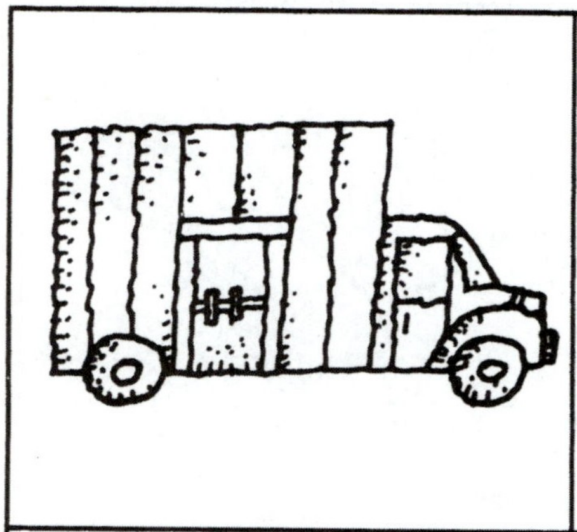

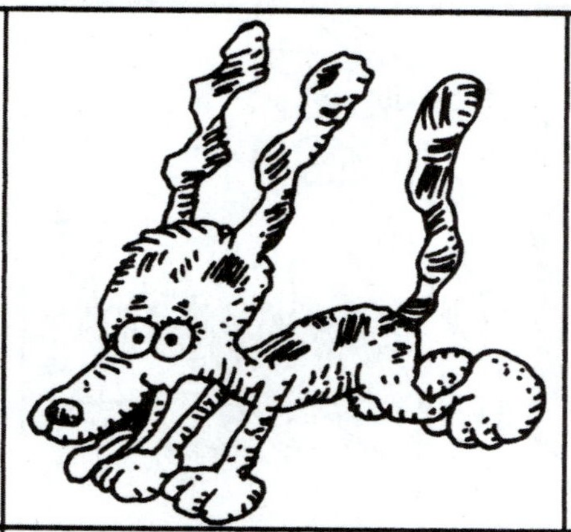

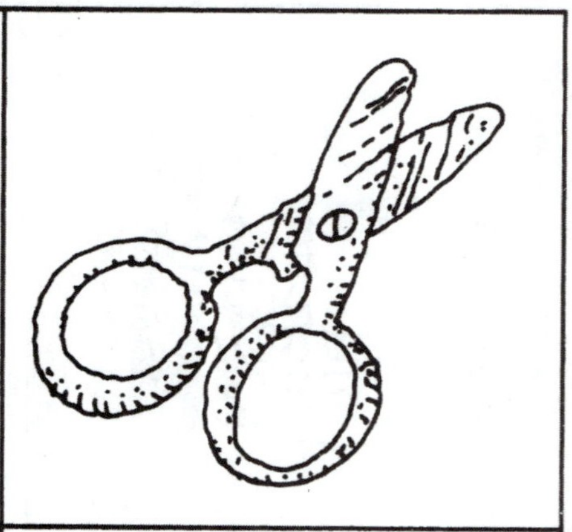

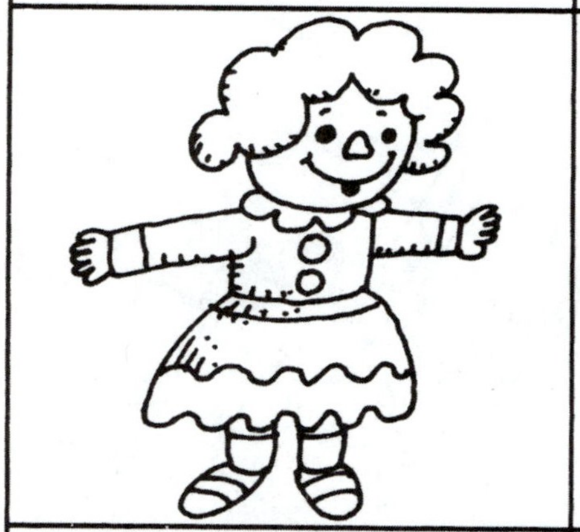

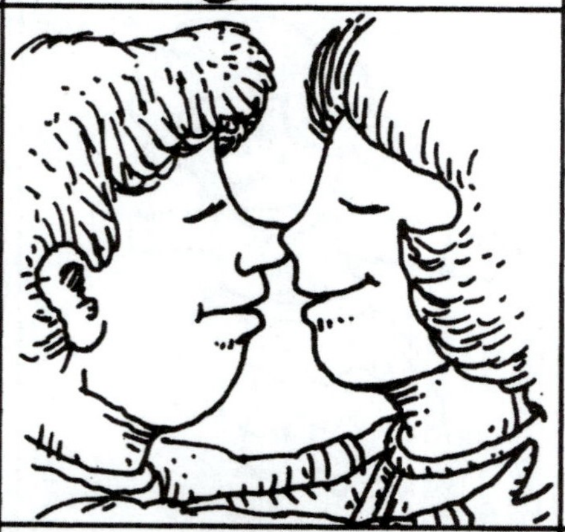

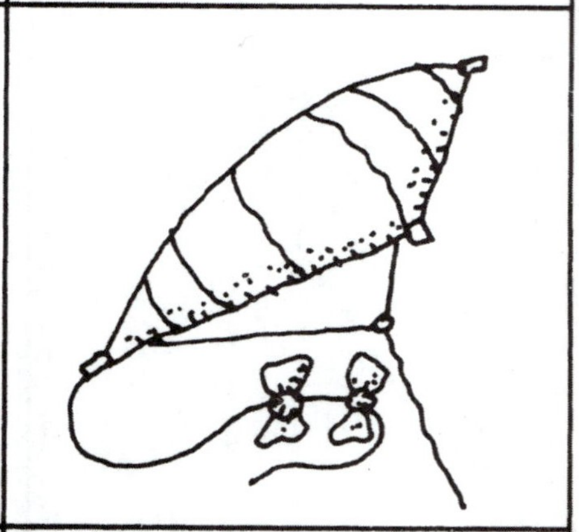

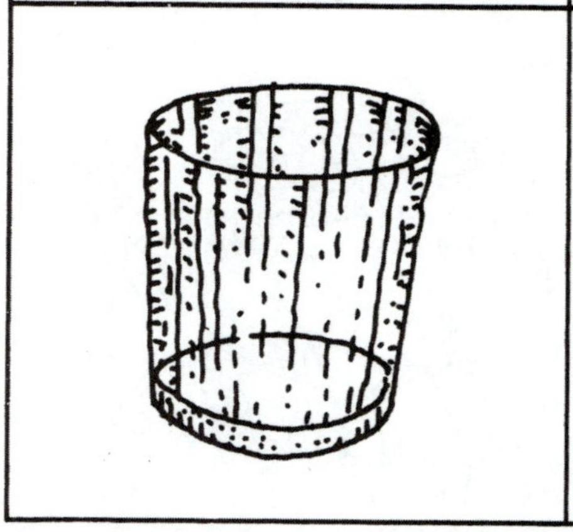

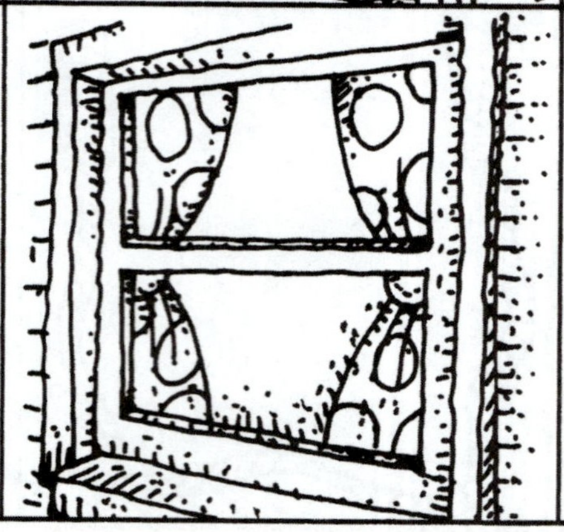

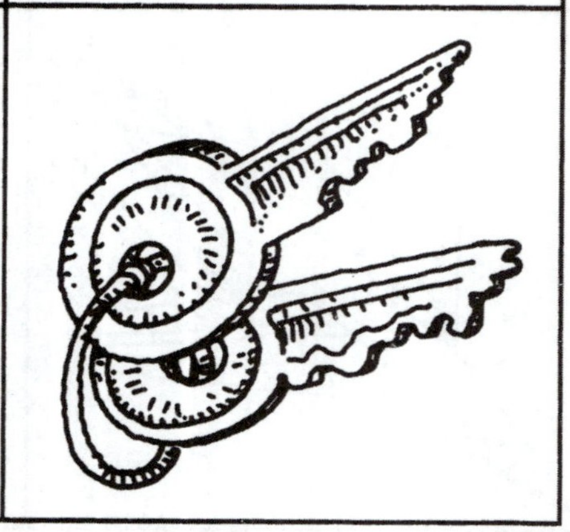

Sounds and Letters

The "l" sound

Ll

Which ones begin with l? Color them green.

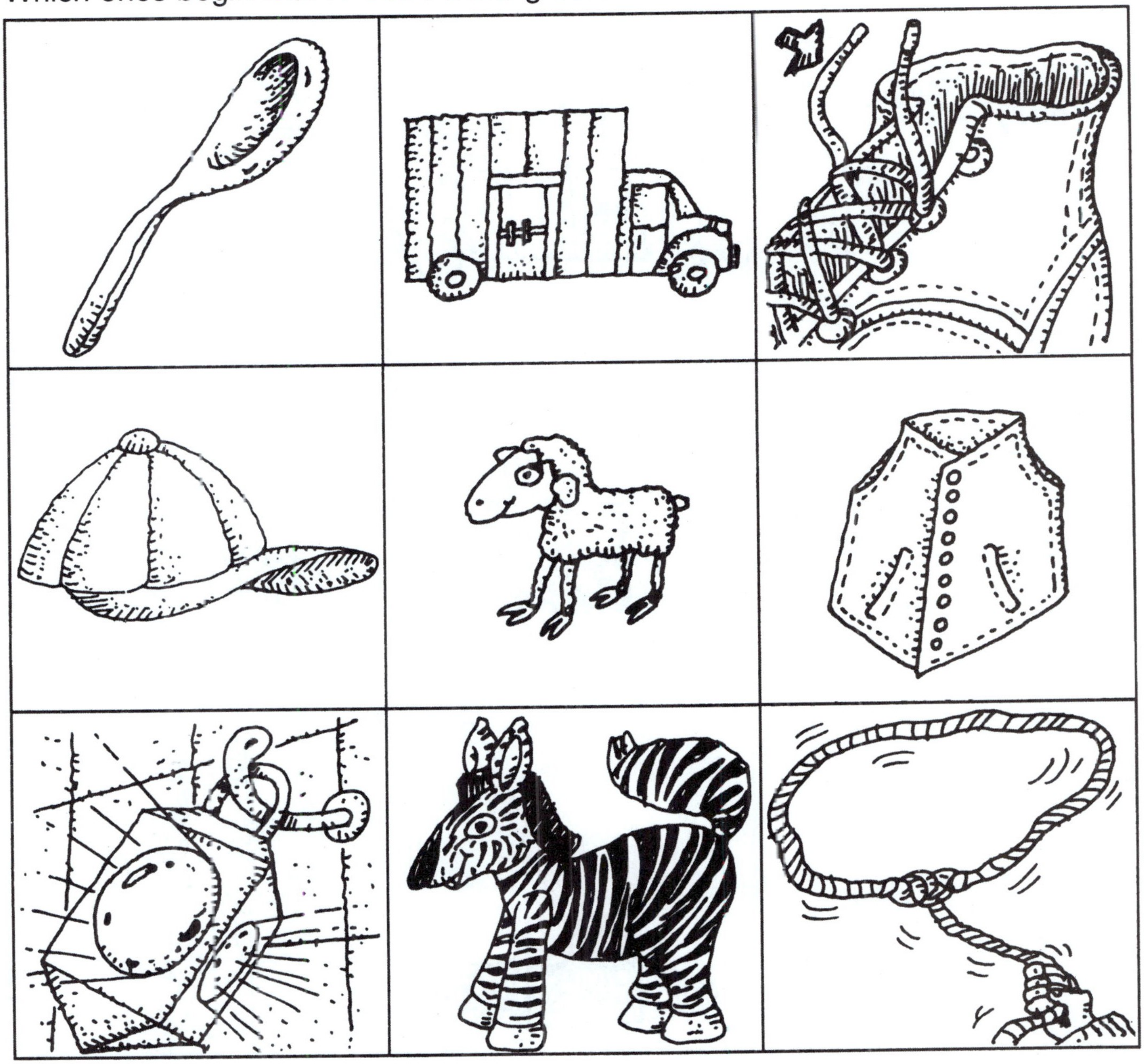

Skills: Auditory and visual discrimination; Recognition of the "l" sound; Sound/symbol association

Sounds and Letters

The "m" sound

Mm

Which ones begin with m? Color them orange.

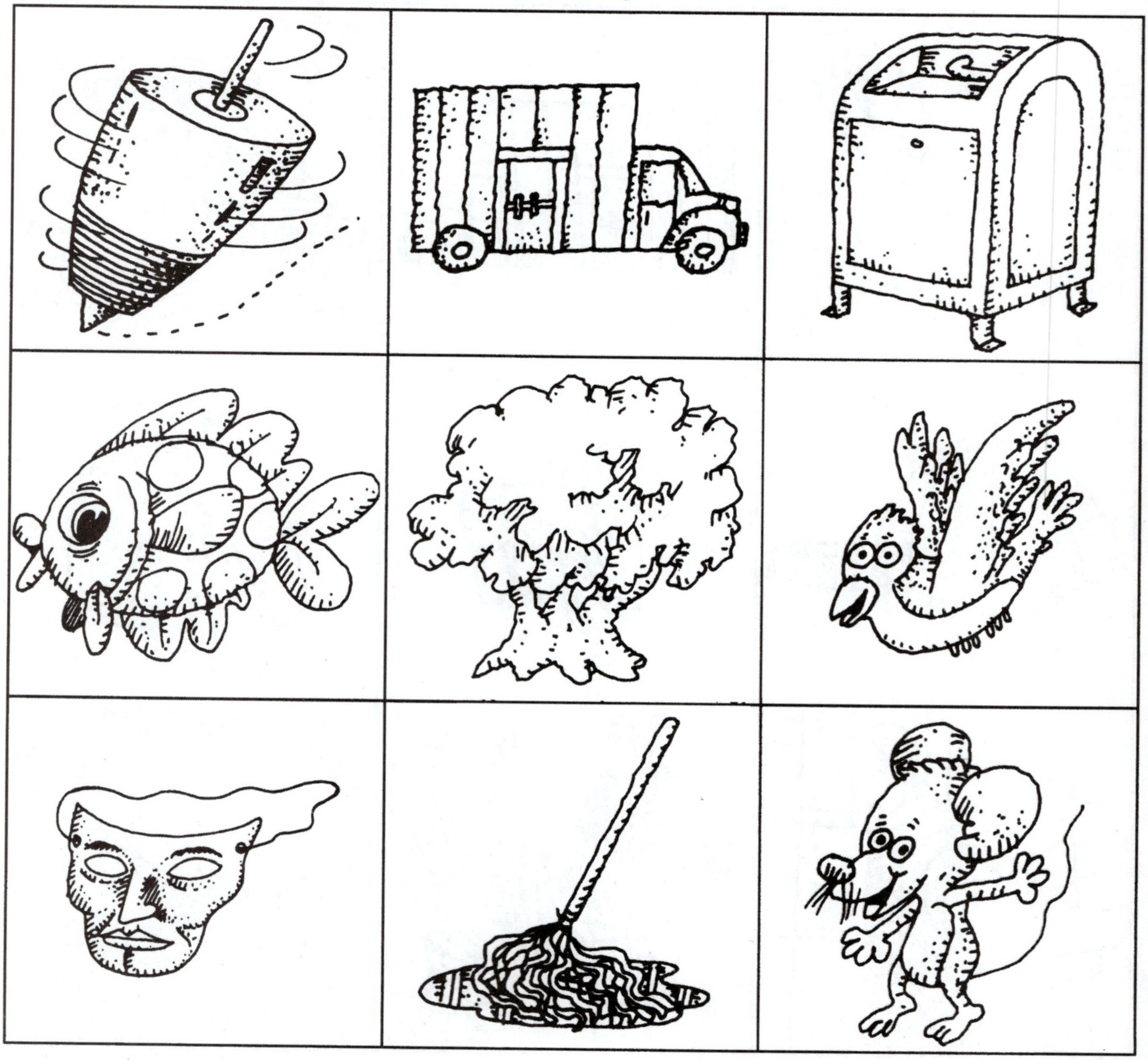

Skills: Auditory and visual discrimination; Recognition of the "m" sound; Sound/symbol association

Sounds and Letters

The "n" sound

Nn

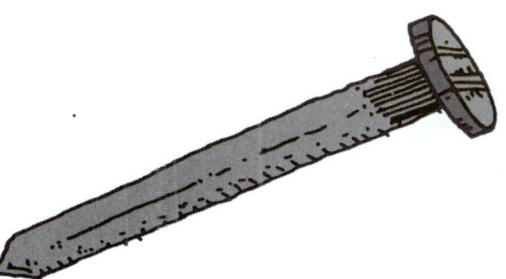

Which ones begin with n? Color them red.

Skills: Auditory and visual discrimination; Recognition of the "n" sound; Sound/symbol association

Sounds and Letters

The "p" sound

Pp

Which ones begin with p? Color them purple.

Skills: Auditory and visual discrimination; Recognition of the "p" sound; Sound/symbol association

Sounds and Letters

The "q" sound

Qq

Which ones begin with q? Color them green.

Skills: Auditory and visual discrimination; Recognition of the "q" sound; Sound/symbol association

Sounds and Letters

The "r" sound

Rr

Which ones begin with r? Color them blue.

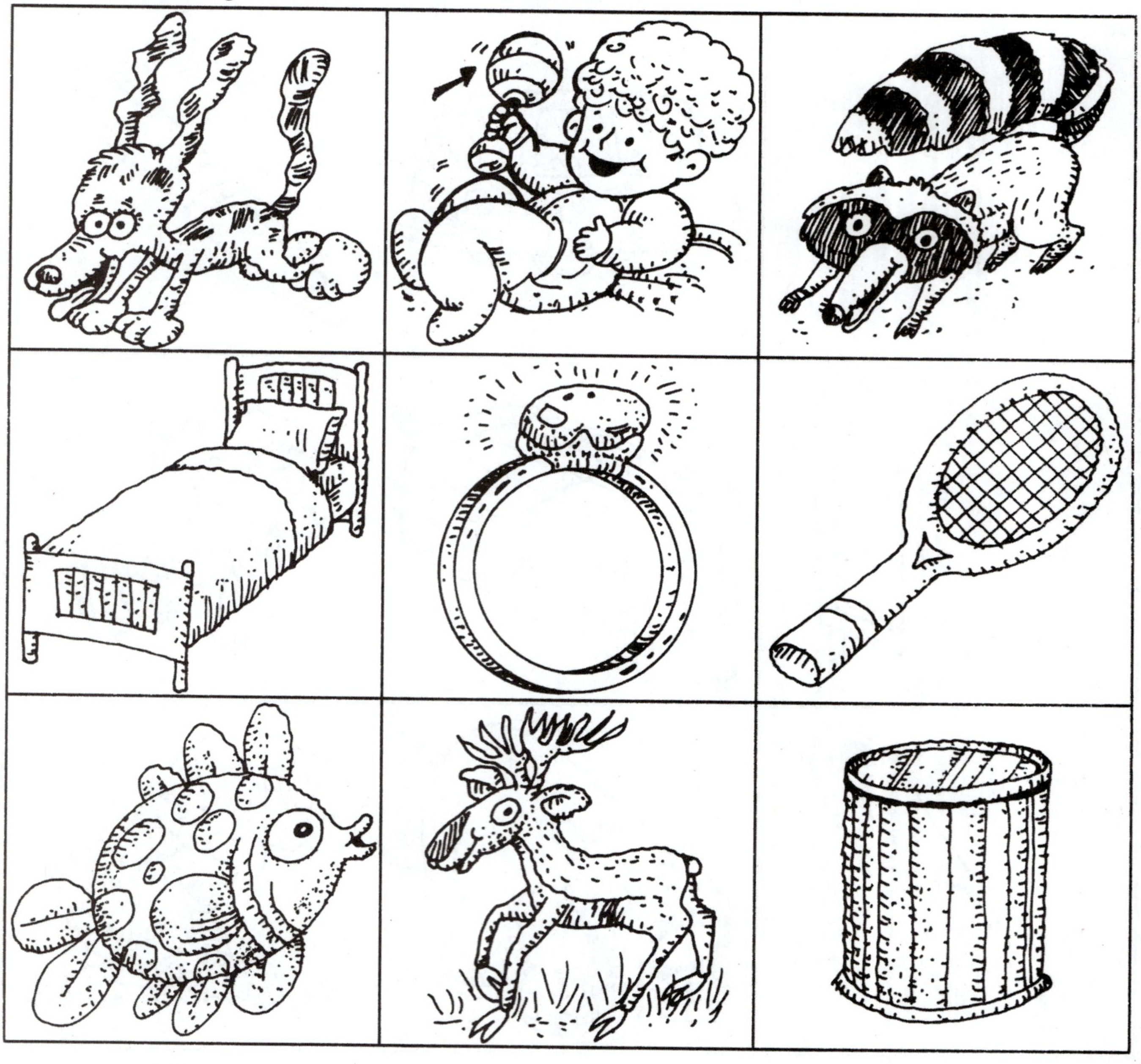

Skills: Auditory and visual discrimination; Recognition of the "r" sound; Sound/symbol association

Sounds and Letters

The "s" sound

Ss

Which ones begin with s? Color them brown.

Skills: Auditory and visual discrimination; Recognition of the "s" sound; Sound/symbol association

Sounds and Letters

The "t" sound

T t

Which ones begin with t? Color them orange.

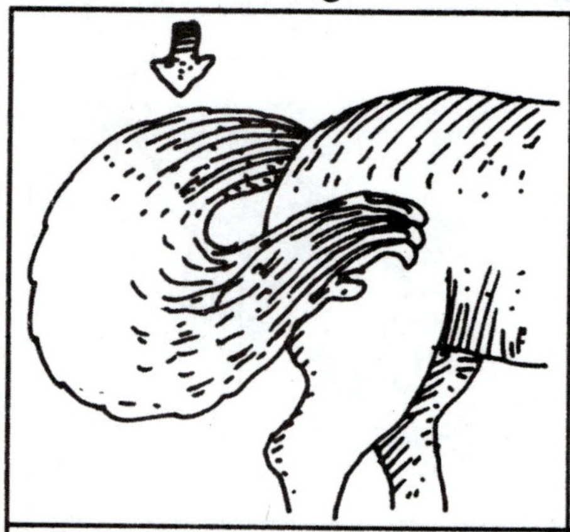

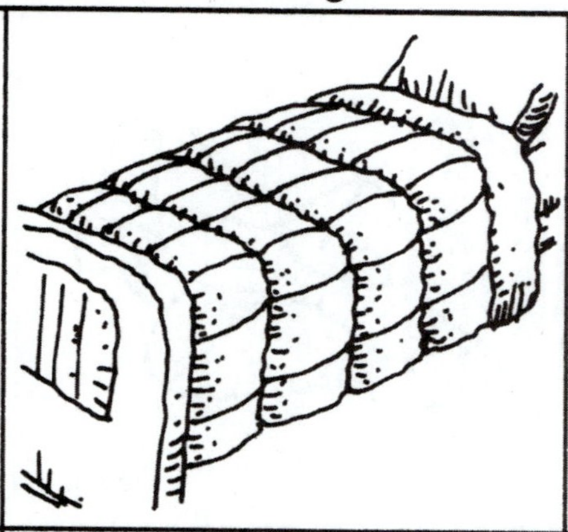

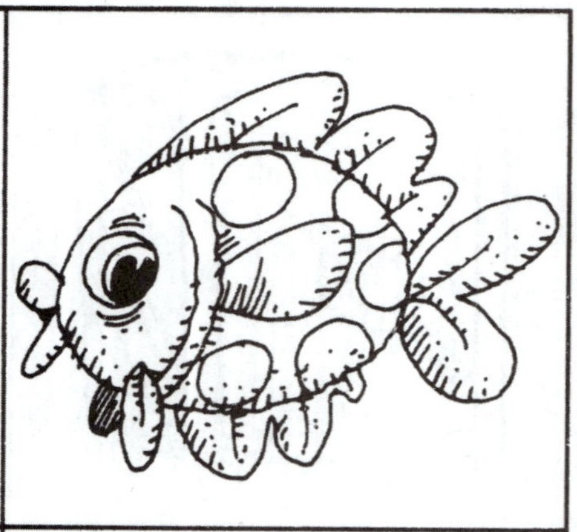

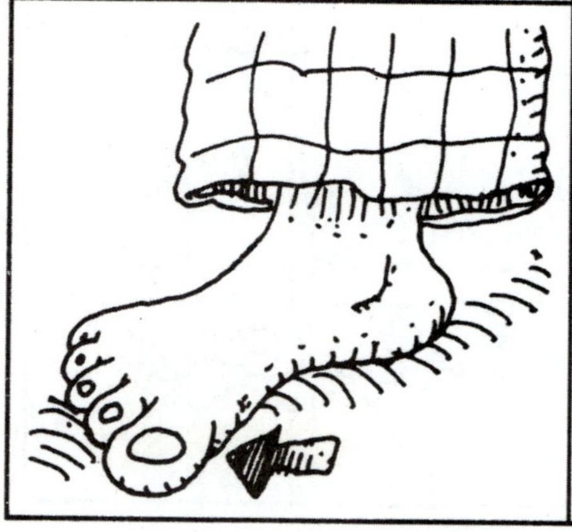

Skills: Auditory and visual discrimination; Recognition of the "t" sound; Sound/symbol association

Sounds and Letters

The "v" sound

Vv

Which ones begin with v? Color them yellow.

Skills: Auditory and visual discrimination; Recognition of the "v" sound; Sound/symbol association

Sounds and Letters

The "w" sound

Which ones begin with w? Color them black.

Skills: Auditory and visual discrimination; Recognition of the "w" sound; Sound/symbol association

Sounds and Letters

The "y" sound

Yy

Which ones begin with y? Color them yellow.

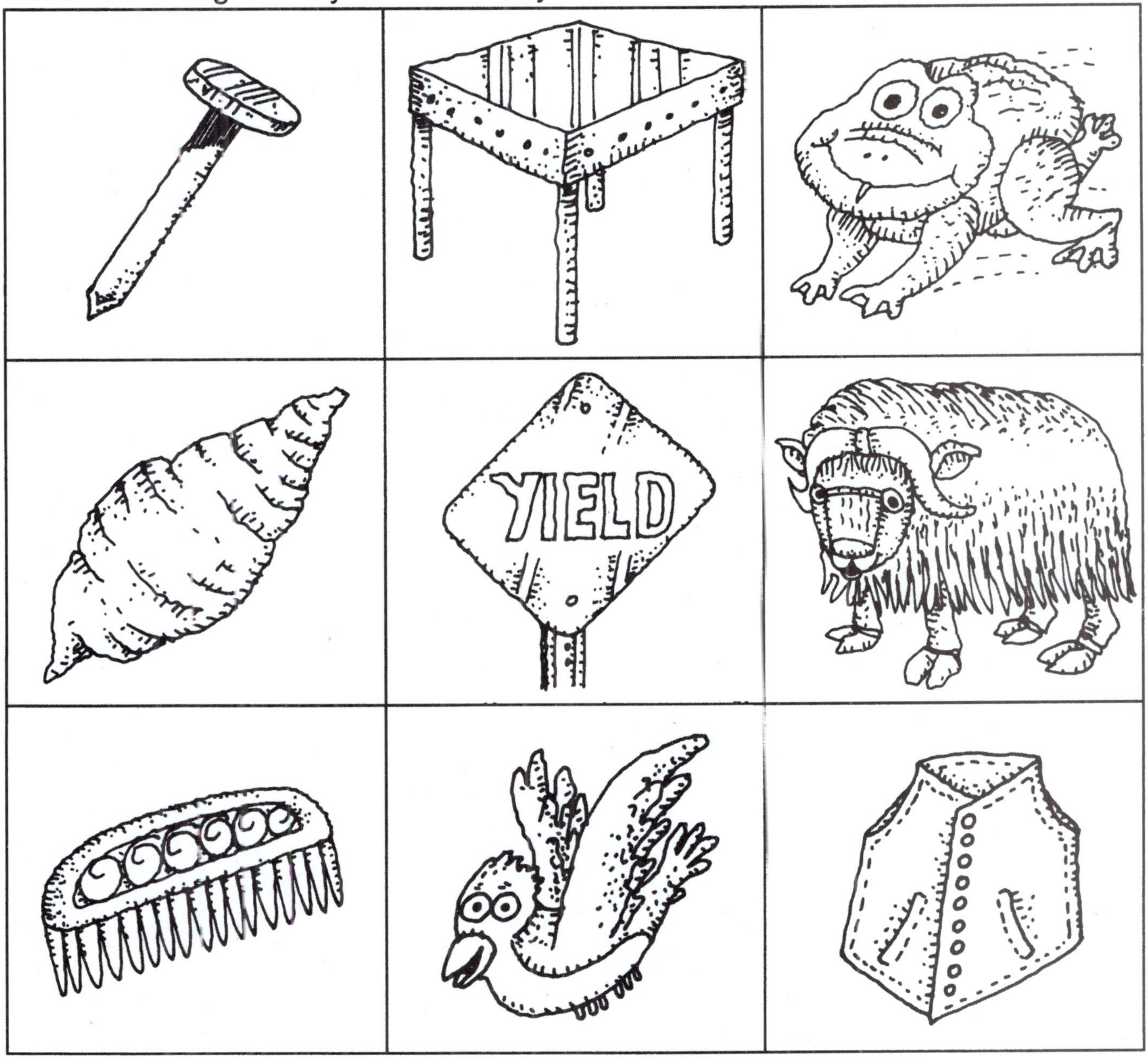

Skills: Auditory and visual discrimination; Recognition of the "y" sound; Sound/symbol association

Sounds and Letters

The "z" sound

Zz

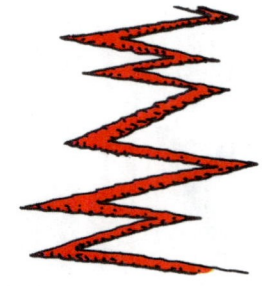

Which ones begin with z? Color them orange.

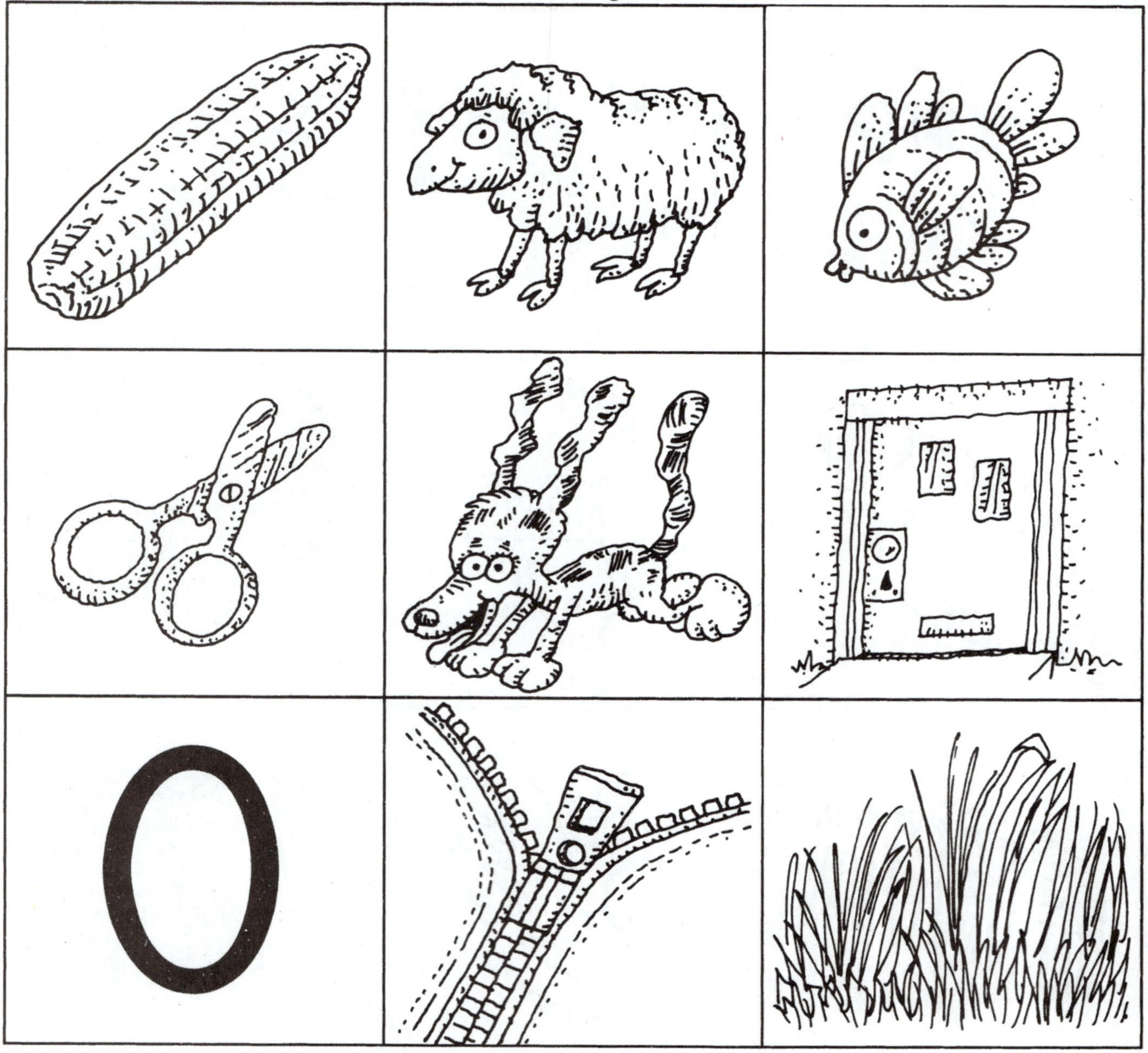

Skills: Auditory and visual discrimination; Recognition of the "z" sound; Sound/symbol association

Sounds and Letters

Say the name of each picture. Listen to the first sound.
Then circle the letters with that sound.

Mm Pp Yy 	Hh Pp Yy 	Cc Mm Yy 
Cc Hh Pp 	Cc Hh Yy 	Cc Mm Pp 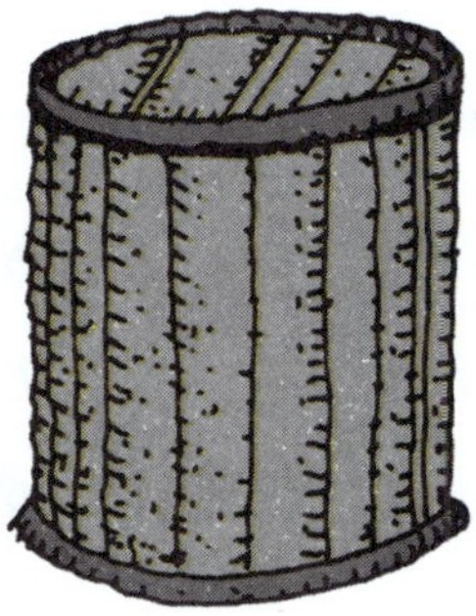
Hh Mm Yy 	Hh Pp Yy 	Mm Pp Yy 
Cc Mm Yy 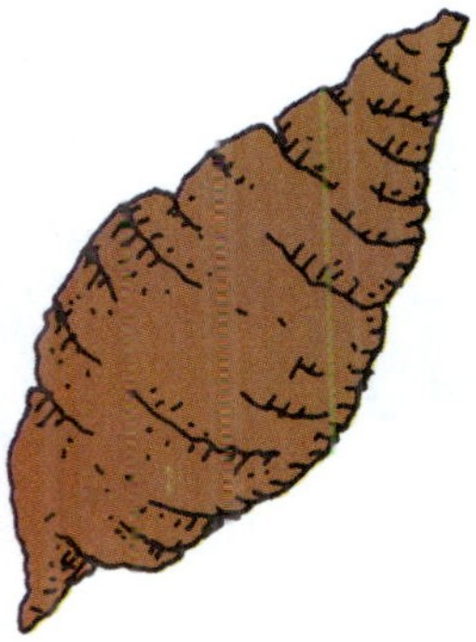	Cc Mm Pp 	Hh Pp Yy 

Skills: Auditory and visual discrimination; Recognition of sounds and their symbols

Sounds and Letters

Say the name of each picture. Listen to the first sound.
Then circle the letters with that sound.

Jj Ww Zz 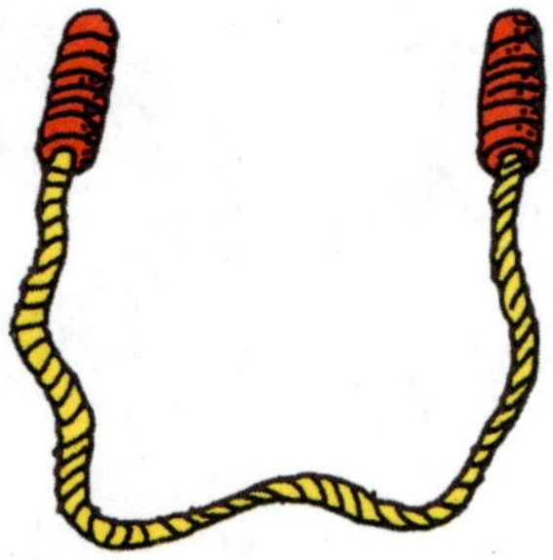	Dd Jj Ll 	Jj Ww Zz 
Ll Ww Zz 	Dd Jj Zz 	Jj Ll Ww 
Dd Jj Ww 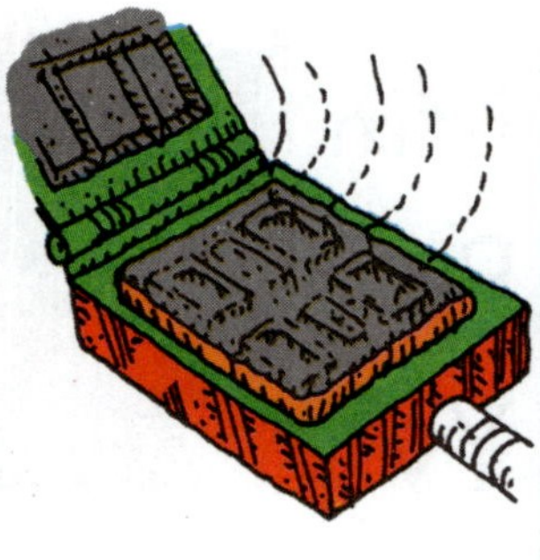	Jj Ll Ww 	Jj Ww Zz 
Dd Nn Zz 	Dd Jj Zz 	Dd Jj Ww 

Skills: Auditory and visual discrimination; Recognition of sounds and their symbols

Well Done!

Give yourself a star!

Math Readiness

Math Readiness

Look at the pattern in each row. Circle the picture at the end of the row that continues the pattern. Then color the pictures.

Skills: Observing and continuing patterns; Visual memory

Math Readiness

Look at the pattern in each row. Circle the picture at the end of the row that continues the pattern. Then color the pictures.

Skills: Observing and continuing patterns; Visual memory

Math Readiness

Look at the pattern in each row. Circle the picture at the end of the row that continues the pattern. Then color the pictures.

Skills: Observing and continuing patterns; Visual memory; Size discrimination

Math Readiness

Look at the pattern in each row. Draw the picture at the end of the row that continues the pattern. Then color the pictures.

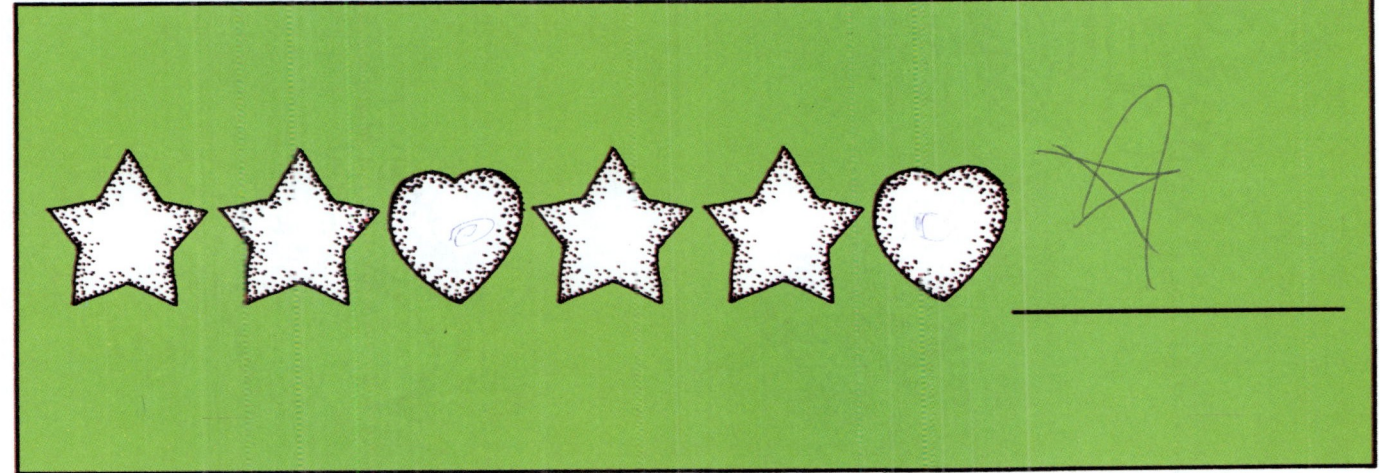

Skills: Observing and continuing patterns; Visual memory; Fine motor skill development

Math Readiness

Look at the pictures in each box. Color the **small** pictures red. Color the **large** pictures blue.

Skills: Making comparisons; Following directions

Math Readiness

Look at the pictures in each box. Color the **small** pictures green.
Color the **large** pictures yellow.

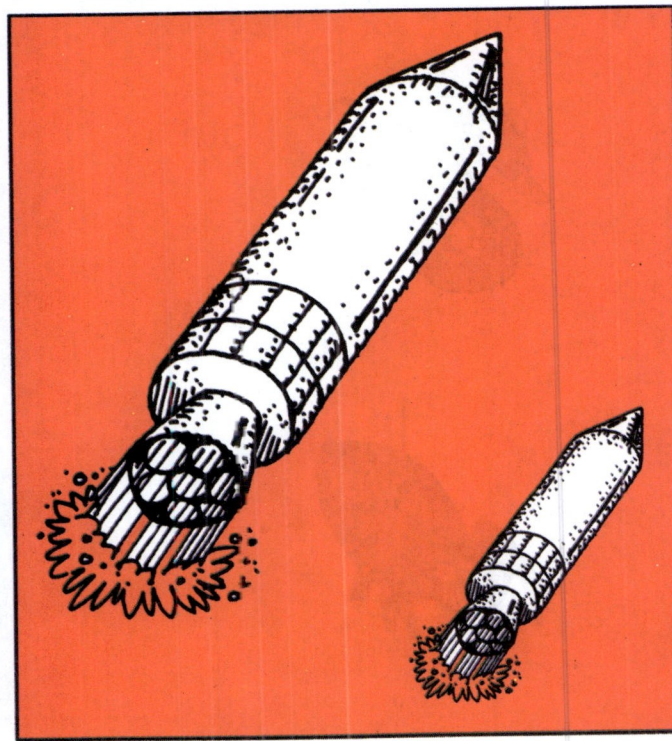

Skills: Making comparisons; Following directions

Math Readiness

Which one is **small**? Which one is **large**?
Draw a line from each small creature to the large creature that matches it.

Skills: Visual matching; Making comparisons

Math Readiness

Look at the pictures in each box. Draw lines to match the number of objects on one side to the number of objects on the other side. Then color the pictures.

Skills: One-to-one correspondence; Association

Math Readiness

Look at the pictures in each box. Circle the group that shows **less**. Then color the pictures.

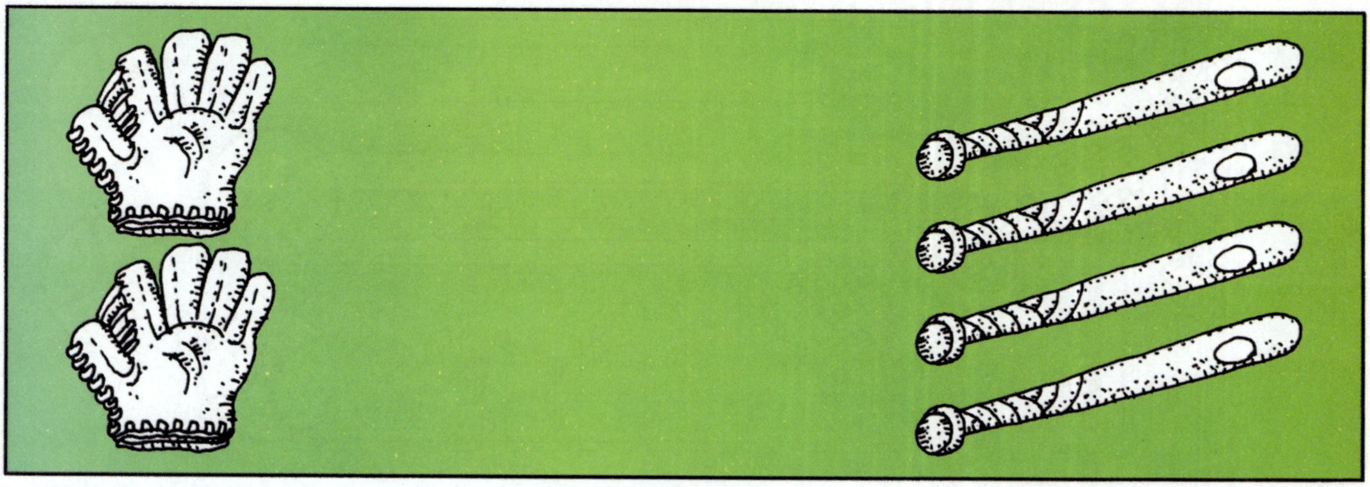

Skills: Making comparisons; Counting

Math Readiness

Look at the pictures in each box. Circle the group that shows **more**. Then color the pictures.

Skills: Making comparisons; Counting

Math Readiness

Look at the pictures in each box. Circle the smaller picture.
Draw a line under the larger picture.

Skills: Making comparisons; Following directions

Math Readiness

Look at the pictures in each box. Circle the smaller picture.
Draw a line under the larger picture.

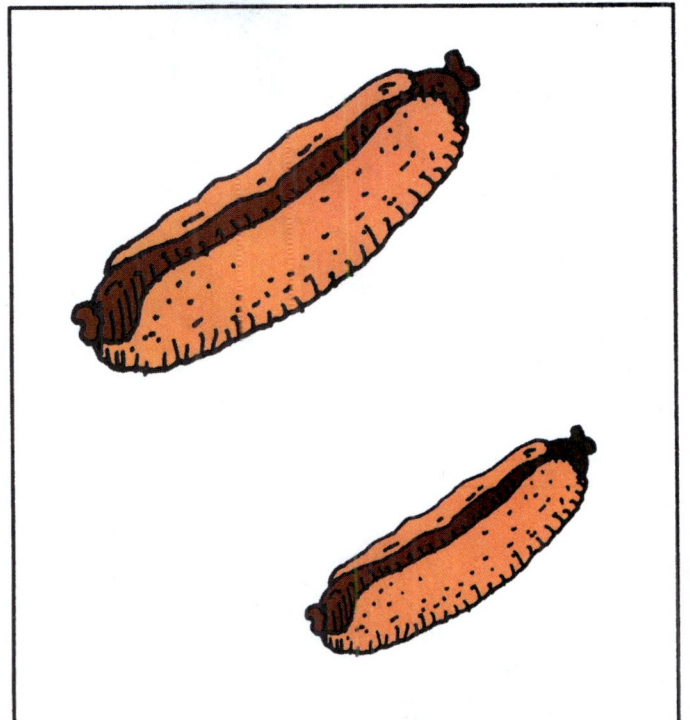

Skills: Making comparisons; Following directions

Math Readiness

Look at the pictures in each box. Circle the set that shows **less**.

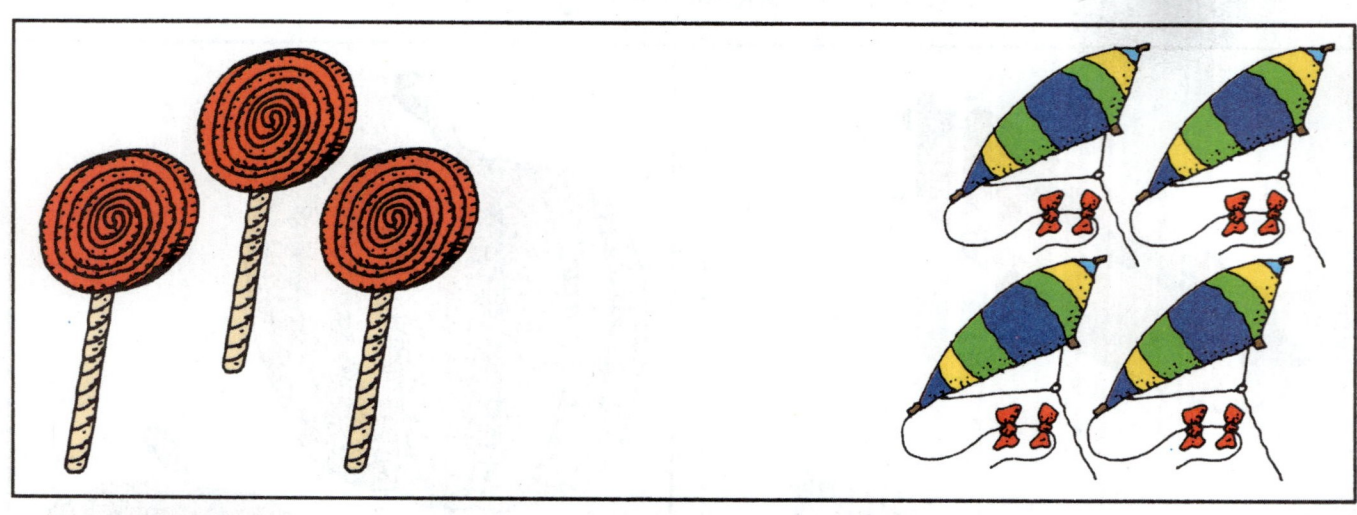

Skills: Making comparisons; Counting

Math Readiness

Look at the pictures in each box. Circle the set that shows **more**.

Skills: Making comparisons; Counting

Math Readiness

How can you help clean up the house?
Connect the dots from 1 to 10 to find out.

Skills: Number order; Recognition of numbers 1 to 10

Math Readiness

There are so many foods to count and eat!
Circle the number that tells how many are in each box.

muffins: (3) 4 5	pears: (7) 8 9
apple: (1) 2 3	grapes: 2 3 (4)
popsicles: 4 (5) 6	ice cream cones: 1 2 (3)
sausages: 5 (6) 7	peanuts: 8 9 (10)

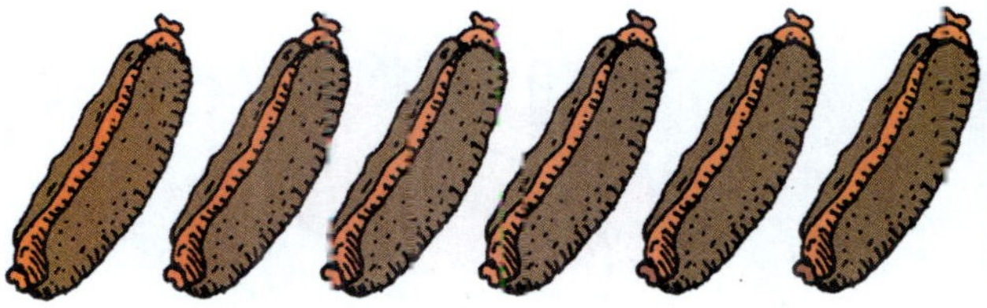

Skills: Following directions; Recognizing sets of objects and the corresponding number

Math Readiness

Rub-a-dub-dub! It's fun to be in the tub!
Look at the pictures at the top of the page. Count those objects in the large picture.
Then write how many objects there are.

 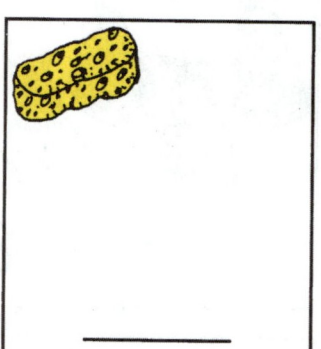 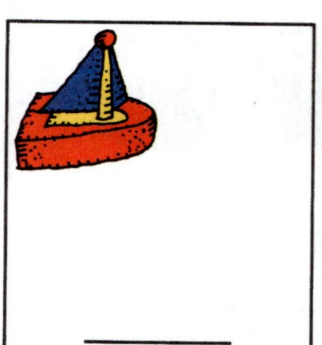 

Skills: Recognizing sets of objects; Classifying and recording information; Writing numbers

Math Readiness

How many animals live on the farm? Look at the pictures at the top of the page.
Count those objects in the large picture.
Then write how many of each animal you see in the picture.

Skills: Recognizing sets of objects; Classifying and recording information; Writing numbers

Math Readiness

Look at the sets in each box. Draw a circle around the sets that show 1.

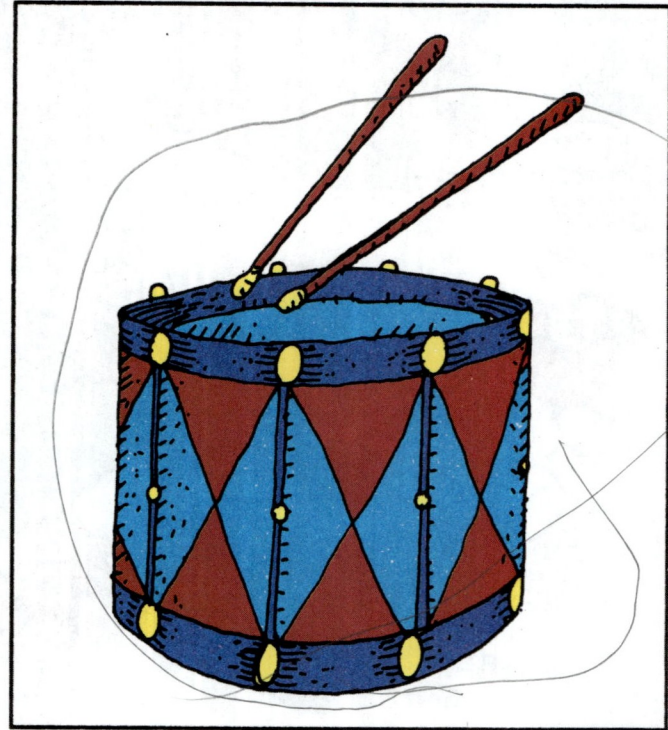

Skills: Identifying sets; Following directions

Math Readiness

Look at the sets in each box. Circle the number that tells how many. Put an X on the sets that show 2.

(1) 2 3

1 (2) 3

(2) 3 4

(1) 2 3

Skills: Identifying sets; Following directions

Math Readiness

Look at the pictures in each box. Circle three of each object.

Skills: Creating sets of 3; Recognizing sets; Following directions

Math Readiness

Look at the set in each box.
Circle the number that tells how many creatures there are.

③ 4 5

2 3 ④

④ 5 6

3 ④ 5

Skills: Identifying sets; Following directions

Math Readiness

Look at the set in each box.
Circle the number that tells how many.

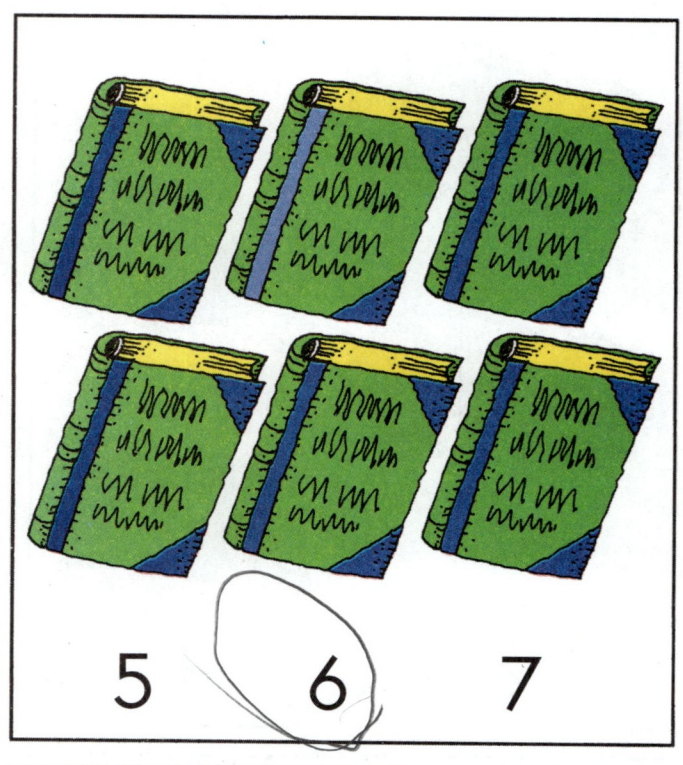

5   6   7

3   4   5

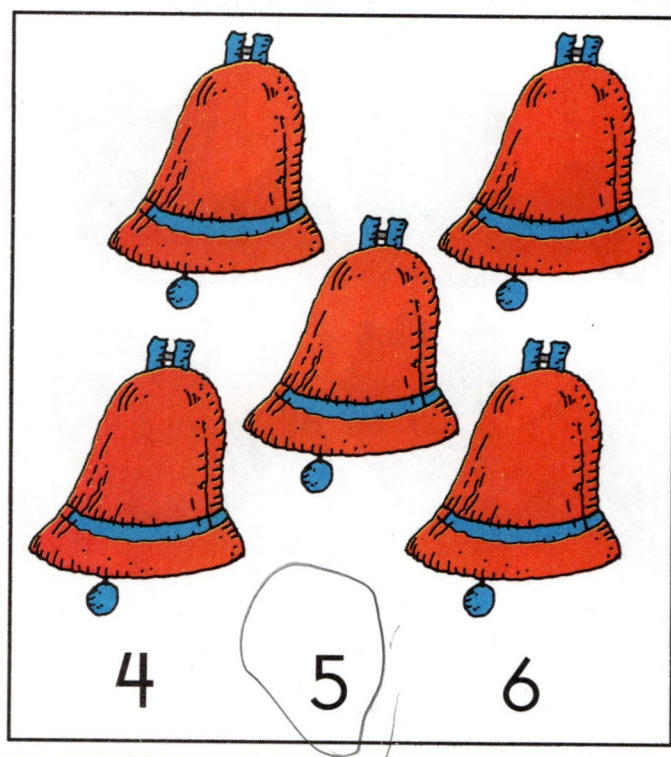

4   5   6

3   4   5

Skills: Identifying sets; Following directions

Math Readiness

Look at the set in each box.
Circle the sets that show 6.

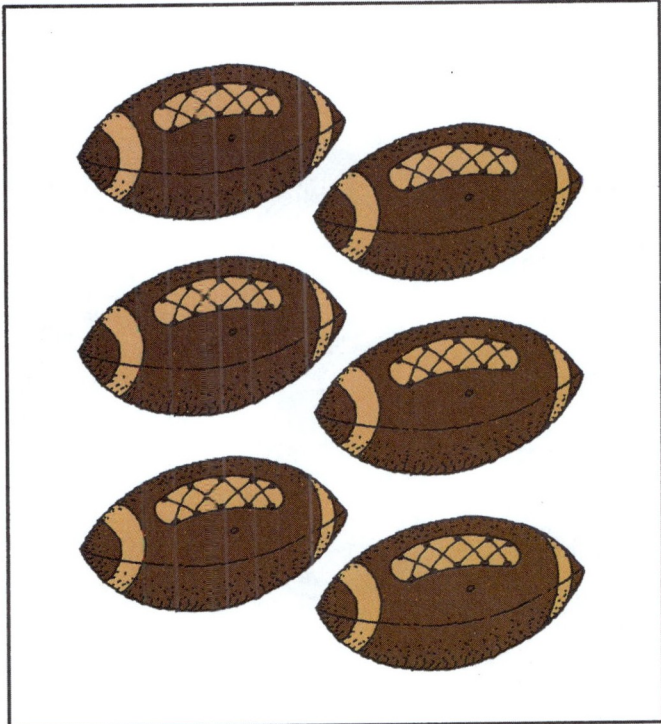

Skills: Identifying sets; Following directions

Math Readiness

How many objects do you see in each big box? Write the number in the small box. Circle the sets that show 7.

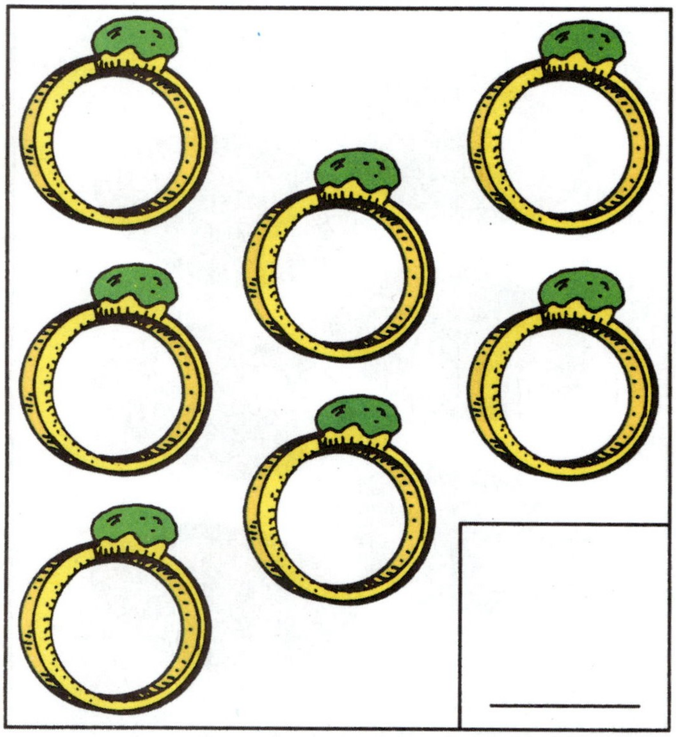

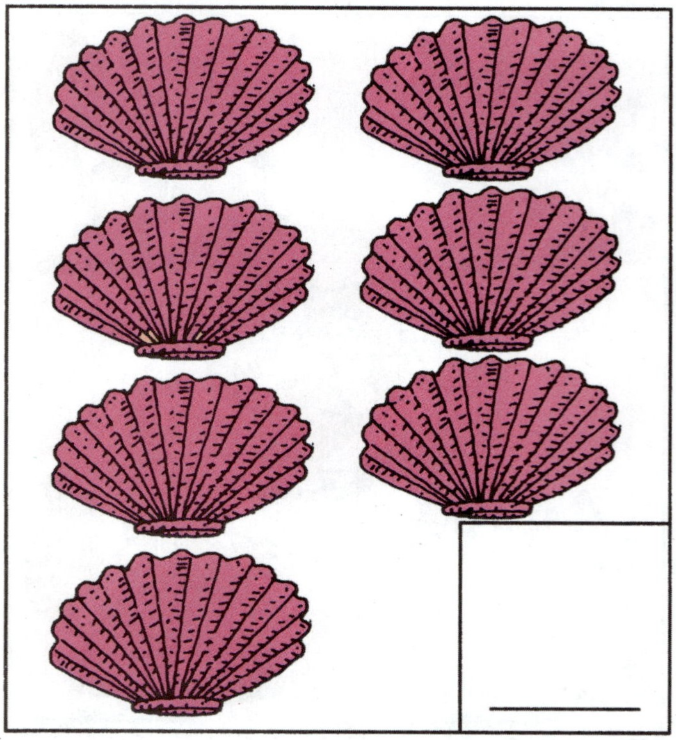

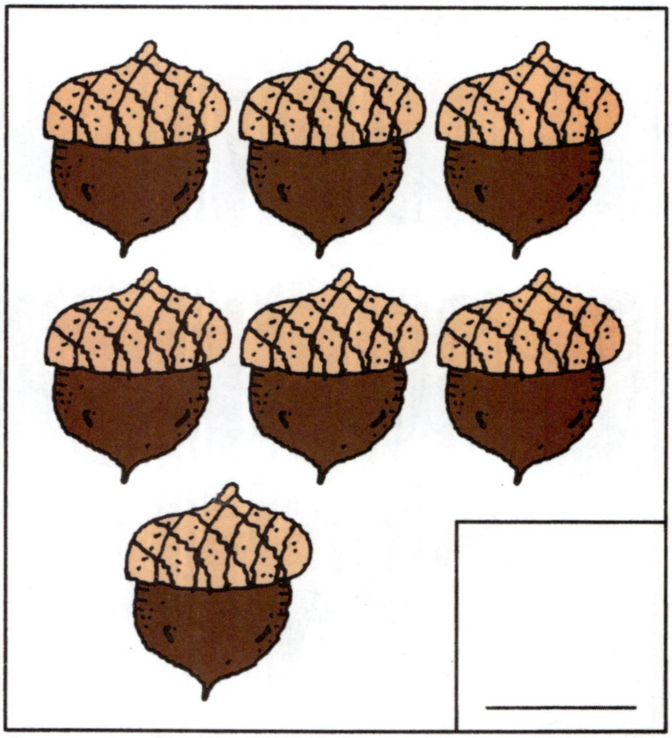

Skills: Identifying sets; Following directions; Writing numbers

Math Readiness

How many jacks do you see on each table? Write the number in each small box. Then circle the sets that show 8.

Skills: Identifying sets; Following directions; Writing numbers

Math Readiness

Look at the pictures in each box. Circle the sets that show 9.

Skills: Identifying sets; Following directions

Math Readiness

Look at the number of bats in this set.
Draw a set of balls in the empty box to show the same number.

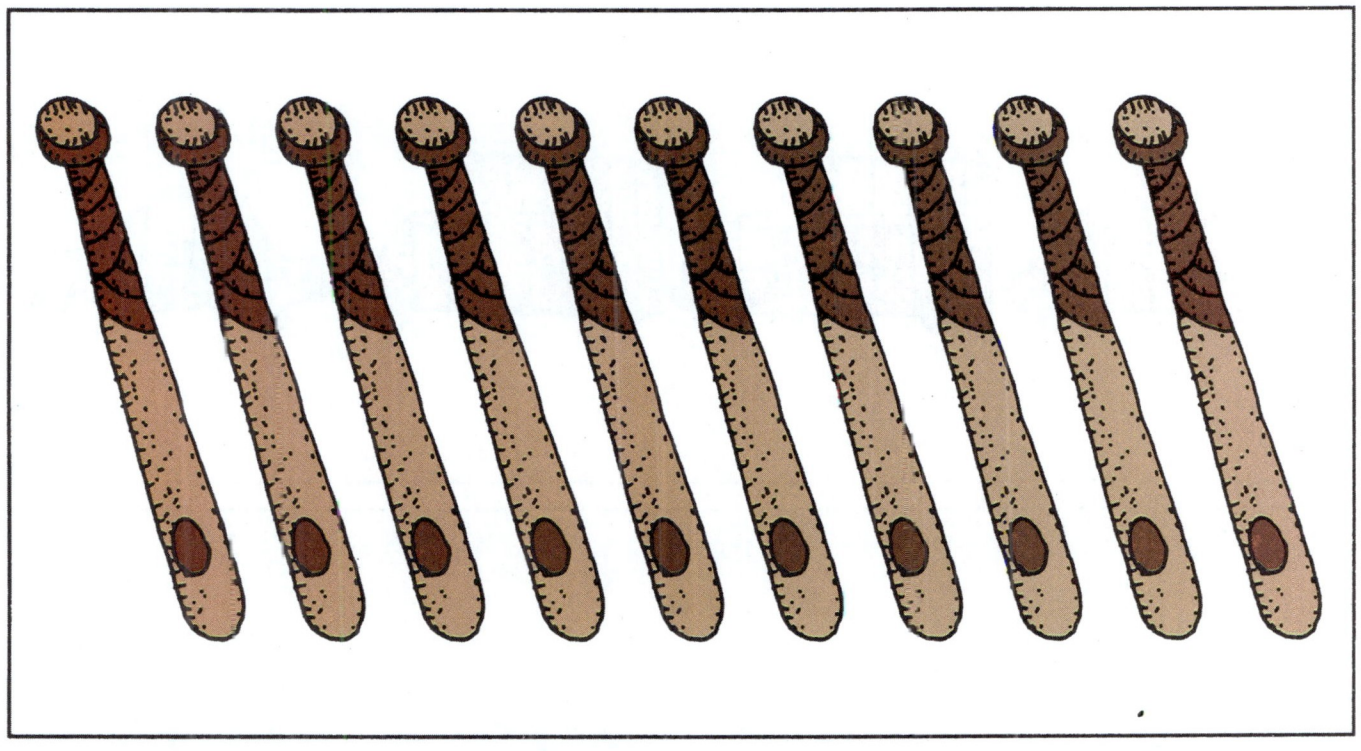

Skills: Recognizing sets; Creating a set of 10 objects

Math Readiness

Look at the pictures in each row.
Put an X on the one that is **different**.

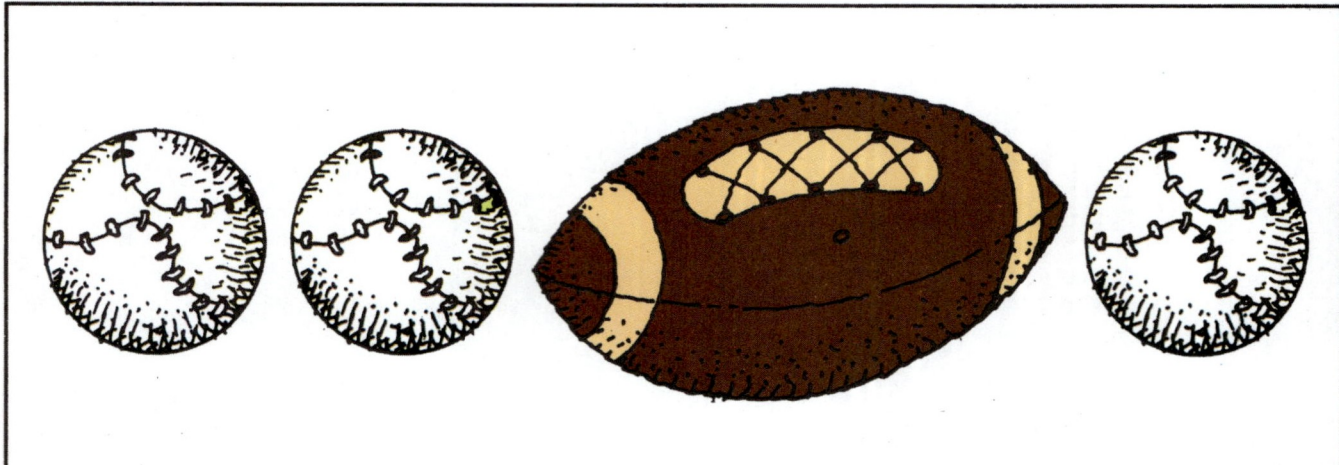

Skills: Understanding same and different

Math Readiness

Draw circles around the pictures in each row that belong together.

Skills: Association; Classification; Logical reasoning

Math Readiness

Look at the socks on each clothesline. Sort them into pairs.
Draw a line to connect the matching socks.

Skills: Understanding pairs; Visual matching

Good Job!

Give yourself a star!

Numbers Concepts

Number Concepts

How many birds do you see? Trace the number. Color the picture.

Skills: Recognizing a set of one; Forming the numeral one

Number Concepts

Look at the set in each box. Color the sets that show "1".

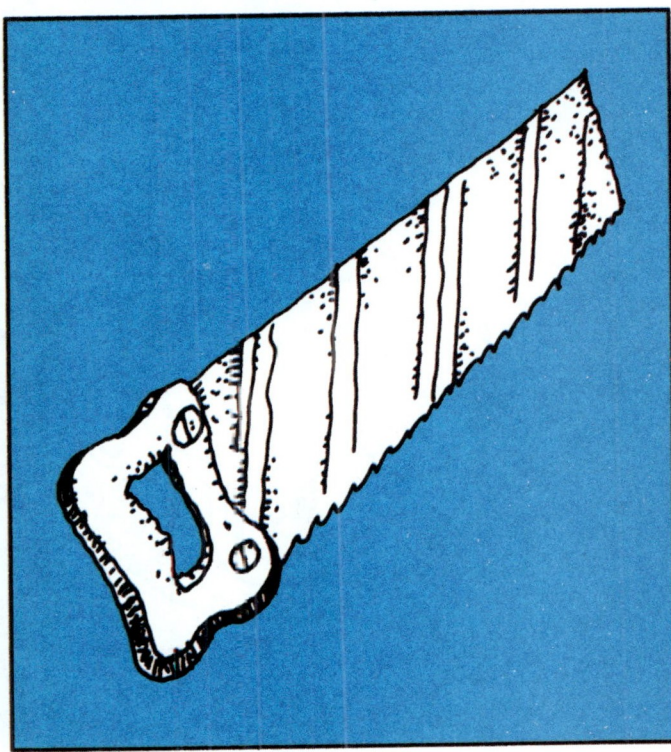

Skills: Identifying sets of one; Following directions

Number Concepts

How many suns do you see? Trace the number. Color the pictures.

2

Skills: Recognizing a set of two; Forming the numeral two

Number Concepts

Lock at the sets in each box. Color the sets that show "2".

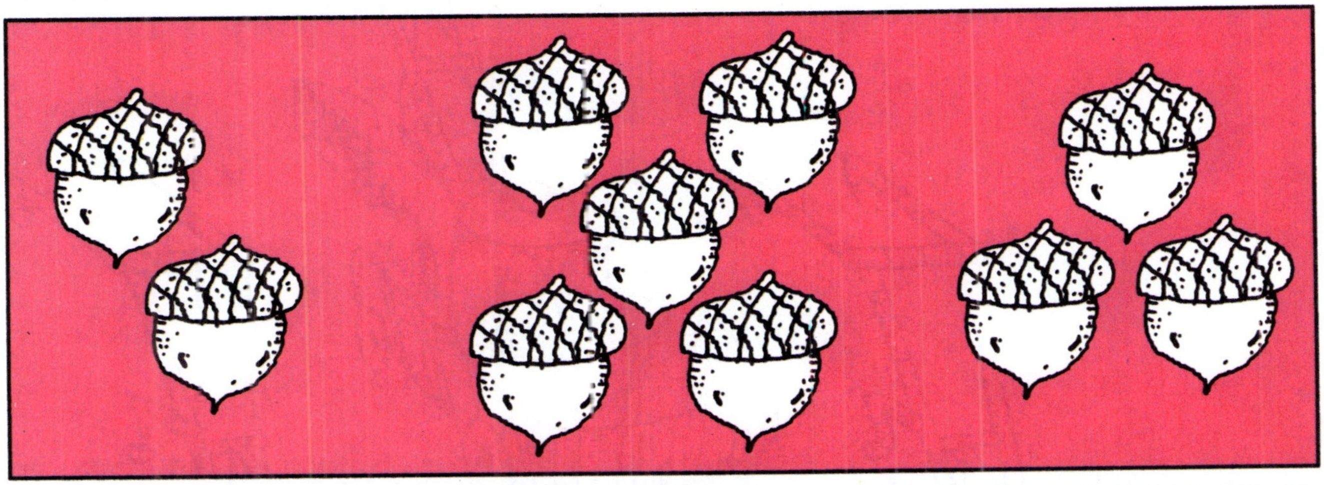

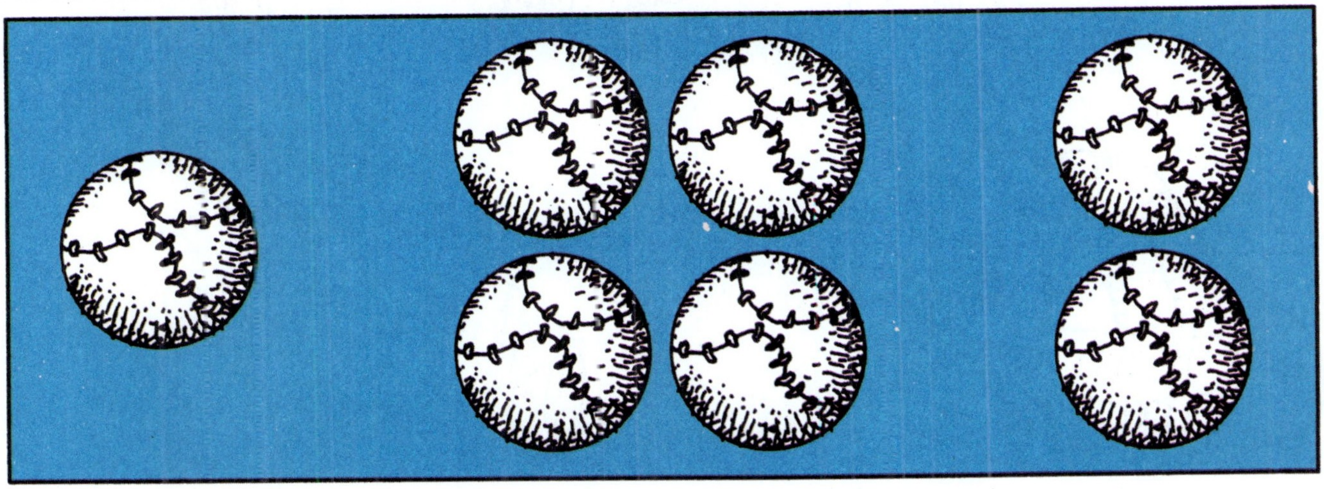

Skills: Identifying sets of two; Following directions

Number Concepts

How many lawn mowers do you see? Trace the number. Color the pictures.

3

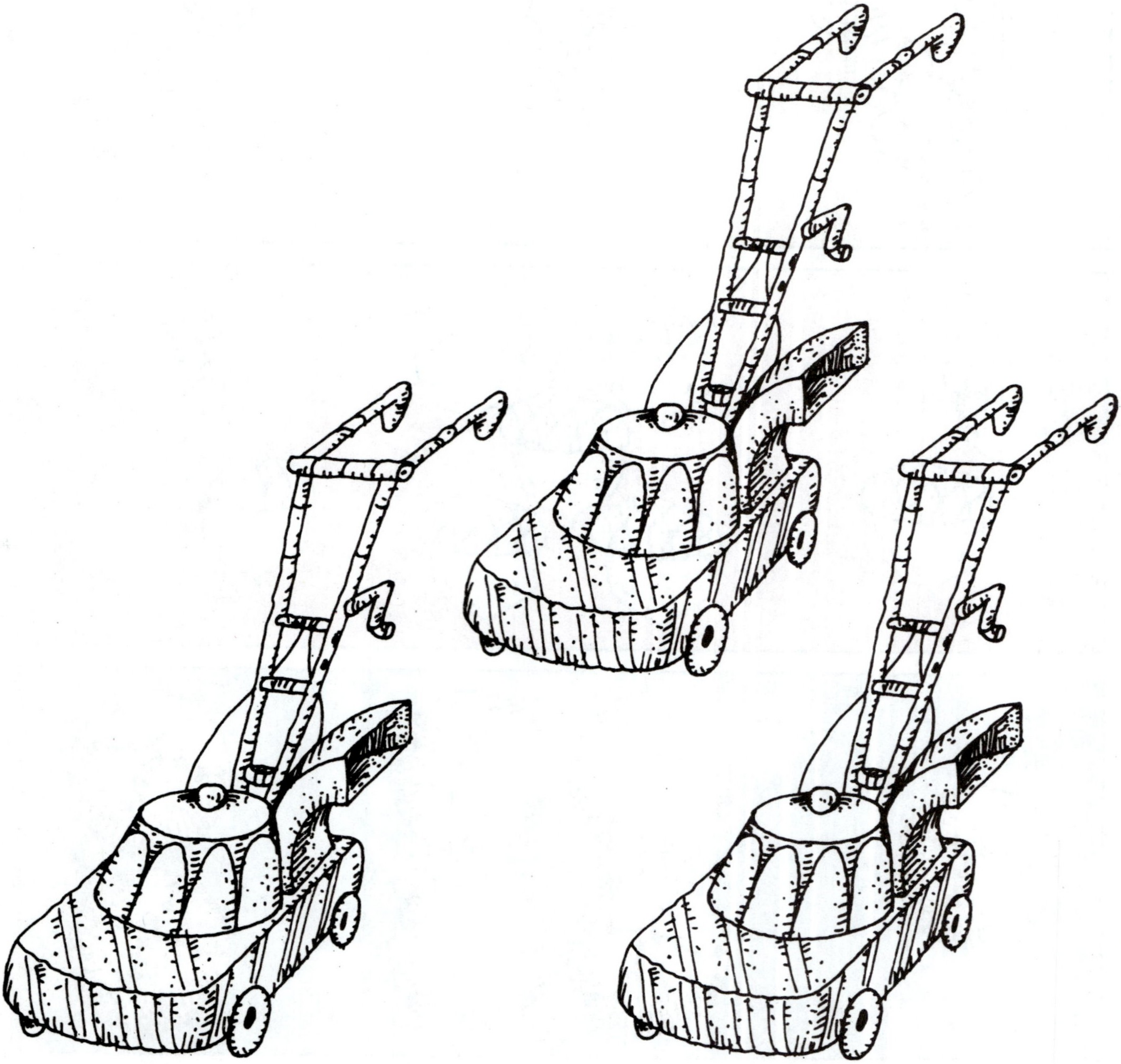

Skills: Recognizing a set of three; Forming the numeral three

Number Concepts

Look at the number of triangles in this set.
Draw another set to show the same number.

Skills: Recognizing sets; Creating a set of three objects

Number Concepts

How many tricycles do you see? Trace the number. Color the pictures.

4

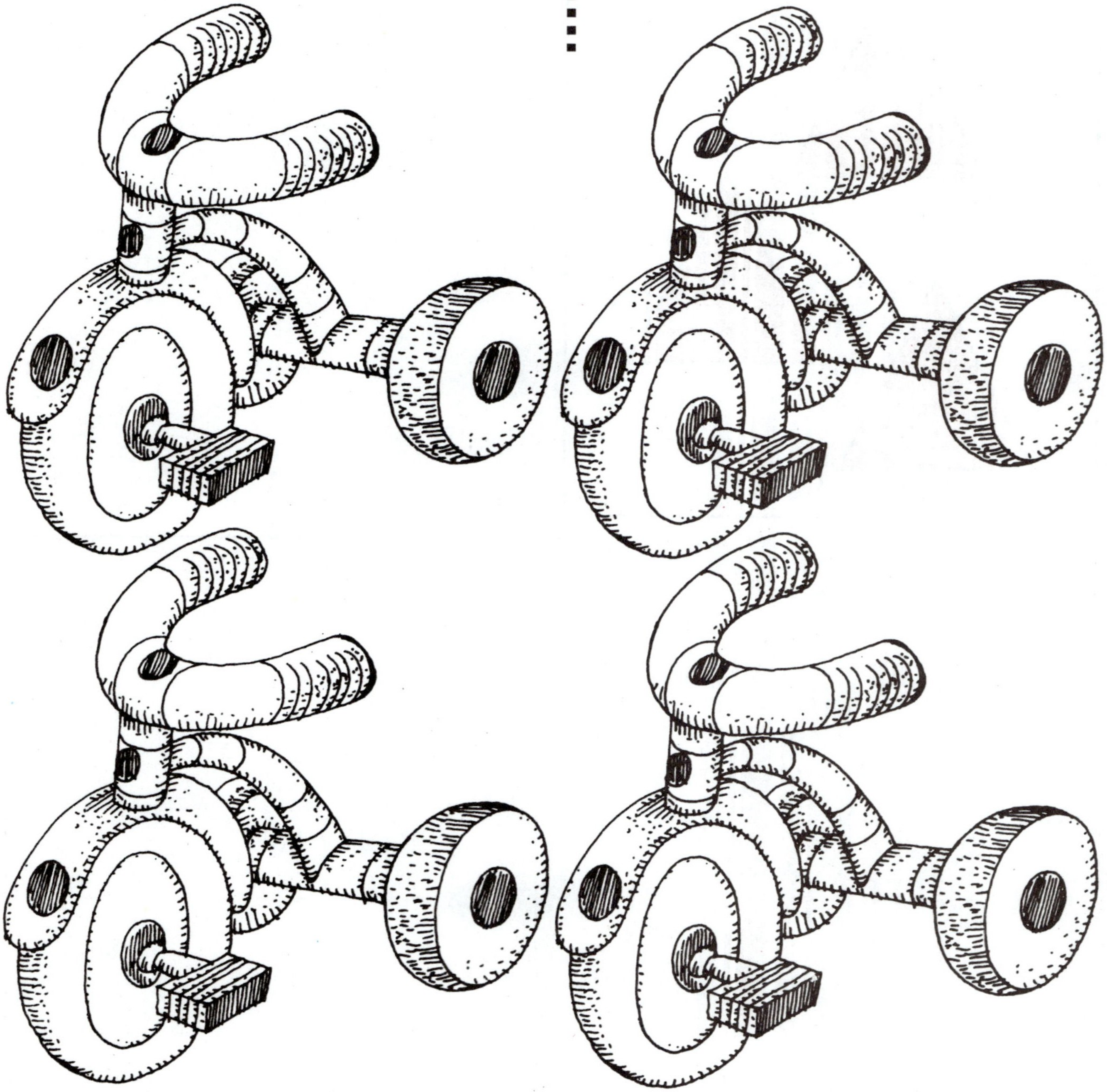

Skills: Recognizing a set of four; Forming the numeral four

Number Concepts

Look at each set. Then color the sets that show "4".

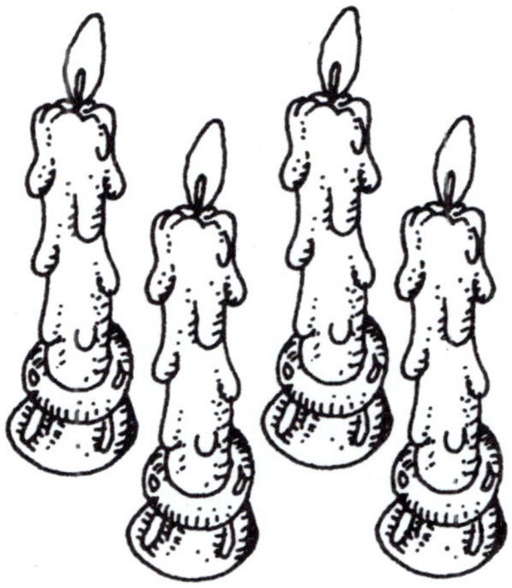

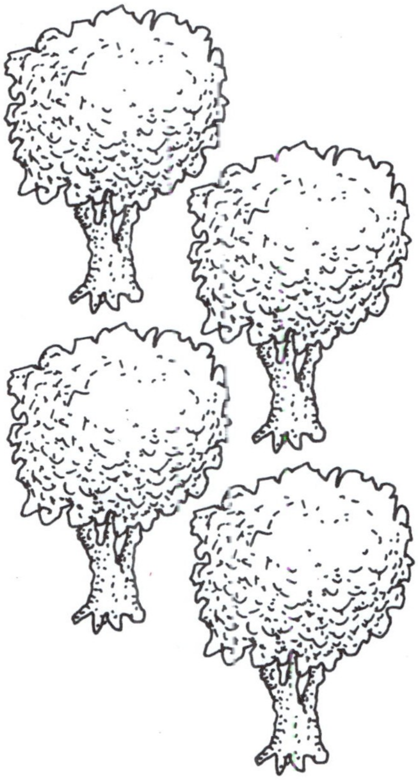

Skills: Identifying sets of four; Following directions

Number Concepts

How many mice do you see? Trace the number. Color the pictures.

5

Skills: Recognizing a set of five; Forming the numeral five

Number Concepts

Look at each set. Then color the sets that show "5".

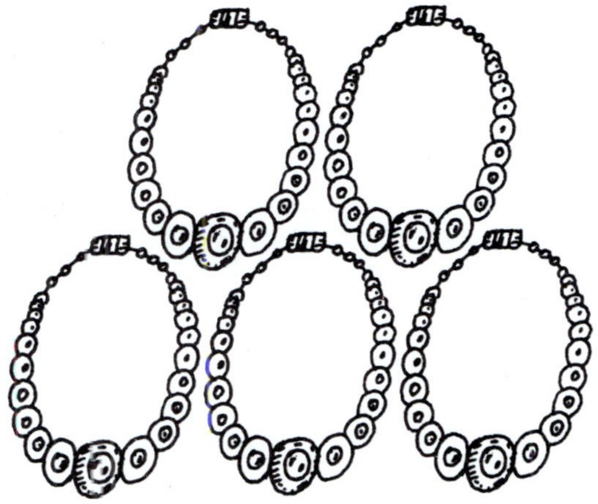

Skills: Identifying sets of five; Following directions

Number Concepts

How many jackets do you see? Trace the number. Color the pictures.

Skills: Recognizing a set of six; Forming the numeral six

Number Concepts

Look at the sets in each box. Circle the sets that show "6".

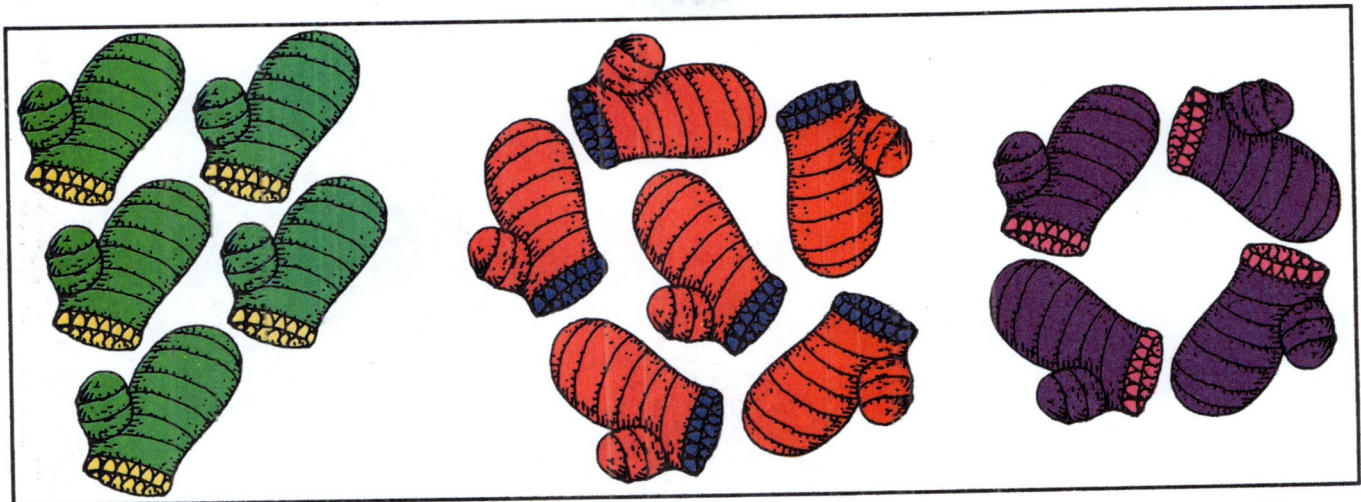

Skills: Identifying sets of six; Following directions

Number Concepts

How many seashells do you see? Trace the number. Color the pictures.

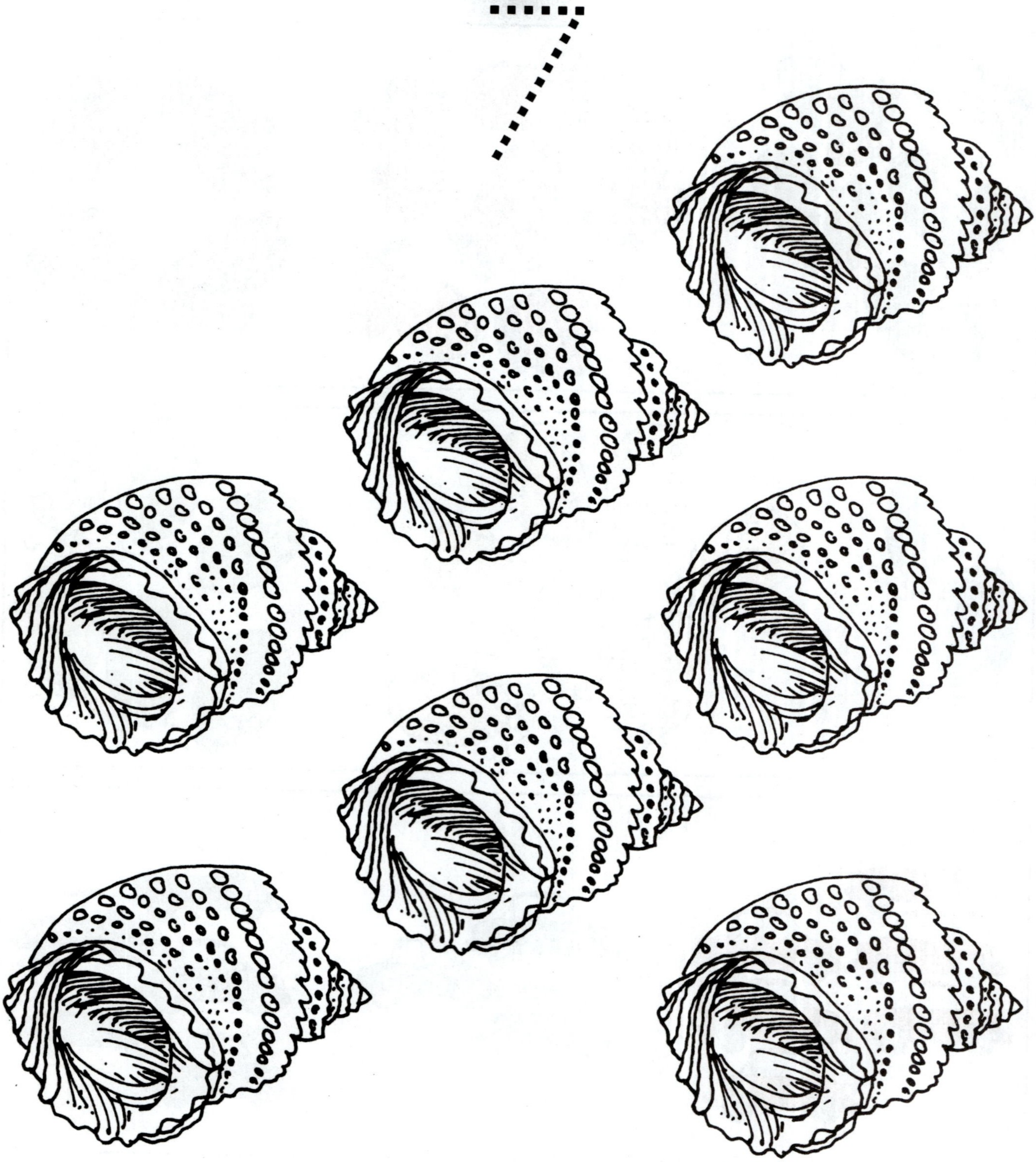

7

Skills: Recognizing a set of seven; Forming the numeral seven

Number Concepts

Look at each set.
Draw a line from the number to the sets that show "7".

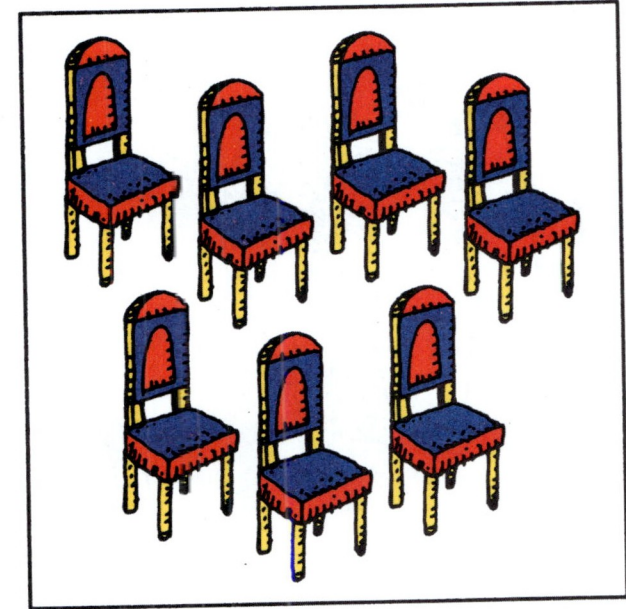

7

Skills: Identifying sets of seven; Following directions

Number Concepts

How many pumpkins do you see? Trace the number. Color the pictures.

8

Skills: Recognizing a set of eight; Forming the numeral eight

Number Concepts

Look at the set in each box. Color the sets that show "8".

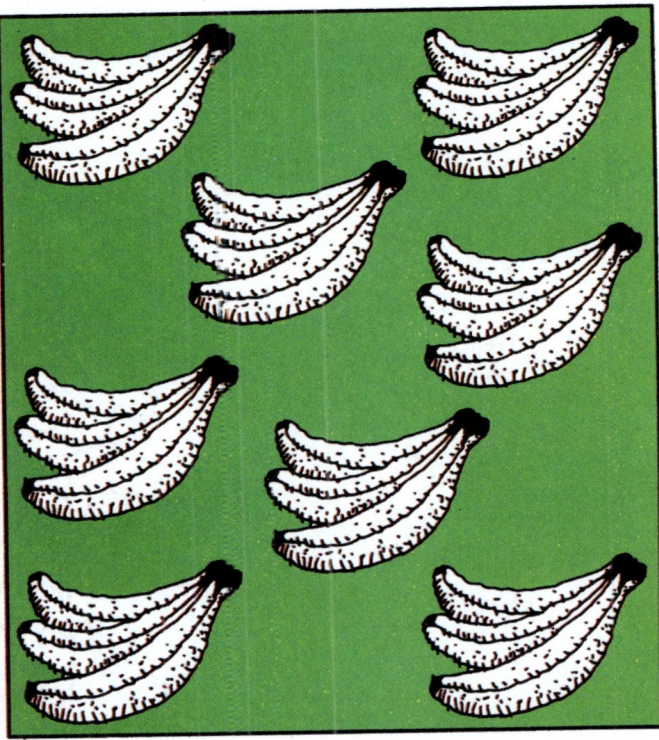

Skills: Identifying sets of eight; Following directions

Number Concepts

How many dolls do you see? Trace the number. Color the pictures.

Skills: Recognizing a set of nine; Forming the numeral nine

Number Concepts

Look at the number of guitars in this set.
Draw another set in the empty box to show the same number.

Skills: Recognizing sets; Creating a set of nine objects

Number Concepts

How many frames do you see? Trace the number. Color the pictures.

10

Skills: Recognizing a set of ten; Forming the numeral ten

Number Concepts

Look at each row of pictures.
Color each row to show sets of "10".

Skills: Identifying sets of ten; Following directions

Number Concepts

Look at the number in each box.
Draw a set that shows that number.

| 1 | 2 | 3 |

| 7 | 8 |

Skills: Recognizing numerals; Creating sets to show an amount

Number Concepts

Look at the number in each box.
Draw a set that shows that number.

| 4 | 5 | 6 |

| 9 | 10 |

Skills: Recognizing numerals; Creating sets to show an amount

Number Concepts

How many objects are in each set?
Draw a line to match the sets with the same number of objects.

Skills: Identifying sets; Matching

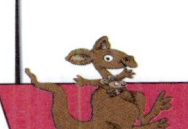

Number Concepts

Trace each number.
Draw the correct number of boxes.

6	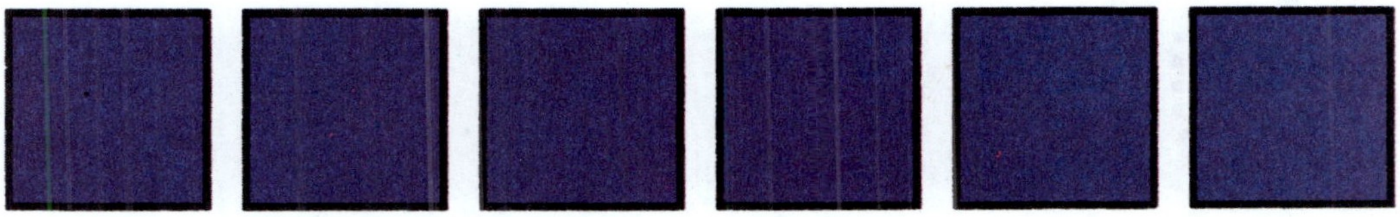
7	
4	
9	
1	

Skills: Forming numerals; Creating sets of objects; Fine motor skill development

Number Concepts

Trace each number.
Draw the correct number of boxes.

10	
5	
3	
8	
2	

Skills: Forming numerals; Creating sets of objects; Fine motor skill development

Number Concepts

How many stars are in each box? Write the number on the line. Then color the stars.

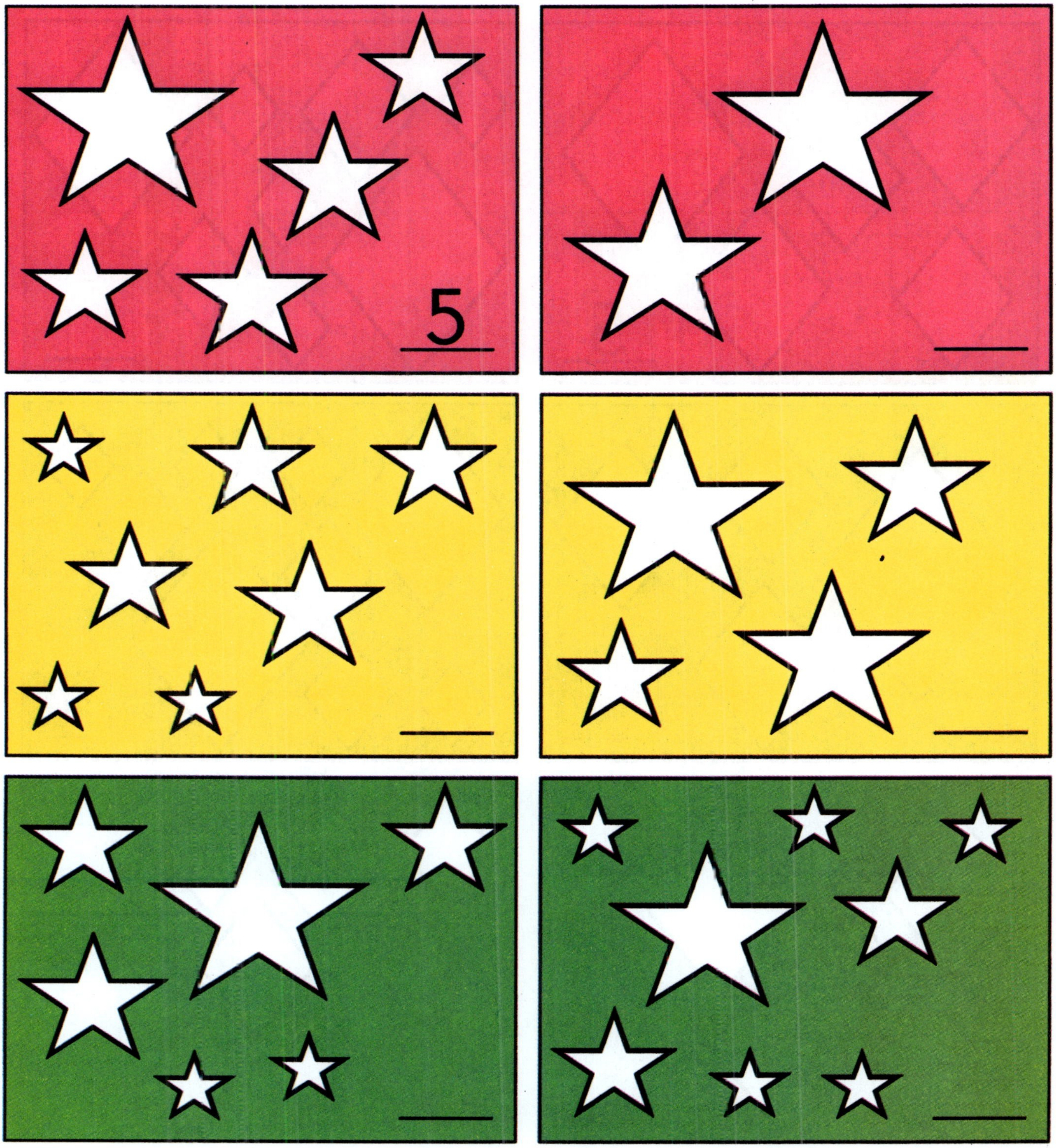

5 ___

___

___

___

___

___

Number Concepts

How many diamonds are in each box? Write the number on the line. Then color the diamonds.

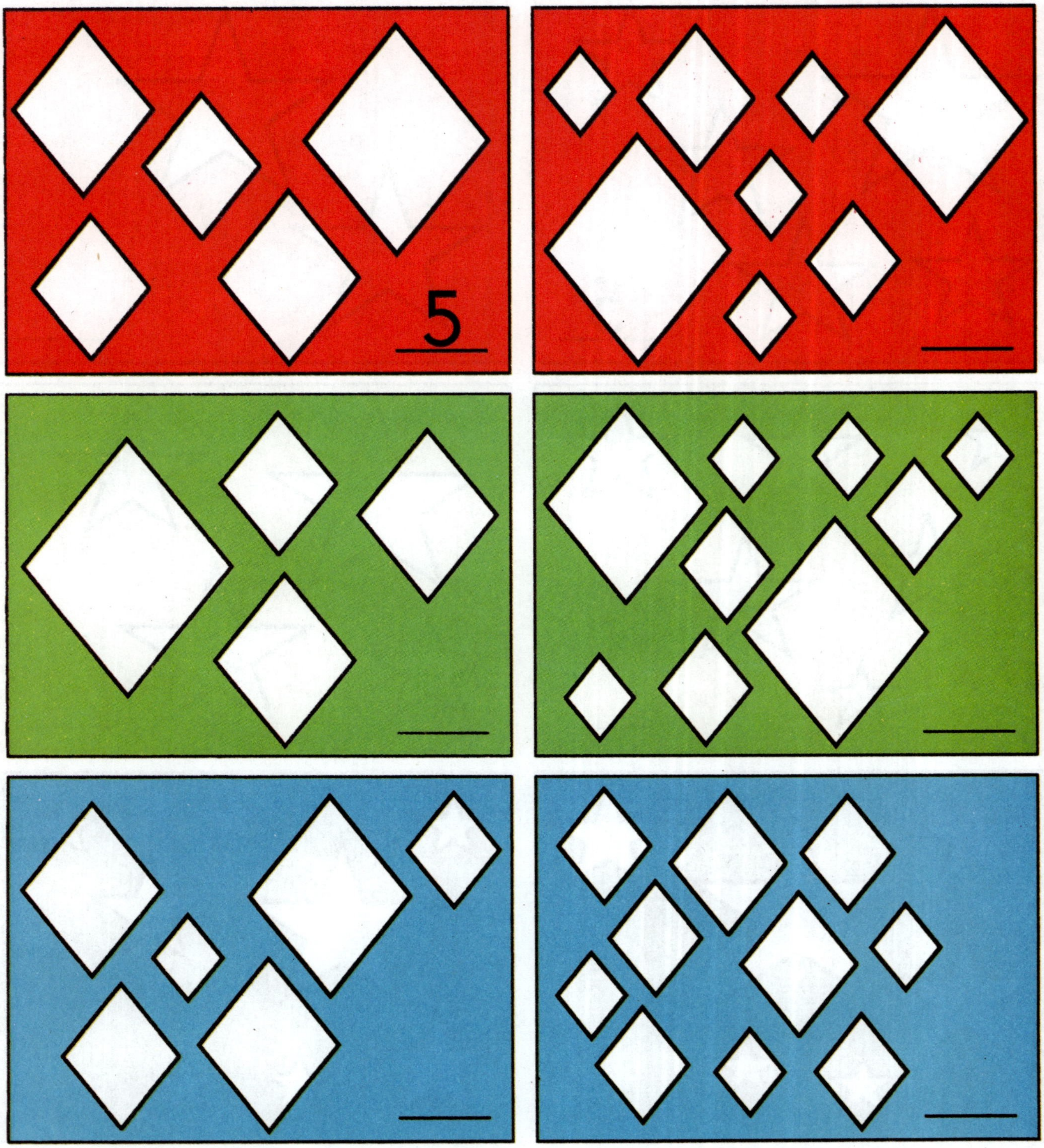

_5_

Number Concepts

How many half circles are in each box? Write the number on the line. Then color the half circles.

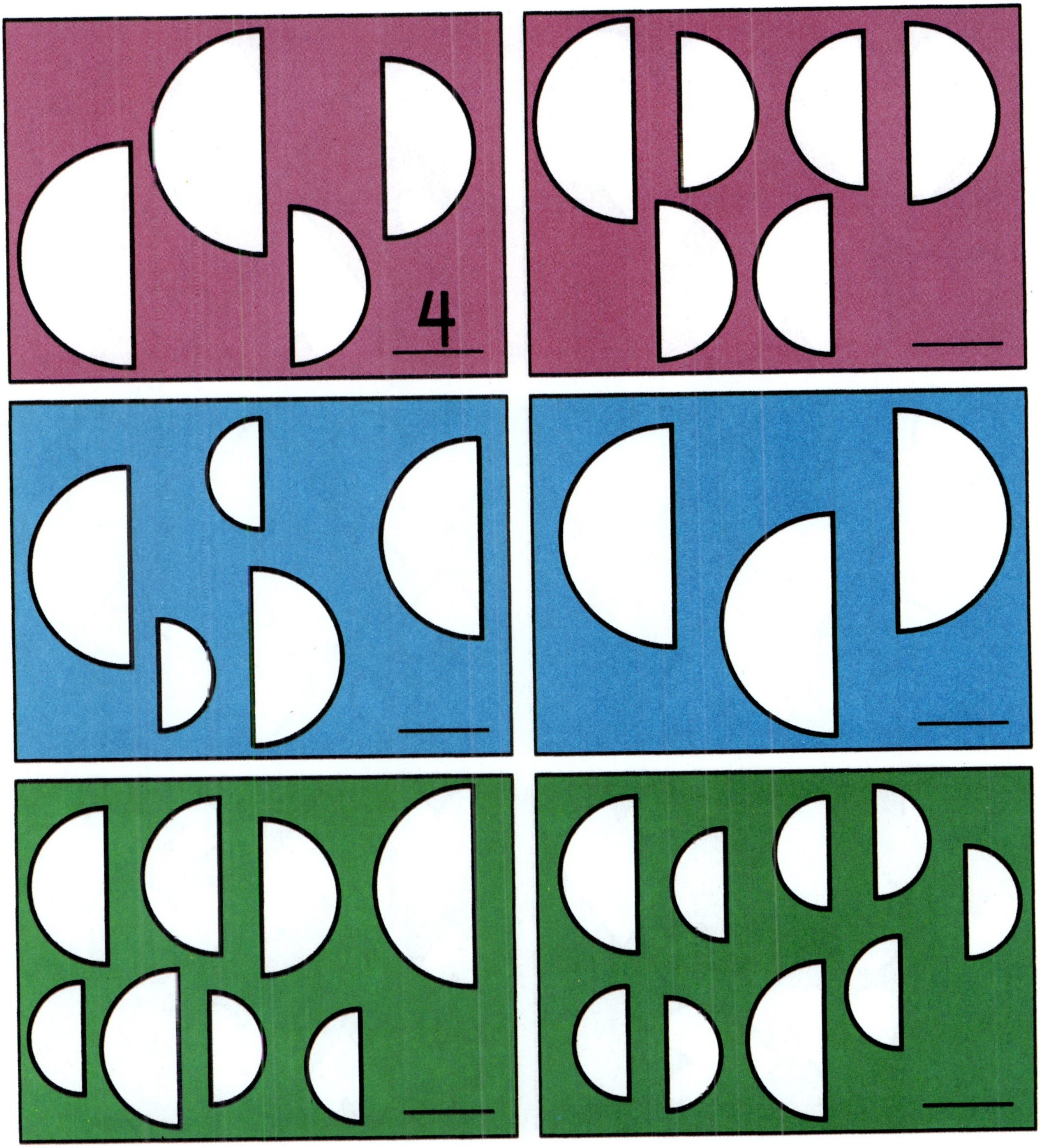

_4_

Number Concepts

How many hearts are in each box? Write the number on the line. Then color the hearts.

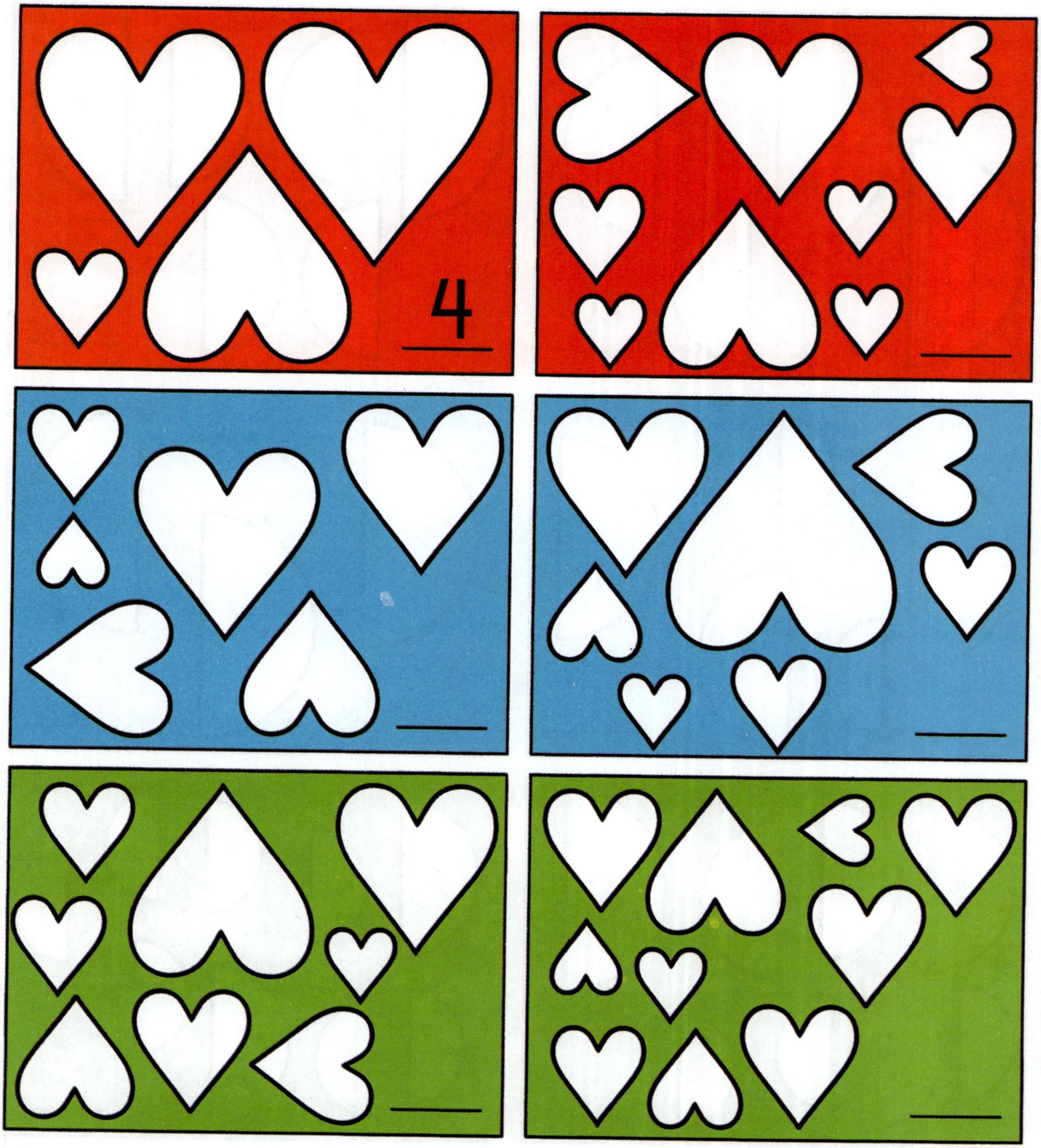

4

Number Concepts

Count how many and write that number in each box.

Skills: Recognizing sets of objects; Classifying and recording information; Writing numerals

Number Concepts

Count the number of each object you see and write the numbers in the boxes. Then color the picture.

Skills: Recognizing sets of objects; Classifying and recording information; Writing numerals

Number Concepts

Look at the number at the beginning of each row.
Circle the picture that shows the correct number.

Skills: Recognizing sets of objects and the corresponding numerals

Number Concepts

Look at the number at the beginning of each row. Circle the picture that shows the correct number.

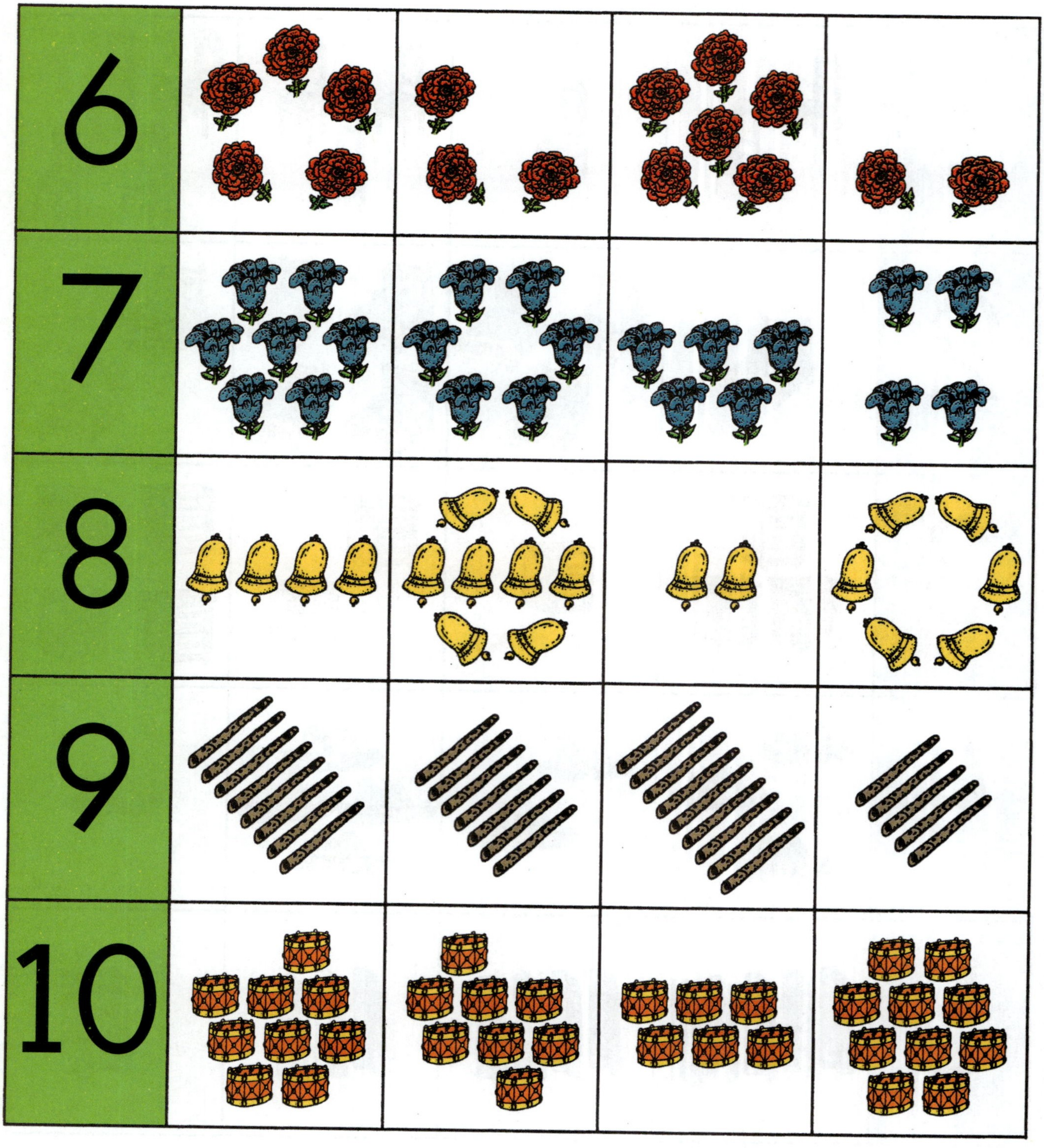

Skills: Recognizing sets of objects and the corresponding numerals

Number Concepts

Look at the numbers and number words.
Color the squares in each row that show the correct number.

1	one
3	three
5	five
7	seven
9	nine

Skills: Creating sets of objects; Recognizing numerals and number words

Number Concepts

Look at the numbers and number words.
Color the squares in each row that show the correct number.

2	two	▢▢▢▢ ▢　▢ ▢▢▢▢
4	four	▢▢▢▢ ▢　▢ ▢▢▢▢
6	six	▢▢▢▢ ▢　▢ ▢▢▢▢
8	eight	▢▢▢▢ ▢　▢ ▢▢▢▢
10	ten	▢▢▢▢ ▢　▢ ▢▢▢▢

Skills: Creating sets of objects; Recognizing numerals and number words

Number Concepts

Circle the number that tells how many objects are in each box.
Then color the pictures.

⑤ 4 7	2 3 8
2 8 3	7 3 6
9 10 6	2 5 1
9 4 8	2 4 10
4 3 5	6 9 2

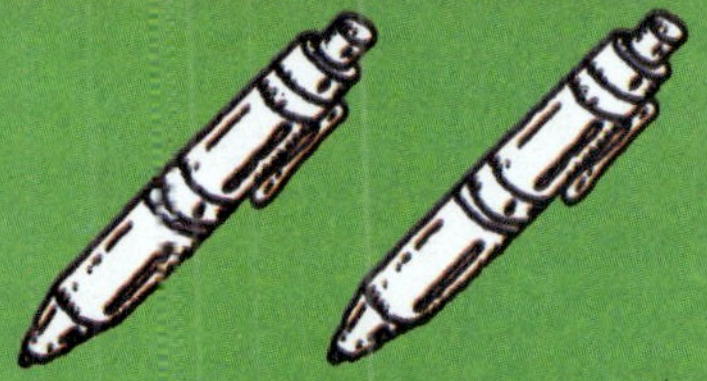

Skills: Following directions; Recognizing sets of objects and the corresponding numeral

Number Concepts

Circle the number that tells how many animals are in each box. Then color the pictures.

5 4 1	9 7 8
10 3 8	2 3 5
7 5 8	4 7 8
2 6 5	6 9 5
8 7 6	7 1 9

Skills: Following directions; Recognizing sets of objects and the corresponding numeral

Number Concepts

Trace the number in each box.
Draw a line to the picture that shows the same number of fruits.
Then write the numbers on the lines.

Skills: Writing numerals; Following directions; Matching numerals to corresponding sets

Number Concepts

Trace the number in each box.
Draw a line to the picture that shows the same number of objects.
Then write the numbers on the lines.

Number Concepts

Look at the set in each box.
Circle the sets that show "1".

Skills: Identifying sets of one

Number Concepts

Look at the set in each box.
Circle the sets that show "2".

Skills: Identifying sets of two

Number Concepts

Circle three objects in each row.

3	
3	
3	
3	
3	

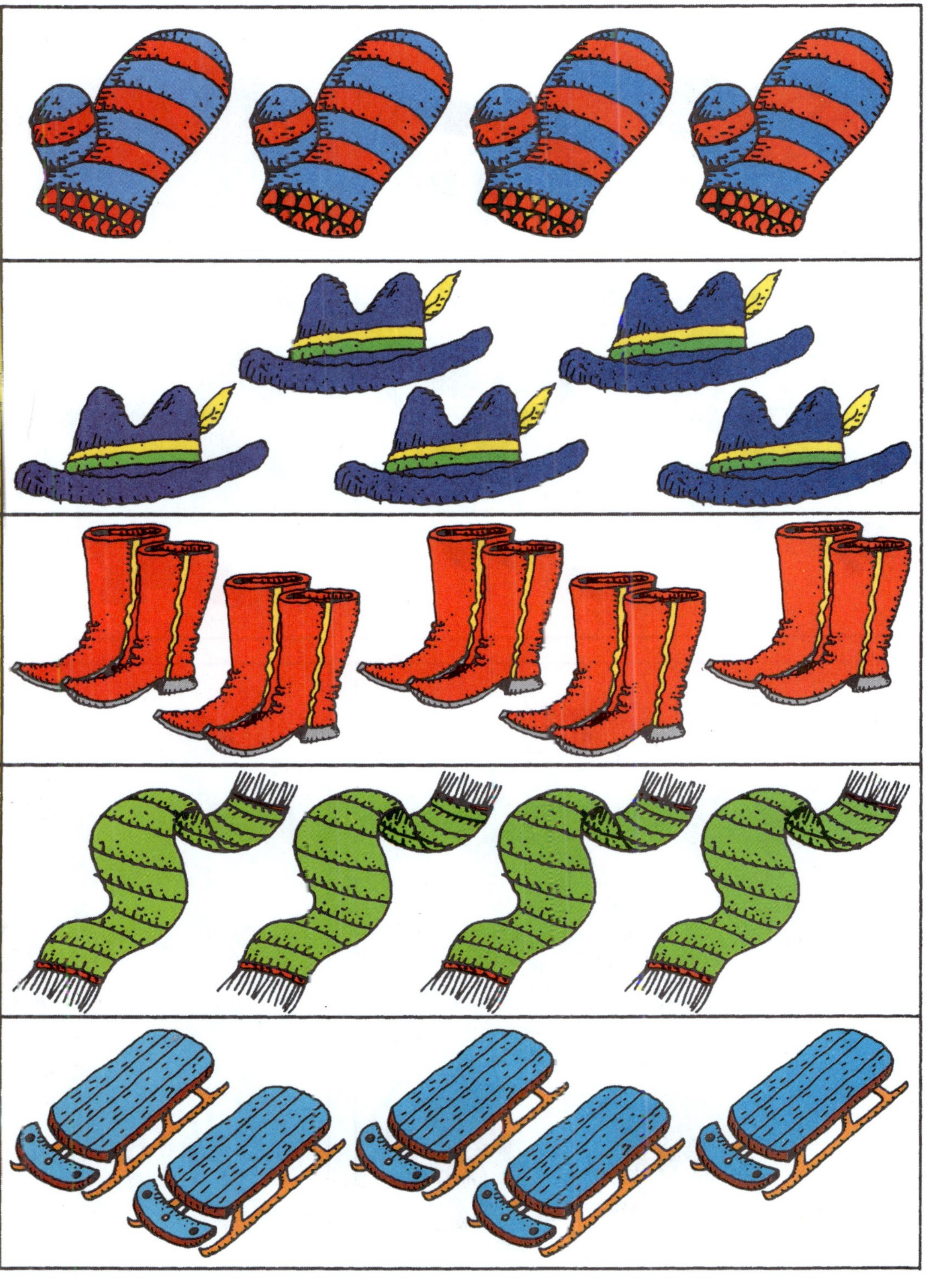

Skills: Creating sets of three; Recognizing sets

Number Concepts

Look at the set in each box. Circle the sets that show "4".

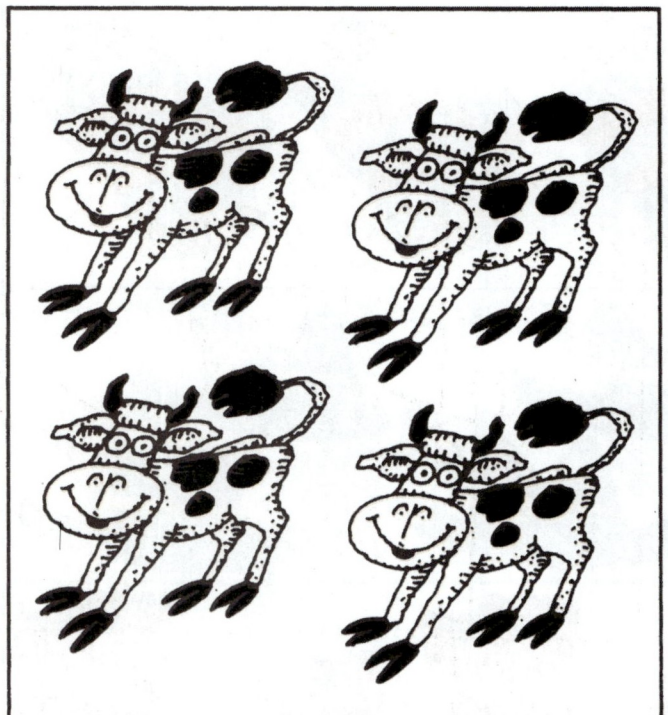

Skills: Identifying sets of four

Number Concepts

Look at the set in each box.
Circle the sets that show "5".

Skills: Identifying sets of five

Number Concepts

Look at the set in each box.
Circle the sets that show "6".

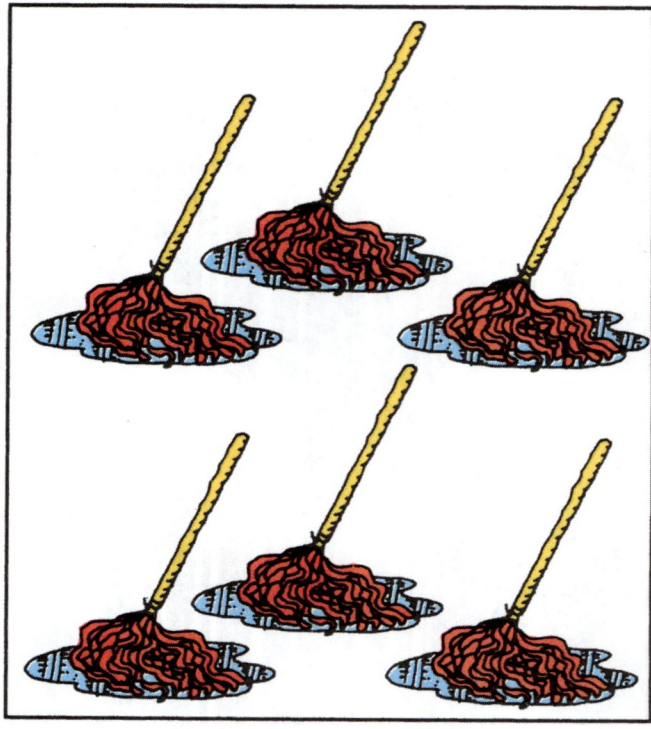

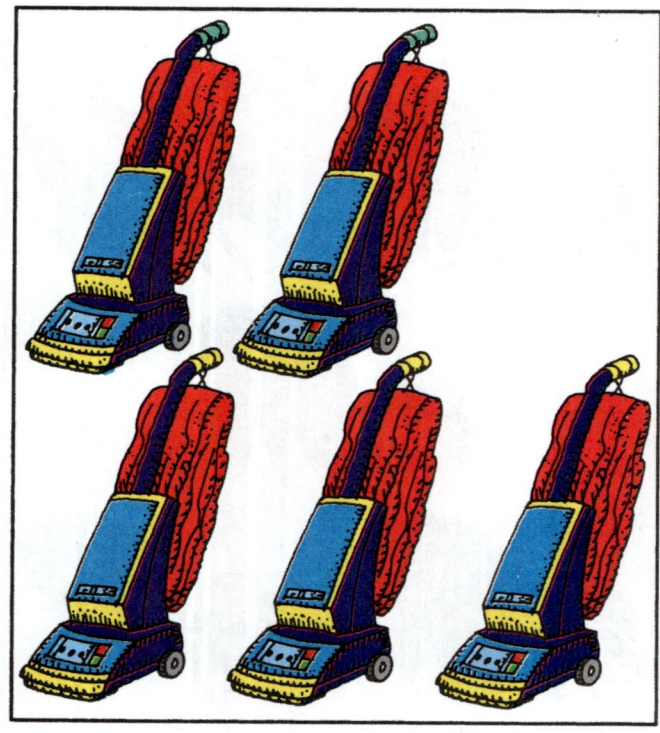

Skills: Identifying sets of six

Number Concepts

Look at the set in each box.
Circle the sets that show "7".

Skills: Identifying sets of seven

Number Concepts

Look at the set in each box.
Circle the sets that show "8".

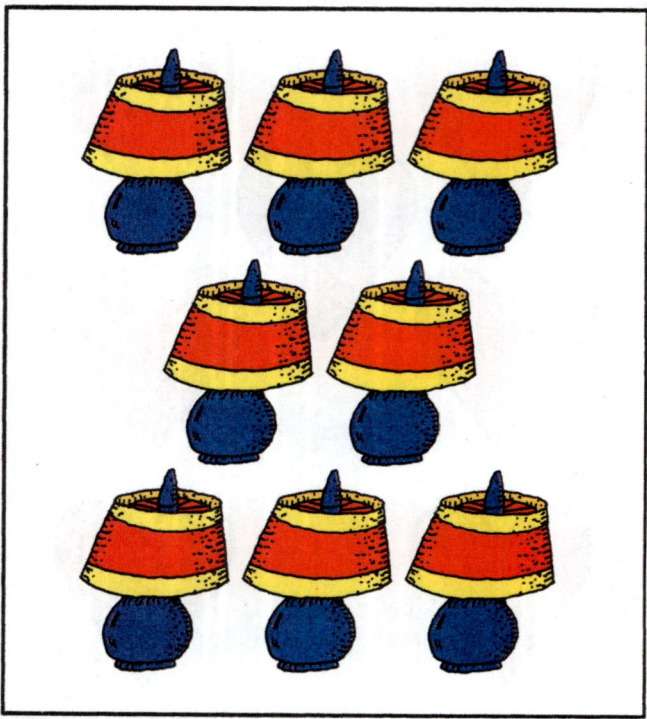

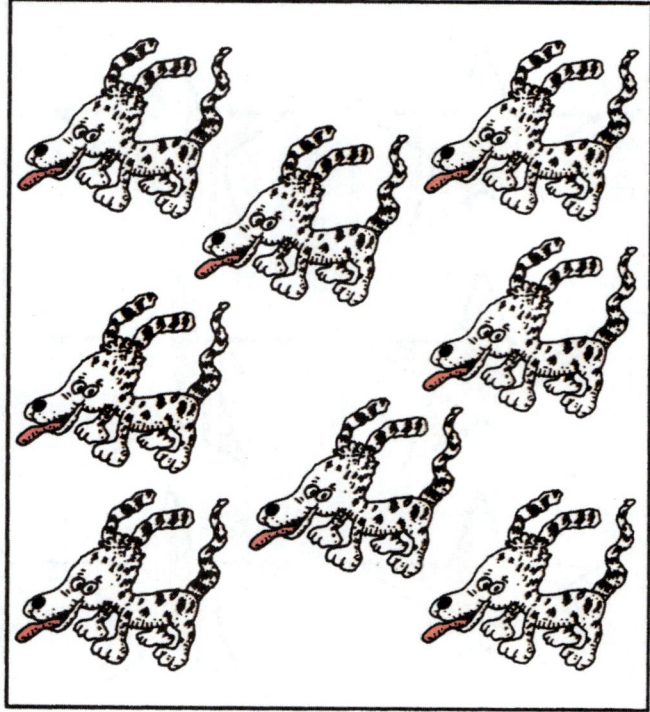

Skills: Identifying sets of eight

Number Concepts

Look at the set in each box.
Circle the sets that show "9".

Skills: Identifying sets of nine

Number Concepts

How many objects do you see in each box?
Circle the sets that show "10".

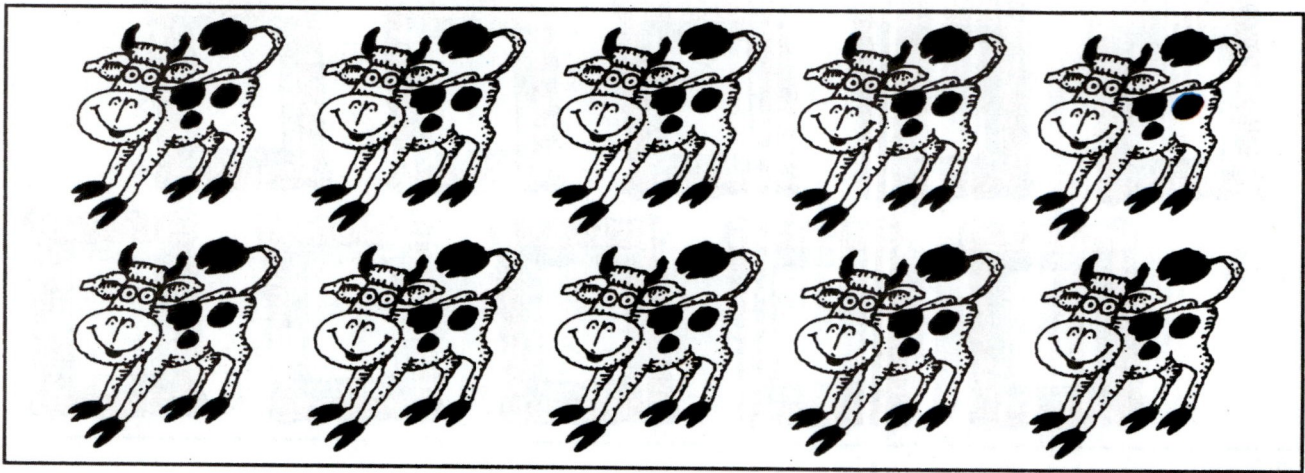

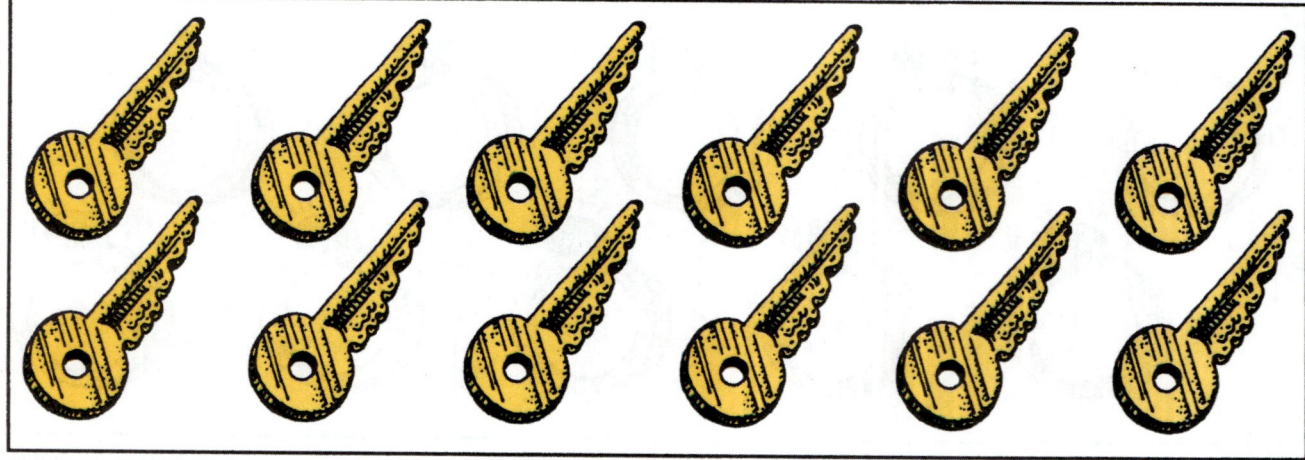

Skills: Identifying sets of ten

Number Concepts

Look at the numbers in each box.
Draw objects that show a set of each number.

1	6
2	7
3	8
4	9
5	10

Skills: Number order; Recognizing numbers 1 to 10; Identifying number sets

Practice Page

Use this page and the next page to practice writing numbers.

Practice Page

Practice Page

Use this page to practice drawing **large** and **small** objects.

Practice Page

Use this page to draw sets that show **more** and **less**.

Practice Page

Use this page to create sets of objects showing the numbers 1 to 10.

Excellent!

Give yourself a star!

Achievement Checklist

Use the checklist below after each session with this book. If your child had trouble with a page, find the problem skill and list the page number in the middle column. You will want to return to it later. If your child successfully completed the pages containing a skill, put a check mark in the "Mastered" column. Your child can watch with pride as the column fills up with skills he or she has mastered.

BASIC SKILLS	Needs Work	Mastered!
BEGINNING WRITING		
Fine motor skills		
Eye/hand coordination		
Tracing		
Forming vertical lines		
Forming diagonal lines		
Forming open curves		
Forming closed curves		
Forming horizontal lines		
Forming letters: Aa		
Forming letters: Bb		
Forming letters: Cc		
Forming letters: Dd		
Forming letters: Ee		
Forming letters: Ff		
Forming letters: Gg		
Forming letters: Hh		
Forming letters: Ii		
Forming letters: Jj		
Forming letters: Kk		
Forming letters: Ll		
Forming letters: Mm		
Forming letters: Nn		
Forming letters: Oo		
Forming letters: Pp		
Forming letters: Qq		
Forming letters: Rr		
Forming letters: Ss		
Forming letters: Tt		
Forming letters: Uu		
Forming letters: Vv		
Forming letters: Ww		
Forming letters: Xx		
Forming letters: Yy		
Forming letters: Zz		
Letter order		
COLORS AND SHAPES		
Recognizing/Forming Shapes: circles		
Recognizing/Forming Shapes: rectangles		
Recognizing/Forming Shapes: triangles		
Recognizing/Forming Shapes: ovals		
Recognizing/Forming Shapes: squares		

Achievement Checklist

BASIC SKILLS	Needs Work	Mastered!
COLORS AND SHAPES		
Distinguishing Colors: yellow		
Distinguishing Colors: red		
Distinguishing Colors: green		
Distinguishing Colors: black		
Distinguishing Colors: blue		
Distinguishing Colors: orange		
Distinguishing Colors: purple		
Distinguishing Colors: brown		
Visual discrimination		
Color matching		
READING READINESS		
Matching		
Association		
Classification		
Noticing details		
Logical reasoning		
Sorting		
Understanding direction		
Following directions		
Visual memory		
Reproducing sounds		
Spatial orientation		
Fine motor skill development		
Observing / continuing pattern		
Eye / hand coordination		
Visual perception		
SOUNDS AND LETTERS		
Recognizing sounds		
Sound / symbol association		
Auditory discrimination		
MATH READINESS / NUMBER CONCEPTS		
Number recognition		
Number order		
Reproducing patterns		
Observing and continuing patterns		
Size discrimination		
One-to-one correspondence		
Understanding more and less		
Counting		
Recognizing and creating sets		
Writing numbers		
Understanding same and different		
Logical reasoning		

Diploma

Awarded to

_____

- - - - - - - - - - - - -

_____

for extraordinary achievement in Preschool Basic Skills

on this date,

_____

- - - - - - -

_____

CONGRATULATIONS!

Smart Kid

This book belongs to:

MEG
....

Illustrated by Arthur Friedman
Educational Consultants: Shereen Gertel Rutman, M.S.
Mary Mclean Hely, M.A. in Education, Design and Evaluation of Educational Programs
Colorization and page design by Creative Quotient

Copyright ©2005 by Modern Publishing,
a division of Unisystems, Inc.

™Revised and Expanded Giant Basic Skills Preschool Workbook
is a trademark of Modern Publishing, a division of Unisystems, Inc.

®Honey Bear Books is a trademark owned by Honey Bear Productions, Inc.,
and is registered in the U.S. Patent and Trademark Office.
No part of this book may be reproduced or copied without written
permission from the publisher. All Rights Reserved.

Printed in India

MODERN Preschool GIANT BASIC SKILLS™ Workbook

Modern Publishing
A Division of Unisystems, Inc.
New York, New York 10022
Series UPC: 49130

Essential Skills

The repetitive activities within each chapter have been designed to help children learn the organizational skills necessary for learning and thinking.

CHAPTER 1 BEGINNING WRITING SKILLS

Learning to control the small muscles of the hand (**fine motor skill development**) allows the child to make the precise movements necessary for forming letters, while activities such as **writing from left to right, tracing,** and **forming lines** help to refine **eye/hand coordination.**

CHAPTER 2 COLORS AND SHAPES

Grouping things according to common attributes such as color, size and shape (**classification activities**) encourages development of a child's ability to reason and make **logical connections.**

CHAPTER 3 READING READINESS

Before learning to read, children must be able to distinguish same and different. For example, children usually recognize the difference between a cow and a horse before they recognize different letters. The emphasis in this chapter is on various visual skills – **noticing details, comparing, matching figures, understanding directionality, etc.**

PICTURE DICTIONARY

This special section will help expand children's vocabulary by introducing and reinforcing knowledge of simple words that are part of their world.

CHAPTER 4 SOUNDS AND LETTERS

Children practice **identifying sounds with letters**, and associating them with familiar words.

CHAPTER 5 MATH READINESS

By **observing, reproducing,** and **continuing patterns**, children develop **visual memory** skills, which prepare them for learning to recognize numbers. Various activities that focus on **making comparisons** also aid in the development of number sense and an understanding of mathematical order.

CHAPTER 6 NUMBER CONCEPTS

The emphasis in this chapter is on identifying and **creating sets of objects and their corresponding numerals**, and on **recognizing numerals and number words**. These activities prepare children for basic math.

To the Parents

Dear Parents,

As your child's first and most important teacher, you can encourage your child's love of learning by participating in educational activities at home. Working together on the activities in this workbook will help your child build confidence, learn to reason, and develop skills necessary for early childhood education.

The following are some suggestions to help make your time together enjoyable and rewarding.

- ▶ Choose a time when you and your child are relaxed.

- ▶ Provide a writing tool that your child is familiar with.

- ▶ Don't attempt to do too many pages at one time or expect that every page be completed. Move on if your child is frustrated or loses interest.

- ▶ Discuss each page. Help your child relate the concepts in this book to everyday experiences.

- ▶ Encourage your child to use the practice pages provided at the end of the BEGINNING WRITING and NUMBER CONCEPTS sections to work independently and reinforce skills.

- ▶ Use the Achievement Checklist to keep track of the pages you need to revisit. When the "Mastered" column is full, your child has earned the diploma at the back of the book!

Happy Learning!